American Diner

Then and Now

American Diner

Then and Now

Richard J. S. Gutman

The Johns Hopkins University Press
Baltimore and London

All photographs are from the collection of Richard J. S. Gutman unless otherwise credited.

Parts of chapter 13 previously appeared in *Automobile Quarterly*, vol. 30, no. 3 (Spring 1992).

Originally published by HarperCollins Publishers, Inc., 1993

Johns Hopkins Paperbacks edition, 2000

9 8 7 6 5 4 3 2 1

Designed by Ingalls & Associates

Designer: Tracy Dean

The Johns Hopkins University Press

2715 North Charles Street

Baltimore, Maryland 21218-4363

www.press.jhu.edu

Library of Congress Cataloging-in-Publication Data

Gutman, Richard.

    American diner then and now / Richard J.S. Gutman.

      p. cm.

    Originally published: New York : Harper Collins, 1993.

    Includes index.

    ISBN 0-8018-6536-0 (pbk. : alk. paper)

    1. Diners (Restaurants)—United States.   I. Title.

NA7855.G87   2000

647.9573—dc21

00-030202

A catalog record for this book is available from the British Library.

To my wife, Kellie,
whose name should also appear on the title page,
and to the dinergirl, my daughter, Lucy

Contents

Acknowledgments

Over the years many people have shared with me information, photographs, anecdotes, and their enthusiasm for diners. These are people in the diner industry, people who run diners, and people who love diners. The network of diner people is ever growing, and I've been in touch with so many people it would be impossible to name all of them.

Closest to home are a group of friends and colleagues who are always willing to talk about diners and the latest developments: Larry Cultrera, Dave Hebb, Norma Holmes, Paul Gray, Dave and Lynn Waller, and Randy Garbin. Separated by a greater physical distance, my oldest diner comrade, John Baeder, has always shared his experiences and encouraged my pursuits. Special thanks to Brian Butko for reading the manuscript, offering suggestions to make it better, and sharing his research. Also thanks to Don and Newly Preziosi for the use of some of their outstanding diner postcard collection.

Many people have kept me informed on diner whereabouts and happenings, in addition to sending me pictures, articles, and ephemera: Jim Heimann, Gordon Tindall, Jim Baker, Dick Parkinson, Mike Bennett, Chuck Biddle, Barbara Marhoefer, Blake Hayes, Tania G. Werbizky, Jerry Berta, Dennis Scipione, James J. Foley, Daniel J. Fitzpatrick, Ruth Hopfman, Ruth Ann Penka, Winifred Fleming Gengel, Donald A. LaPlante, Donald W. Parks, Mrs. John D. Murray, Walter Bramble, Katie Armitage, Kenrick A. Claflin, Barry and Nancy Garton, John B. Levine, John E. Rau, Donald J. Parker, Marc C. Wagner, Paul Downey, and Lynne Spiegel.

Others have helped track down elusive photographs and information: Elizabeth Polucci, Dave Noyd, Henry R. Timman, Mrs. Shirley Kupp, Jeffrey Hoyt, Alexander B. Cumming, Steve Tankanow, Bill Giavis, George Poirier, Nathan Silver, James Cucci and Dorothy Moore.

The following people at their respective institutions have been very helpful: William D.

Wallace, Gail T. Randall, Beverly H. Osborn, Joan Bedard, and Wallis H. Darnley at the Worcester Historical Museum; Nancy Gaudette at the Worcester Public Library; Cynthia Read-Miller and Judith E. Endelman at Henry Ford Museum & Greenfield Village; Robert Eskind at the Atwater Kent Museum; Craig A. Gilborn at The Adirondack Museum; Fred Dahlinger, Jr. at the Circus World Museum; Carl A. Rakich at the Summit County Historical Society; Charlotte and John McCarron at the Merrimac Town Museum.

Of the many diner owners who have helped, fed, and encouraged me over the years, extra-special thanks go to Jack Mulholland, Mayfair Diner; Fred and Joe Casey, Casey's Diner; Charles and Nicholas Georgenes, Victoria Dining; and Don Levy, Blue Diner.

People connected with the diner-building industry have aided me in my search to document their history. Thanks to Harold and Robert Kullman and Amy S. Delman at Kullman Industries, who have helped me over the past twenty years; Mrs. Joseph W. Swingle and her late husband; Erwin Fedkenheuer, Jr., of Erfed, who gave me his entire company archives; Pat Fodero, who, beginning in my college days, always had the time to talk about diners, and gave me the use of his photographic archives. Fred Crepeau, Laurence LeBlanc, and Wilfred Bernard, of the Worcester Lunch Car Company, shared their time and memories, as did Elbert "Amby" McConnell of the J. B. Judkins Company, Frank Bonifanti of the Jerry O'Mahony Company, and Joe Montano, whose long career found him working at many companies. Also thanks to Philip DeRaffele of DeRaffele Manufacturing, Herbert Y. Enyart of Paramount Diners, Ralph Musi of Musi Dining Car Company, and Vincent Giannotti of Manno Dining Car Company.

And to the editors at HarperCollins, especially Hugh Van Dusen and Stephanie Gunning, who gave me the freedom to write the book I wanted to write, I extend my greatest thanks.

Introduction to the Johns Hopkins Edition

The S & C group was a chain of nine diners in the Detroit area before World War II that beat Starbucks to the coffee shop idea by at least half a century. Another matchcover of the era erroneously predicted the look of diners at the new millennium. Though ultimate streamlining is not the rage it was in 1940, diners of the twenty-first century have happily returned to a classic styling.

The diner renaissance is twenty years old—and still going strong. In the late 1970s the first diner books appeared, and people began to appreciate diners for more than just the food they served. Diners were recognized for their unique atmosphere and appearance, as well as their place in the American psyche. People feel good about diners.

When this book first appeared in 1993, the trend toward new old-style diners was nascent. The Silver Diner chain, out of Rockville, Maryland, had four units and its impact was strong and immediate. Most new diners, and renovations of older ones, imitated the Silver Diner look, with its landmark entrance tower. In the year 2000, there are thirteen Silver Diners, with no end in sight to the chain's growth.

Chain operation has always been a small but significant alternative to the mom-and-pop operation. From the turn of the last century, the greatest diner builders, Tierney and O'Mahony, operated their own chains in addition to manufacturing. For example, Jerry O'Mahony had thirteen Club Diners operating in three states in 1926.

The newest manufacturer, Starlite Diners, in Ormond Beach, Florida, is now turning out more diners per year than any of the old-line builders and shipping them throughout the United States (plus two to Moscow). Their sales are bolstered by an arrangement with Denny's to supply them with Denny's Classic Diners. At the same time, Denny's has planned to spend more than $30 million to remodel 150 of their restaurants, making them look more like diners.

Chain operation is also taking hold in Germany, where a handful of vintage diners has been imported. The latest trend is the multiunit chain, Sam Kullman's Diners, the buildings for which are being built by Sam's son and grandson, Harold and Robert of Kullman Industries, in Lebanon, New Jersey. Kullman is the oldest manufacturer and still the trendsetter in the business.

Europe remains fascinated with this American icon. Much to the dismay of the locals, the occasional American diner has been loaded onto a ship and sent abroad. Spain has a pair, England has a few, and the Clarksville Diner, whose loving restoration is recorded herein, is now part of the scenery in a Paris suburb. Sometimes even the most beautifully restored diner doesn't succeed, however, especially if its neighborhood won't support it.

While brand-new diners are being delivered on a regular basis, there remains great interest in restoring the best of the old. Individual entrepreneurs restore their diners, but one man deserves recognition for buying, restoring, and installing a host of them: Steve Harwin, head of Diversified Diners, of Cleveland, Ohio, has saved more than a dozen diners from the wrecking ball and brought them back to life, from Massachusetts to Colorado.

The diner's place in history is further guaranteed by the growing number of museums that are adding them to their collections. The pioneer in this effort was Henry Ford Museum & Greenfield Village, in Dearborn, Michigan, which wasn't content with only a horse-drawn lunch wagon; they also acquired a classic, streamlined Worcester Lunch Car to add to their collection of historic buildings. Most recently, the Strong Museum, in Rochester, New York, restored and now operates the Skyliner Diner, a 1956 Fodero. It sits next to a 1918 carousel, within a new wing of the museum built to house these artifacts.

The twenty-first century looks good for diners—and that's a good sign for people who eat in diners, who work in diners, and who build them. With the reissue of this book, and its updated listing, "Where the Diners Are," those who love diners will be able to savor both their history and their fare.

The Diner's Humble Beginnings

Walter Scott's cart. (*Providence Journal*)

The classic stainless steel, streamlined diner could not have been a glint in the eye of Walter Scott, of Providence, Rhode Island, when he trundled down Westminster Street in 1872 in a light horse-drawn wagon laden with tasty sandwiches, boiled eggs, pies, and coffee. This first "night lunch wagon" would undergo many stylistic changes as it evolved into the familiar roadside diner of the twentieth century. But the diner's history had to start somewhere. ¶ The problem was that nighthawks, late-night workers, and carousers couldn't get anything to eat anywhere in town after eight P.M., when all the restaurants closed for the evening. At least that was the case in Providence before the appearance of Walter Scott. At the age of eleven, in 1852, Walter sold newspapers, fruit, and homemade candy on the street to help support his family. ¶ This connection with the newspaper business eventually caused Scott to realize that newspaper workers with large appe-

tites toiled all night to put out the morning editions. When he later got a job working as a compositor and pressman, he started making the rounds of all three Providence papers—the *Journal,* the *Star,* and the *Herald*—peddling sandwiches and coffee between editions.

After the Civil War, Scott built himself a small handcart to carry more provisions. While he made his rounds, people would stop him on the street to make purchases. In 1872, in order to concentrate only on the night lunch business, Scotty quit his job, bought a horse (named Patient Dick), hooked the horse up to a small freight wagon, and pulled up to the front of the *Journal* office.

This first wagon was merely a converted freight wagon. It provided shelter for Scott alone, who sat inside on a wooden box (while Patient Dick stood outside in all weather). He had installed a cover, out of which he cut window openings to face both the sidewalk and the street. When customers ordered from both sides at once Scotty could hand out the victuals and collect the money with both hands.

In what became the hallmark of diner cuisine, Scotty served only homemade items. Except for chicken, a nickel could buy any order: a ham sandwich; perhaps a boiled egg with a slice of buttered bread; or a piece of pie—apple, mince, squash, huckleberry, or cranberry And for your nickel, you didn't just get a slice of pie; a regulation cut was *half* of a small pie. For the "dude" trade (dudes being those who could afford it), there was a plate of sliced chicken at thirty cents. To avoid waste, Scotty invented the "chewed" sandwich, consisting of scraps left over on the cutting board, chopped still finer, and spread with butter or mustard between two slices of bread. For twenty-five years Scotty baked his own bread, and for close to forty his own pies.

At the time of his retirement in 1917, he proudly told the *Providence Sunday Journal:* "For my chicken sandwiches, rooster fowl was always good enough. I bought the best of native birds and

An Ethiopian named Tom Jay was Scott's first competitor, peddling food at night in the streets of Providence. *(Providence Journal)*

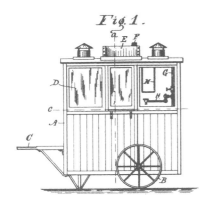

When Scott outgrew his basket, he constructed a street vending cabinet similar to Edgar Miller's patented design of 1891.

cooked them under the best condition. Nobody ever kicked at a chicken sandwich that I passed out."

As one might expect, the early days on the dusk-till-four-A.M. shift were rough-and-tumble, and Scotty had to devise ways to protect himself against the sorts of rowdies who would eat and run, without paying. Over the years he developed a good eye for whether a customer was apt to pay or not. If he distrusted the fellow, Scotty would reach out from the wagon and grab his hat, holding it as security until the bill was paid. He also kept a stout hickory club in case of emergency. In 1917 Scott reminisced:

If a man got too gay I had a spring billy that took some of the gayness out of him. Nobody ever wanted more than one taste of the billy. . . . ¶ On another occasion one of the Fox Point roughs tried to beat me out of 10 cents. I took his hat and he took a shot at me with his fist. We clinched and rolled to the ground. I fell on top and pounded his head on the pavement until he cried enough. When he got up he asked for his hat. ¶ He didn't get it. My son, who watched the fight, was holding the hat; and he became so nervous that he tore it to pieces without knowing what he was doing. I gave the fellow the pieces and told him that he was lucky to escape so lightly. I heard afterward that he'd served a sentence in State Prison for biting off a man's nose in a fight. I was thankful that he didn't get hold of mine while we were wrestling.

In fact, Scotty's slogan became "Get a hat, or give a sore head." Precious space in his small wagon was taken up by a box storing stolen bowlers and top hats, testimony of unpaid bills.

Competition picked up. One of the first entrepreneurs with an eye toward expansion was a Providence patrolman named Ruel B. Jones. Eight years of night duty in the constabulary convinced Jones that there was a better way to make a living and that there were other lucrative

The *Providence Journal* was impressed with the large number of hats Scott had claimed.

spots in town for a night lunch operator. So, sometime in 1883, he turned in his badge and nightstick, and by August of that year he was operating a healthy business making the rounds by horse and wagon to clubrooms and saloons.

Later that year, Jones contracted a local wagon builder named Frank Dracont to construct a wagon for him—the first one specifically designed as a lunch cart. It was bright red, with windows bearing the name of Jones, and an open counter along one side. Business boomed, and by 1887 Jones had a chain of at least seven wagons in Providence. Daily, a caravan of them could be seen winding its way to the Jones house to be stocked up for the night's business. Ruel's son George spent his youth baking pies by the hundreds for the family's wagons.

During a year Jones's wagons went through 4,000 pounds of sugar, 1,400 pounds of coffee, 10,000 quarts of milk, 5,500 pounds of chicken, and 12,000 pounds of ham.

Other proprietors sprung up. Mike Stapleton, in his wagon at Snow and Westminster streets, was the first to introduce hot dogs, also in the 1880s, causing many lunch carts to be known as dog wagons. Other operators began offering a free slice of onion with an egg sandwich, or catsup, or even mustard, at no extra charge. When Walter Scott finally retired in 1917, at the age of seventy-six, he complained of the high cost of those extras:

But if some of the early patrons were tough customers, few of them wanted the earth for every nickel they spent. If they bought an egg sandwich they didn't demand a slice of onion to go with it. They didn't swamp their beans in catsup or slather mustard on a "dog" until you couldn't see the "dog." In the last few years downtown I lost several dollars a week in free onions, wasted mustard and excess catsup. ¶ I don't know who invented the slice of onion with the fried egg. I know I didn't. With eggs and everything else high, there wasn't much profit in a sandwich at five cents, especially if you added the piece of onion. . . . ¶ I'd

Sam Jones as a prominent Springfield citizen in 1895. (Connecticut Valley Historical Museum)

probably be in business still if things weren't so high. . . . I guess I've done my share in putting the night lunch on the map, and I'm perfectly willing to step back and let others do the scratching for the dollars that came pretty easy in the old days.

With that, Walter Scott left the lunch cart business.

Sometime in late 1884, Samuel Messer Jones, thirty, a cousin of Ruel B. Jones, moved from Providence, Rhode Island, to Worcester, Massachusetts, and made a name for himself there. Although he is often incorrectly credited with conceiving the lunch wagon, Sam Jones did introduce the first one to Worcester, and it also appears that he was the first one to build a wagon that a customer could enter.

As a jobless mechanical engineer in Providence in 1884, Sam Jones walked home from a lodge meeting one dreary rainy night and spied a lunch wagon with a crowd of people standing around gobbling down some sandwiches and pie. He bought a snack himself, and while he was eating, the night lunch business made a convert. Something else struck him as well, and he wondered why no one had thought of it before: Why make people stand out in bad weather to eat? Sam Jones wanted a lunch cart big enough for people to come inside.

With $200 borrowed from a friend, Jones bought an old express wagon, which he modified as a lunch cart. But he still didn't have enough money to carry out his idea completely, and his first customers stood outside just like everyone else's.

Moving to Worcester shortly afterward, Jones opened for business on October 20, 1884. On Main Street, at the corner of Front, Sam Jones operated the first lunch cart in Worcester. Shortly thereafter, Frank A. McKenzie opened a competing wagon on Front Street, at the corner of Main.

Over the next several years, Jones's profits went to pay off his college-education debts, but

Trying to get customers when he opened his business, Jones placed his first and only ad, in the Worcester City Directory. (Worcester Public Library)

when he had accumulated $800, he invested in a new wagon of his own design. In the fall of 1887 Jones's "first distinctive night lunch wagon" appeared at the New England Fair in Worcester, and, for the first time ever, customers entered a mobile building constructed especially as a lunch cart. The new eatery had a complete kitchen inside, standing room for the customers, intricate woodwork, and stained-glass windows. A newspaper article some years later described them: "Its colored windows were a triumph of the glazier's art, with a bill of fare incorporated in the decorations—-sandwiches, pie, cake, coffee and milk." Such a window became a standard feature in lunch wagon design for the next twenty years.

The idea was an instant success, and Jones expanded his business by adding more wagons at different locations. Before moving to Springfield, Massachusetts, in October 1889, he sold all his wagons but one to Charles H. Palmer of Worcester.

It was in Worcester that the lunch wagon business mushroomed into an industry. On September 1, 1891, Charles H. Palmer received the first patent given for a lunch wagon design. The patent described what was to become the standard configuration for nearly twenty-five years: The wagon had an enclosed body with the forward portion extending over a set of small front wheels, and the rear made narrower to stand between the tops of the high back wheels.

The rear of the wagon was the "kitchen-apartment," with a counter separating it from the "dining-room space," where stools or chairs could be installed. Over one of the high rear wheels was a window for passing out food to those customers standing on the curb; the other side had a carriage window, to which you could drive up to place an order.

Palmer manufactured two models, with an average size of six feet by sixteen. One was a "fancy night café" replete with an elegant ornamental paint job and ringed with stained-glass windows etched with designs. The other model was described as a "night lunch wagon" and was much

Palmer's Sterling Junction lunch wagon factory is visible behind the baskets that brought down his empire. *(Sterling Historical Society)*

simpler in appearance, with fewer, unadorned windows, etched only on the door. Evidently these enclosed carts were extremely popular on cold and stormy nights. They could hold about twenty patrons standing. During the summer the crowd preferred to stand out in the open air.

In 1895, Palmer moved the manufacturing operation about fifteen miles north of Worcester, to the small town of Sterling Junction. He kept the office in Worcester. The office had demonstration wagons on view and also served as a supply station, preparing the food for the many night lunch wagons operated by Palmer. In an 1896 advertisement, Palmer offered a selection of lunch wagons always in stock, as well as wagons to lease.

In 1898, Palmer moved to a house on Fairbanks Street across from his factory, a large wooden two-story structure. He rented out space in the factory to the Brooks Basket Company, which had been burned out several times in previous locations. Fire struck again on the night of December

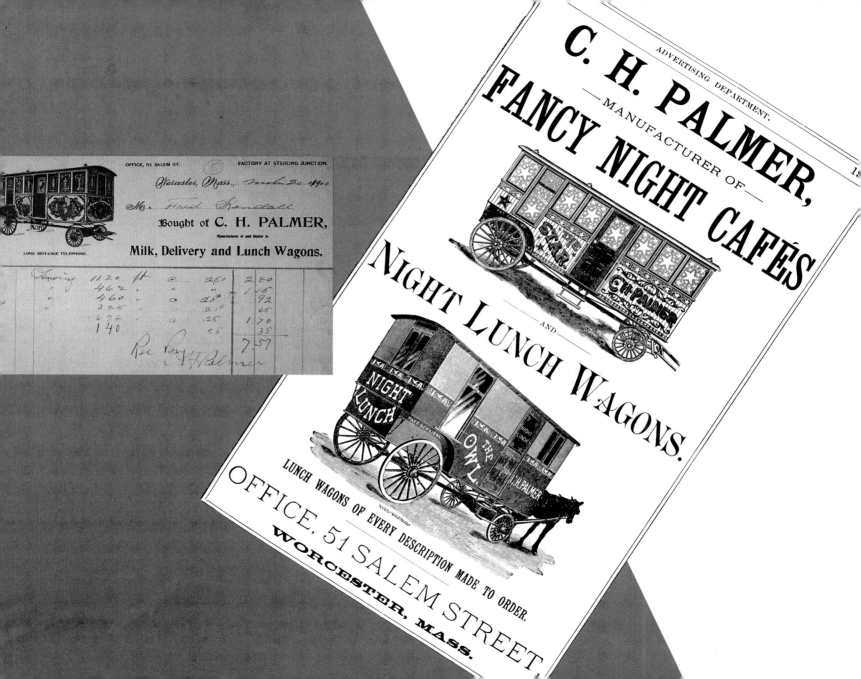

13, 1901, and the building was destroyed. Palmer collected $4,500 insurance for the building, but had no coverage on the wagon stock. In 1905, the Commonwealth of Massachusetts bought the factory site in a land-taking for a nearby reservoir.

Meanwhile, back in Springfield, Massachusetts, Sam Jones introduced the night lunch wagon concept to that town with his wagon, The Owl, and had immediate success. "The Owl" became a popular name for lunch wagons selling to the night-owl trade. By the time Jones had two wagons in operation, one on Court Street and the other on Hampden, an ex–letter carrier named W. L. Clough muscled in on his night business by opening a conventional lunchroom that he kept open "two dozen hours out of the twenty-four." Then, a former Smith & Wesson employee named Wilson Goodrich opened what was described as a "gorgeous" lunch cart, complete with stools for customers to get off their feet. Goodrich soon started building wagons right down the street from Jones's house on Wilcox Street.

As Jones was the original lunch wagon man in town, many asked him to build wagons for them. He did and called his new design the Pioneer Lunch; it cost $1,400 in the spring of 1894. One of his first customers was Walter Scott of Providence. Jones's manufacturing concern at Union Street grew rapidly, until he had built forty carts, one single order being for sixteen carts. Unfortunately, the city of Springfield got fed up with the roving lunch wagons and passed a law banning them from the streets. This shut down Jones's manufacturing business overnight, and, after finally selling off the last of his stock (presumably to an out-of-towner), he retired in 1905 a well-respected man in town. He was also a Knight Templar, a Knight of Pythias, an Odd Fellow, and a socialist.

At one point in Jones's career, he was operating twenty-two carts in Springfield alone, and had wagons leased out in other cities in New England. But this story is nothing compared to that of Thomas H. Buckley, the "Original Lunch Wagon King."

Wilson Goodrich advertised briefly in the Springfield City Directory. (Connecticut Valley Historical Museum)

Opposite, left

An original bill for lumber, signed by Palmer in 1900. (Sterling Historical Society)

Opposite, right

This advertisement shows Charles H. Palmer's 1890s offerings.

T. H. Buckley, the "Original Lunch Wagon King"

Fame and fortune could be made and lost within a few short years in the lunch wagon business, and Thomas H. Buckley, of Worcester, Massachusetts, was without a doubt the preeminent example of a meteoric rise. ¶ Buckley was born on October 21, 1868, in New London, Connecticut. At ten, he moved to Worcester, where he was, successively, a hack driver, an assistant janitor, and a lunch wagon counterboy. In 1888, he built himself a lunch wagon called The Owl. As in the Sam Jones models of the same name, customers could enter Buckley's wagon; the dining area boasted four stools. After opening for business opposite the Soldiers' Monument in Worcester on January 7, 1889, and operating for a number of years at that location, the first Buckley wagon was taken to Denver, Colorado, where, under the management of W. A. Bowen, it introduced the quick-lunch business to the West.

T. H. Buckley's patented lunch wagon body.

Tom Buckley almost always included himself in promotional photographs. This wagon was festooned with a painting of a lunch wagon.

(Worcester Historical Museum)

Preceding page

Kenny's White House Café, one of the last Buckley wagons, featured a new interior layout.

(E. B. Luce, photographer)

The reason Buckley built a lunch wagon in the first place was to market his famous oyster stew. As assistant janitor at Horticultural Hall in Worcester, he'd gained quite a reputation dishing up his stew at the dances held there. He soon decided there was more of a future in constructing lunch carts than in selling stew.

So Tom Buckley committed himself to the manufacture of wagons, and continued to oversee their operation as well. On October 2, 1891, a reporter for *The Record* in Worcester noted the launching of Buckley's latest car, The Palace Café, with the following comment: "I question if there is another night lunch car in America to equal it." With hyperbole typical of the times, the journalist remarked that within a week's time, the car had been "visited and inspected by thousands of persons."

By 1892 Buckley's firm, the New England Night Lunch Wagon Company, had built more than seventy-five wagons. After several reorganizations, the outfit emerged in 1898 as the T. H. Buckley Lunch Wagon Manufacturing and Catering Company, with factory and offices at 281 Grafton Street in Worcester. The shop afforded space to work on twelve wagons at once, and was capable of turning out six to eight wagons a month. Each wagon took three to five weeks to build. In case of emergency—if you absolutely, positively had to have a wagon immediately—the Buckley outfit promised one in *twenty-four to thirty-six hours!*

In addition to building lunch carts, the company also dealt in lunch cart supplies, including dishes and urns, Sabatier knives "specially imported for Lunch Wagon Business," French plate mirrors and decorated glass, linoleum, wagon jacks, and standard fire pails. It was Buckley's innovation to add cooking stoves to lunch wagons, thus expanding the menu considerably from sandwiches, frankfurts, and pies to include hamburgers, baked beans, clam chowder, poached eggs, and waffles.

White House Café 439 was located on Bass Point Road in Nahant, Massachusetts, not far from Lynn. It may well be a Hamel wagon.

(Larry Cultrera)

T. H. Buckley's most famous series of lunch wagons, the White House Cafés, was first introduced on September 4, 1890. The cafés were generally sixteen feet long, six or seven feet wide, and ten feet high.

Buckley was granted two patents on his lunch wagon designs, which were original in that they featured windows encircling the entire wagon. The first patent, dated January 10, 1893, was one-half assigned to Ephraim L. Hamel, of Lynn, Massachusetts.

A native Canadian, Hamel moved to Lynn as a young boy. He was working in the shoe industry as a dinker, or leather cutter, when he became distracted by the lunch wagon business. In 1891, he operated a night lunch from his house at 49 Wheeler Street. The following year he

Buckley posed proudly both outside and in the unbelievable Tile Wagon. (Worcester Historical Museum)

entered into a business arrangement with Tom Buckley and began to manufacture "White House night lunch wagons" in Lynn. Other members of his family, Alexander and Walter, operated wagons for the next twenty years. Ephraim continued his manufacturing concern at Wheeler Street until 1910.

The White House Cafés were quite unlike any other lunch wagons of their day. As one contemporary remarked, "These wagons are perfect little palaces and are admired by all who see them." Each wagon was ringed with windows of frosted glass and red-and-blue flash glass. Using this combination of "the national colors" produced a very pleasing light inside the wagon. In the plainer models the window glass was etched with scroll designs. More elaborate wagons had "pictured lights," as the stained-glass windows were called, some with the four goddesses of music, flowers, day, and night. Others were etched with portraits of the presidents: Washington, Lincoln, Grant, Garfield, Harrison, and Cleveland. Still others featured famous pugilists of the day.

The wagons were painted brilliant white on the outside, and Buckley employed a local artist and sign painter, Charles K. Hardy of Worcester, to embellish them further. Mr. Hardy had many themes: festive hunting scenes, florid landscapes, marine paintings, and works of historical interest. One wagon boasted on the street side a sixteen-foot painting of the battle of New Orleans. All of the views were surrounded by heavy blue-and-gold scrolling. The name White House Café was done in heavy block letters.

Back when Tom Buckley began to manufacture lunch wagons, he had the idea of building himself the most elaborate and gorgeous wagon ever made, and on September 28, 1892, after nearly a year's work, the famous Tile Wagon was completed. It was used for many years for promotional purposes and sent all over the country to compete in wagon exhibitions at county and state fairs, where it garnered over 140 prizes and premiums.

Flash glass was made by fusing colored glass to clear glass. Designs were etched into the color with acid. This window is in the Worcester Historical Museum.

Truly a wonder, the Tile Wagon was constructed on the inside entirely of tiling. As Buckley himself described it, "The floor is laid in mosaic tile of fine design, and the entire ceiling and walls are covered with a bright, glistening opal tiling, inserted in which are artistic designs of numerous flashing brilliants."

The interior was lit by lamps with bases incorporating ivory and gold statuettes of historical figures, mounted on ebony pedestals. The patrons sat on nickeled stools with glass tops as they ate their food and appreciated what Buckley called the "fine workmanship in the historical art. . . . Washington with his cloak thrown carelessly about him, stands as though viewing his army; Lincoln with his pen in hand has just signed the Emancipation Proclamation; . . . and Columbus, gazing into the distance, points down at a revolving globe by his side." Other statuettes included an American newsboy and a violinist.

"The most elaborate cash register ever built" was prominently located behind the counter, which had a top of heavy polished brass. Spittoons made of brass helped complete the interior appointments.

The exterior was covered with heavy beveled German and French plate-glass mirrors inlaid with lacework tracery. A pair of hammered-silver carriage lamps adorned the front of the wagon.

Buckley claimed that the Tile Wagon, built at a cost of $5,440, was worth to him a quarter of a million dollars in advertising. It certainly did help the public open its eyes and take a second look at lunch wagons, although it was far too costly and elaborately decorated to serve practically as an eating establishment. According to Jim Harrington, who ran a Buckley cart in Waterbury, Connecticut, in the 1890s, "People thought the man was crazy to put so much money into a cart."

Other Buckley lunch wagons received publicity in an unusual way. Early on, several were sold to the Church Temperance Society in New York City, under whose proprietorship they offered

A rare interior photo of a lunch wagon with the operators in action. *(Don and Newly Preziosi)*

Hamel's letter to Simmons was addressed care of the night lunch wagon. *(Don and Newly Preziosi)*

stiff competition to the free lunch that was offered in most bars during the 1890s. At that time, a man could go into a saloon, buy a couple of beers for a dime, and partake of a free lunch that included pig's feet, ham and beans, bread, and other tidbits. The Church Temperance Society proceeded to serve meat, vegetables, and coffee in Tom Buckley's lunch carts for that same thin dime. The price was far too low to make this much of a business proposition, but it was not too cheap for a moral issue. In fact, a customer who had only a few pennies could get two pancakes and a cup of coffee for three cents, or, for the same sum, buy a serving of rice pudding. Soup and bread without butter cost a mere six cents. The Church Temperance Society was composed of prominent and influential clergy and laymen of the Protestant Episcopal Church. Proceeds from the wagons were used to build free ice-water fountains in the tenement districts of New York City.

It was the Church Temperance Society that, in 1893, introduced the first lunch wagon to the business area of New York City. The sixteen-foot-by-seven-foot wagon had a plain exterior with the name, The Owl, painted on it. The first wagon was so successful, selling 67,600 ten-cent meals in one year, that the society was able to use the profits to purchase a second wagon for $1,000. The first wagon was located at Herald Square, right in front of the Herald Building. It just so happened that the façade of the Herald Building was adorned with decorative owls. The Owl wagon had no connection with the *Herald,* but the scathingly wry comments of publications like *Life* magazine prompted the *Herald*'s management to ask the Temperance Society to move its wagon. Generally the wagons were set up in neighborhoods where those manning cab stands, car stables, or street railways could be enticed to partake of hot coffee instead of liquor to stay warm. The wagons were in use both day and night.

The temperance wagons were made possible by endowments from a number of prominent

New Yorkers, among them Cornelius Vanderbilt, who was quoted in *The New York Times Magazine* of December 24, 1922, as saying, "I like these restaurants on wheels. When you want one come to me." Mr. Vanderbilt provided not only a wagon, which was installed on the east side of Union Square, but also its name "Good Cheer."

By 1898 there were eight temperance wagons in New York City, some of which were called the Way-Side Inn. In a single year they supplied 230,804 ten-cent meals. Unlike the White House Cafés, the temperance wagons were finished in natural wood with heavy lettering in blue and gold. The flash-glass windows had the Church Temperance Society's monogram on each pane.

Although lunch wagon operators enjoyed terrific success in some New England cities, the carts were slow to take elsewhere. To remedy that situation, Tom Buckley would travel around the countryside choosing towns likely to support lunch wagons. If no one local could be induced into buying one of his eateries, he'd set one up himself, under the direction of a capable, handpicked manager. These were owned by a subsidiary of his, the United States Lunch Wagon Company. In 1898, it operated wagons in twenty-five cities.

Between 1893 and 1898 Buckley set up wagons in some 275 towns all over the country. In each one he claimed to have personally appeared before the local council to plead his case for establishing a lunch cart. He was never refused.

Buckley did not seem to advertise that the White House Café wagons were also available from Ephraim Hamel in Lynn, but Hamel also traveled the countryside looking after his own wagons. On September 26, 1899, Hamel (who was on the road in Auburn, New York) wrote to Charles Simmons at his Columbia Café in Franklin, Pennsylvania. Simmons was running a White House Café and was unhappy that he could only make $10.98 profit from a $38.00 take. Hamel offered to drop the rent to $4.00 a week, in advance, expecting Simmons to keep the wagon very clean.

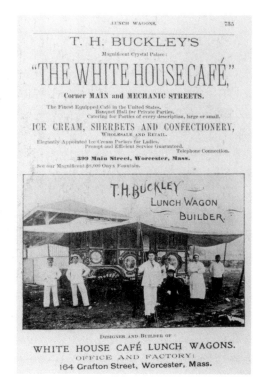

Buckley advertised his stationary and mobile restaurants in the Worcester City Directory.

(Worcester Public Library)

Otherwise, if Simmons was unhappy, he could try to sell the wagon for Hamel.

T. H. Buckley's wagons grew more and more elaborate, and the grand designs no longer always fit the lunch wagon image. In 1897, Buckley opened an incredible restaurant, the White House Café, named after the series of lunch wagons he was promoting at the time. Not a simple wagon but a permanent restaurant, it was informally known as "the Delmonico's of Worcester," in reference to the famous New York City eatery, and was called by the Worcester *Daily Spy* "the boldest and grandest that has ever been attempted in Worcester." The focus was the fantastic soda fountain, made of eighteen thousand square inches of Mexican onyx. Costing $8,000 to build, it sported thirty-six syrup dispensers. According to one view, the White House Café was "so magnificent in its fittings that it awed everyone. Persons fed themselves by viewing it."

This venture of Buckley's failed miserably, setting him back $25,000. On July 15, 1903, at the time of these bankruptcy problems, the Buckley lunch wagon business was reorganized as the T. H. Buckley Car Manufacturing Company.

It was said that the blow of the restaurant's going under broke Buckley's health. In fact, he was such a successful businessman that he still managed to pay off his creditors. In any event, on December 1, 1903, five months after the restaurant went bankrupt, Tom Buckley died of peritonitis at the age of thirty-five. Who knows? Maybe it was his gallivanting around the country to those 275 cities and towns promoting lunch wagons that did him in.

The T. H. Buckley Company continued after his death. By 1905, they had introduced a newly designed wagon with two sets of low wheels, a kitchen area in the center with a U-shaped serving counter, and an eating shelf running around the inside perimeter, with stools along the shelf's length. This interior was a completely new look, but more significant was the change to the outside, which was the beginning of the standard diner shape for years to come.

The Buckley Company's cavernous new factory could accommodate the construction of many new lunch wagons. *(E. B. Luce, photographer)*

The low-wheeled lunch wagons were not designed to trundle around town every night. When wagons were making daily trips through narrow, muddy, rutted streets, high wheels were a necessity, even though they used up valuable kitchen space. The new wagons were built on small wheels used primarily to haul them to their destinations. The wheels remained in case business slacked off and a switch in location was desired.

In their expanded facilities the Buckley company also built electric and steam cars and snowplows. They also had a new slogan: "In this line, we lead the world." But not for long.

Wagons Abound

FIG. 2

When Thomas H. Buckley put lunch wagons on the map, and, indeed, tried to put them in every town, he opened himself up to a lot of competition. Wherever lunch wagons were introduced, there was invariably an established wagon builder or blacksmith ready, willing, and able to knock off a duplicate. ¶ In this fledgling business, the possibilities were so vast that many an entrepreneur could rightly earn the title of pioneer. For example, Wilson Goodrich muscled in on Sam Jones's territory in Springfield, but also sold wagons in Montreal, thus "pioneering" the line of business in Canada. Goodrich himself operated four wagons in Springfield, but would only sell his new $1,200 wagons to "responsible parties wishing to start a night-lunch business in neighboring towns and cities." ¶ An article in *The New York Times Magazine* of February 7, 1926, prompted by the death the previous year of Sam Jones, the lunch wagon pioneer, described the customers and the milieu of the early days:

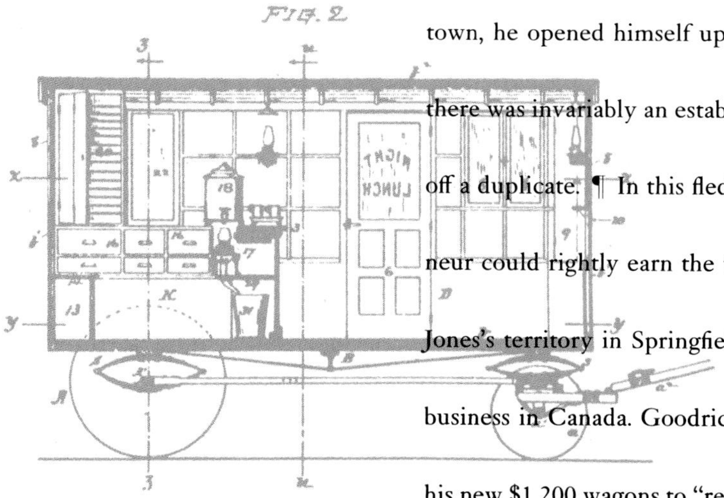

C. H. Palmer's patented night lunch wagon.

J. J. HENNIGAN, Builder of
FRANKLIN CAFE LUNCH WAGONS
22 CUTLER STREET, WORCESTER

WHEN HUNGRY YOU WILL FIND US "ON THE SQUARE"

LINCOLN SQ.   WASHINGTON SQ.   SALEM SQ.   VERNON SQ.

**John Hennigan in a 1907 photograph. He was
another lunch wagon builder in Worcester.
(Worcester Public Library)**

Preceding page
**Miles & Ryan had a unique lunch wagon built for
them. The wooden shelves on the outside
flipped up to make a walk-up counter.**

Into . . . dull-streeted communities came the lunch wagon, its cheery light shining like a hospitable deed in a chilly world. . . . ¶ Here met all sorts and conditions of men on democratic footing. One would be addressed as "Bo" or "Brother" and only the out-of-place and haughtily supercilious person would resent either term, and such a person had no proper title to admittance and companionship. ¶ Here gathered night workers with an hour to spend in eating and chatting, the night owl who sought sustenance before turning in and he who had no place into which he might turn. Often were found in the company dingy men with a suggestion of the eminence from which they had fallen still irremovably upon them—men who could spout Homer in his own tongue; could discuss philosophies that never made them wise and economies that had failed to enrich them. . . . ¶ In the lunch wagon atmosphere one might hear the views of the man on the street on the vital questions—anything and everything from the cross-word puzzle craze to the views of Conan Doyle and Sir Oliver Lodge on life after death and spiritual phenomena. Here gathered the satirist, humorist, raconteur, and over a post-prandial cup of coffee offered leisurely contribution to the discussion.

Art Dawson's lunch wagon in Whitehall, New York, was built by A. H. Closson. Its unusual features included being wired for electricity and having a built-in water tank above the driver's seat, to provide running water in the cart.

(Don and Newly Preziosi)

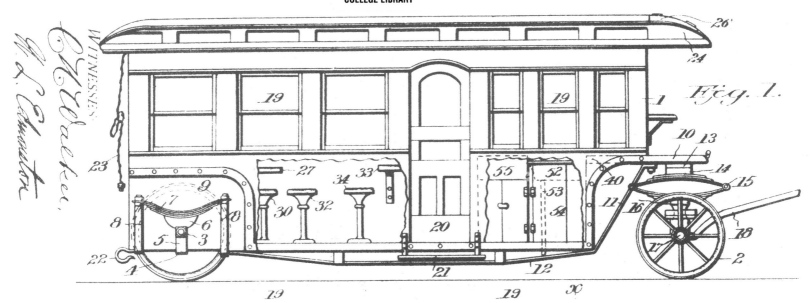

SEEDS ROSS BROS. CO. WHOLESALE
BLANKETS-ROBES FERTILIZERS
ROSS BROS. CO.
M.J. FINNIGAN & CO.
WARREN

And who ruled these roosts? It is well to remember that the night lunch business was a new enterprise. Even around the turn of the century, it was still gathering converts. If Worcester, Massachusetts, is any indication, the lunch cart operators came from every trade. They were men—and only men—who wanted to work for themselves and make their fortunes.

John Hunter, in an unpublished manuscript of 1978, looked at the occupations and ethnic backgrounds of the lunch wagon operators in Worcester from 1900 onward. Of the fourteen listed in the 1900 city directory, only one had been in the same business in 1895. All were from the British Isles or were members of the large French-Canadian immigrant group in Worcester. The number of the latter may be owing to the fact that many of the lunch wagon factory workers were French-Canadian. They had previously held jobs such as shoemaker, carpenter, laborer, wire-worker, stage manager, stonecutter, baker, and foreman. Half were still in the lunch wagon business five years later, and a clerk, a butcher, and a janitor had joined the ranks.

With this diversity of backgrounds, the lunch cart operators provided a milieu that was comfortable for the working-class people who ate there. Lunch wagons became so popular in New England shortly after the turn of the century that in Providence, for example, nearly fifty of the "floating" restaurants were roaming the streets by 1912. It wasn't long, however, before all of those "two frankforts and a cup o' coffee for a nickel" wagons started to become eyesores, their gaily painted exteriors fading and peeling in a few years to a lackluster weatherworn finish. Also, with scores of customers hopping in and out on a nightly basis, the lightweight lunch wagons soon literally opened at the seams.

Citizen complaints began in earnest when some wagons stayed on into the late morning to do more business; this was a clear violation of their operating permits, because the early lunch carts were only allowed to remain on the streets from dusk till dawn because of traffic congestion. So

The only establishments open at night in this view of Worcester were the lunch wagons outside M. J. Finnigan & Company and the one across the street, barely visible under the glare of the streetlight. (E. B. Luce, photographer)

the cities cracked down and declared that the wagons had to be off the streets by ten A.M. A number of operators quickly discovered a good way around the rules. The simplest answer was to pick a good site, off the road, where the lunch carts could set up permanently.

For most owners life was considerably simpler once the wagons became permanently situated and the need to drive them around town was eliminated. Supporting the romantic image of the horse-drawn lunch cart was really a lot of trouble, and soon most everybody was happy to abandon it. Thus occurred the greatest change in the history of the business—the transformation of the wandering horse-drawn wagon into the stationary (yet still portable) lunch car.

Once the wagons were off the streets, they were not restricted to specific hours, and in order to capitalize on the hungry masses, many stayed open around the clock. The menu also expanded at this time. A wagon in Springfield offered the following in 1893:

Corned Beef	.10	Corned Beef and Beans	.10
Corned Beef Hash	.10	Pork and Beans	.10
Ham and Beans	.10	Cold Ham	.10
Beef Stew	.10	Hot Frankfurts	.10
Lamb Tongues	.10	Boiled Eggs	.10
Coffee and Rolls	.10	Coffee and Doughnuts	.10
Sandwiches	.05	Pies	.05
	Tea, Coffee and Milk .05		

T. A. Seamans and his crew posed in front of his stationary Quick Lunch in Sanford, Maine, in a postcard view he sent to his mother in 1911.

In addition there would be clam chowder on certain days, and fruits in their season. Not only did the business profit, but the public appreciated being able to grab a bite, any hour, day or night.

The constantly evolving menu has always been, of course, an integral part of the restaurant business. Some wagons were sought after for their specialties. The Trilby sandwich was named after a counterman in James Harrington's White House Café in Waterbury, Connecticut. This was a chopped-ham sandwich with a slice of Bermuda onion. At the Cornell Café, also known as the Sibley Dog, a lunch cart conveniently placed near the Cornell campus in Ithaca, New York, the local favorite was the Desdemona. This was a handful of hamburg steak stirred up with an egg and fried.

This crowded lunch wagon interior had the bill of fare in plain view. (Don and Newly Preziosi)

The *Worcester Telegram* of February 12, 1900, noted a big menu change in available fare: "Lunch Carts Put the Frisky Bean off Their Lists." Lunch wagon operators had quietly removed pork and beans from their menus. This was purely a profit-making move. The nickel-a-plate servings filled the customers up too quickly. It would take two or three five-cent frankfurts to do the same job, so in the interests of making more money, beans went by the wayside.

The Big Three

There certainly was money to be made dishing out dogs in lunch wagons, but the *big* money was

made by the men with the foresight to manufacture new and improved lunch cars. Starting in the

early 1900s, three companies came into being which transformed the industry—and spawned

from their ranks most of the subsequent companies, including those still building diners today.

Lunch car drawing from *The Diner* Magazine.

These pioneers included the Patrick J. Tierney Company, the Worcester Lunch Car and Carriage

Manufacturing Company, and the Jerry O'Mahony Company. ¶ Patrick Joseph Tierney, the son

of Irish immigrants, was born and raised in New Rochelle, New York. He was twenty-nine in

1895, when he decided that two lunch wagons would earn him twice as much money as the one

he was operating. This way of thinking eventually had him "dotting wagons in good locations here

and there in neighboring towns until he owned a string of thirty-eight—the first lunch wagon

THE BIRTH OF THE BUSINESS

This old horsecar was changed into a lunch wagon. Fancy flash-glass windows were added, but otherwise it was a rather mundane establishment. *(Don and Newly Preziosi)*

The Tierney Company did more than just sell you a lunch wagon; it also helped you find the right location. *(Kullman Industries)*

Preceding page
The Rite-Bite is ready to be hauled to Philadelphia on pneumatic tires. The iron wheels used on the assembly line lay alongside.
(Atwater Kent Museum)

Types of Profitable Locations for Dining Cars

syndicate," as reported in the New York *Herald Tribune*. Tierney placed the wagons in busy spots on leased property and ran them twenty-four hours a day. These Tierney-run wagons were manufactured by T. H. Buckley. By 1905 Tierney was constructing his own "improved" wagons at a rate of three per year in a small garage at his home on Cottage Place in New Rochelle. The wagons sold for $1,000 apiece.

P. J. "Pop" Tierney brought new stability to the lunch wagon business at a crucial time. Just around the turn of the century, the lunch wagon rage suffered its first major setback. In city after city the traditional horse-drawn trolleys were being replaced by electric streetcars, and not only the transit companies' car barns, but empty lots all over town, began filling with these battered old wrecks. Soon the companies began to sell them off for a pittance to anyone who would haul them away. Once the pride of their cities, the discarded horse trolleys were converted by their new owners into chicken coops, newspaper stands, housing, and immobile lunch wagons. With a little elbow grease, some paint, and about fifty dollars' worth of equipment—a counter and stools, a coffee urn, a grill, and some dishes—a fellow had himself a lunch car. Nothing, though, could mask the shoddy state of these scarred old trolleys.

Their effect was absolutely devastating. For the first time, a stigma, growing out of the influx of the disreputable-looking trolley lunches, began to be attached to the lunch wagon. Until the advent of the surplus trolleys, lunch carts had been considered perfectly respectable places to go to for a quick meal and were patronized by all types of people.

It is true that, because of their hours, lunch carts were, right from the beginning, favorite haunts of those who were out drinking the night away. A drawing of an inebriated soul steadying himself against a brick wall accompanied an article entitled "The Night Lunch Business" in the Springfield *Graphic* of April 29, 1893. It began with some verse:

Often on a midnight dreary
Rounders muddle with the query
Where they'll go to get a soberfying, satisfying bite:
White House, Palace, Ruth, Oasis, Nox or wheelless midnight places,
And then unto the nearest one they make erratic flight.

In fact the occasional drunk never really kept the good customers away from the lunch wagons. The converted trolleys, though, with their dark corners, drafts, and leaky roofs, surely did. Unattractive and uninviting to the general public, they began to cater to an even less reputable type of night trade. The police helped to reinforce the bad image of the trolley lunches, as they were always sure to include them on their rounds while looking for shady characters and desperate underworld types who just might have committed crimes.

By the late 1890s, even the "real" lunch wagons were getting a bad reputation, and the business was caught in an uphill battle. When P. J. Tierney embarked on the manufacture of lunch wagons, he built so many good ones that he helped overshadow the bad image and restored to the lunch car its lost respectability.

It wasn't at all long before Tierney was selling more lunch cars than anyone else around. He loved lunch cars and would do practically anything to get someone started running his own. If he liked you, you'd pay one fourth down and the rest on time. If he liked you a lot and you had an old lunch wagon (if you had an old lunch wagon he'd almost surely like you a lot), he'd take the wagon as down payment. And if he loved you, he'd give you a new car, and all you had to do was promise to pay for it.

P. J. Tierney made it his business to get out among the people and sell his lunch cars personally.

The Tierney outfit prefabricated the wall sections and put the lunch cars together on an assembly line. *(Pat Fodero)*

It was for this purpose that he traveled to Greenwich, Connecticut, on January 10, 1917. One Mrs. Benham of Yonkers accompanied him, and they inspected there a lunch wagon similar to one she intended to buy. After supper at the wagon, they returned to Yonkers. Upon entering Mrs. Benham's home, Mr. Tierney complained of gas pains in his stomach. He took a dose of Bromo-Seltzer and was persuaded to lie down while a doctor was summoned. But when the physician arrived, Mr. Tierney was dead. He had died within ten minutes of lying down, and acute indigestion was given as the cause. For lack of contrary evidence, it is assumed Mrs. Benham did purchase her lunch wagon.

When Pop Tierney died a millionaire, his sons Edward J. (Ned) and Edgar T. (Dick), who had grown up with the business, took over. In their advertising they tried to build their father into a legend, and they largely succeeded:

It was Patrick J. Tierney, the founder of the *Dining Car Business of America*, who was the first to take the *Dining Car* off the street and to give it a permanent location. . . . It was Patrick J. Tierney who first conceived the idea of equipping the *Car* with tile. . . . It was he who first installed exhaust fans, skylights and ventilators and who replaced the old kerosene lamps by electric lights.

And it was also Patrick J. Tierney who brought the toilet inside. Although his sons, it appears, were not especially interested in this claim, there is little doubt that many patrons over the years were highly appreciative.

Wendell's Corner Snack Bar in North Falmouth, Massachusetts, is an early-twenties diner with the not-so-celebrated toilet inside.

Back in Worcester, Massachusetts, Wilfred H. Barriere, the carpentry foreman at T. H. Buckley's company, decided to set out on his own. Early in 1906, along with a Worcester blacksmith named Stearns A. Haynes, he began building lunch wagons at Haynes's shop at 69 Franklin Street. One of Barriere's first wagons was built for the Haven brothers of Providence, Rhode Island, cousins of the late Thomas H. Buckley. They had had a White House Café since 1893 and decided to replace it with a brand new Barriere model.

At the same time, Philip H. Duprey of Worcester was looking closely at the lunch wagon business. As an established insurance and real-estate agent, he undoubtedly noticed the city's burgeoning industry. In December 1906 he decided to get into it and formed the Worcester Lunch Car and Carriage Manufacturing Company, with himself as president and Granville M. Stoddard

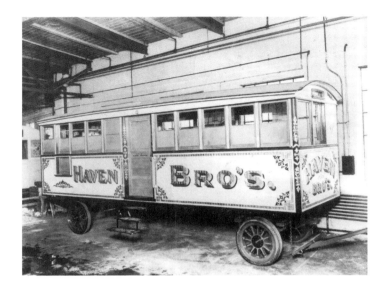

This low-wheeled, barrel-roofed wagon, still in the shop, is ready to move to Providence. *(Worcester Historical Museum)*

Wilfred H. Barriere became the head carpenter at the brand-new Worcester Lunch Car and Carriage Manufacturing Company. *(E. B. Luce, photographer)*

as treasurer. His first move was to buy out the local lunch wagon builder, Barriere. During the week ending December 22, 1906, Barriere's fledgling company was acquired by Duprey and Stoddard. Barriere and Haynes were each paid a salary of $25 a week to run the operation and turn out the wagons.

The small organization of half a dozen carpenters, blacksmiths, and painters, working on and off, was soon joined by another Buckley carpenter, Charles P. Gemme, a French-Canadian who had immigrated with his family from Marieville, Quebec. He started work one month after the others, on January 22, 1907.

Duprey and Stoddard ran the business from their offices downtown. Within a year and a half, Barriere and Haynes had both left, and Gemme was put in charge of the factory on May 23, 1908. Charlie Gemme wasn't officially called foreman until 1910, but he had a hand in the design of every lunch car manufactured by the company. Within a few years, he was recruiting family

The first Worcester Lunch Car was documented before it ever left the plant. The new roofline had a barrel shape when seen from the end, but a monitor, or "railroad"-style, clerestory running the length. (E. B. Luce, photographer)

members (he was one of fifteen children) to work at the plant on Franklin Street. Wilfred Barriere's brother, Napoleon, came to work for Worcester Lunch from the T. H. Buckley Car Company when they folded in 1908. Apparently the company just couldn't make it for long after Thomas Buckley died. Napoleon Barriere continued working for the Worcester Lunch Car Company for decades. Although Wilfred left before his brother joined the company, he was to reappear sixteen years later.

The very first Worcester Lunch Car built, the American Eagle Café, serial number 200 (who would want number 1?) was installed on Myrtle Street, behind the post office, in Worcester in 1907. The most prominent of Gemme's innovations was the roofline: a monitor with a raised clerestory and operable windows to vent the car. Until that time all lunch wagons, except Closson's, were built with barrel roofs. The exterior was elaborately painted in the tradition of the Buckley wagons, right down to pinstriping on the spokes of the two sets of low wheels. On the entrance façade, there were four pictorial flash-glass windows, as well as flash glass in the door depicting a drawn curtain overlooking a veranda, a bill-of-fare window, and one advertising handout service. Two paintings in the style of the Dutch Old Masters flanked the sliding door. The street side featured a painting of a bald eagle in a patriotic motif.

On the inside, the design was based upon the old wagon layout, with the kitchen on the end. Gas lamps provided lighting. The entire interior was finished in highly varnished natural wood, with the ceiling decorated with gold-leaf striping and fleurs-de-lis. A few wooden-topped stools were provided along the eating shelf.

By the time Worcester Lunch had built its ninth wagon, the Buffet Lunch, owned by Peter Neebonne, the size was half again as long, with a center entrance in addition to one at the end. The roofline had been simplified to a barrel style. Windows in the body of the car could be opened

for ventilation. The painting scheme was considerably less elaborate. The interior layout had been changed; the new scheme placed the kitchen along the length of the car, with a long serving and eating counter and a row of stools running down the middle. As the lunch cars grew longer, the size of the kitchen was increased in direct proportion to the seating. The handout window was eliminated. And another innovation had taken place: This car was wired for electricity.

Worcester Lunch was successful right from the start. By 1910 there were twelve workers employed, busy nine hours a day, six days a week.

In 1913 the last of the early pioneers, Jerry O'Mahony of Bayonne, New Jersey, got into the business. While working in his father's bar and grill in Bayonne, Jerry was impressed by the successful lunch car owners who patronized the place. Invariably, they seemed to be rolling in cash. Jerry got the idea to purchase his own wagon and he convinced his brother to join him in the enterprise. It was undoubtedly a Tierney diner at Thirty-fourth Street and Seventh Avenue in New York City that young Jerry O'Mahony purchased at some point after 1910. Its immediate success induced them to purchase a larger car and then acquire a chain of seven already in operation.

But then he had a vision: that of a deluxe car with every conceivable modern convenience, a veritable "Pullman" type of lunch car. He decided to manufacture lunch cars.

In 1913, at the age of thirty-two, Jerry joined in a partnership with John J. Hanf and built two lunch wagons in a small garage in Bayonne. The first wagon was sold before it was completed. A 1922 catalogue stated, "From that day to this he has never caught up with the demand although he has repeatedly enlarged his facilities." A Mr. Kelley bought the first O'Mahony lunch car for $1,900, and he put it into service at Elm and Midway avenues, in Arlington, New Jersey. Mr.

Eriksen's Lunch is an early O'Mahony car.

(George Mahoney)

Opposite

Worcester's second car was wheeled out into the open air for documentation. (E. B. Luce, photographer)

Kelley operated the car for ten years and sold it for $1,500, upgrading to a larger O'Mahony diner.

Jerry vowed to construct the most beautiful and the most rugged lunch cars available. When a customer from northern New England came to the O'Mahony plant, he wanted solid proof that their product could withstand a harsh climate with heavy snow. Jerry didn't hesitate. He called his workers and ordered them onto the roof of a finished car. The skeptic, having seen all he needed, left with a new O'Mahony model.

The lunch cars built by Jerry O'Mahony in the teens were all barrel-roofed models. They all had the same general appearance and size, though custom models were always available. Standard size was approximately ten feet wide by twenty-six feet long. There was usually a center entrance through a sliding door, and a symmetrical façade of five windows flanking. The narrow end had four "bays," consisting either of four windows or of three windows and a side entrance. There were two operable transom windows at each narrow end. Prior to the 1920s, the windows were flash-glass, etched with fancy geometric floral designs. Sometimes a menu or other signage was

From the beginning, Jerry O'Mahony's lunch cars had the counter running the full length of the car. *(George Mahoney)*

featured at one end. A popular window was etched to read: "PURE FOOD. CLEANLINESS. QUICK SERVICE AND POPULAR PRICES." This stained-glass window also summed up the whole philosophy of the lunch car business.

The exterior sheathing was built of three-quarter-inch beaded pine paneling. In a detail taken directly from the horse-drawn wagons, the earliest O'Mahony cars had fancy painted and molded corner posts. The cars were custom painted with the business names in elaborate block letters and floral borders.

The O'Mahony company built only low-wheeled, permanently installed cars, and eventually became the largest manufacturer of the time. Soon Jerry was unabashedly proclaiming a slogan remarkably similar to that of T. H. Buckley: "In our line, we lead the world."

A Diner-a-Day

Sometime between March 1923 and March 1924, the lunch car became a "diner." History does

not record which company was the first to use the word "diner," but as soon as that happened,

the nomenclature began changing. In a 1922 Jerry O'Mahony catalogue, one page pictured eleven

"lunch cars" heading for their destinations from the factory. There was not a "diner" in the bunch.

Two years later, the new catalog showed a similar page with thirteen cars en route, ten of which

were called "diners." ¶ The name "lunch car" had outlived its usefulness. Born in the days of

night lunches, it wasn't enough to describe the expanded fare of breakfast, lunch, and dinner

available in the twenty-four-hour cars. In a September 1924 article promoting the first Jerry

O'Mahony lunch car in Chicago, the author warned those unfamiliar with O'Mahony cars not to

An O'Mahony advertisement.

(George Mahoney)

be confused by the name "lunch car." This was a complete restaurant in every detail with an

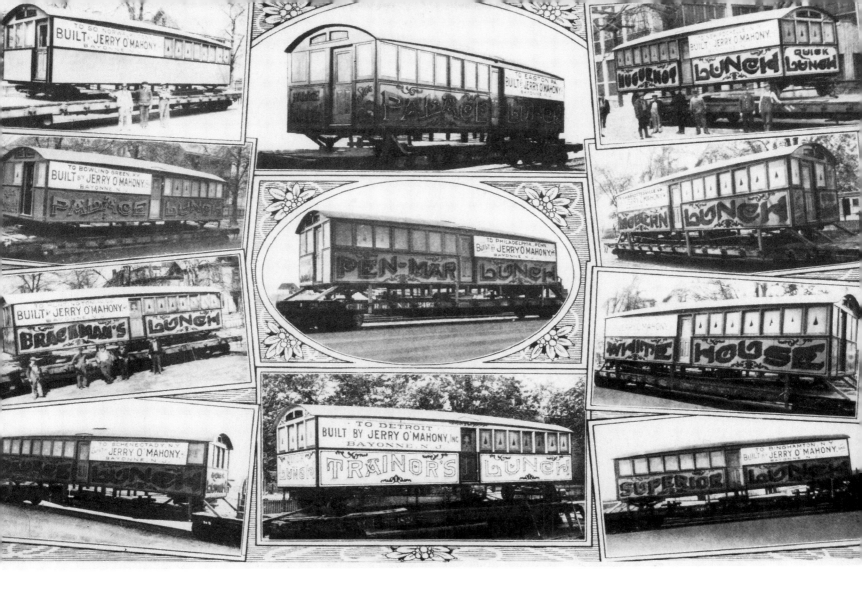

By the mid-1920s, Jerry O'Mahony had moved to his fifth, largest, and last plant in order to keep up with the demands for his diners. *(George Mahoney)*

Preceding page

Eleven Jerry O'Mahony lunch cars are ready for delivery by rail. *(George Mahoney)*

The O'Mahony Factory at Elizabeth, N. J.

Partial view of the cabinet shop where all doors, sash and wood trim are assembled and finished. All finished lumber is carefully dry-kilned before coming to this department.

Loading Platform at the Jerry O'Mahony Plant

A corner of the mill where the most modern wood-working machinery cuts and planes the wood to be used in O'Mahony Dining Cars.

Section of an erection aisle showing the various stages of O'Mahony Dining Car construction.

Looking through one of the erection aisles. Note how superior lighting and plenty of open space give the men better opportunity to do their best work.

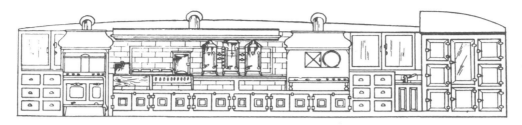

interior that compared favorably to any high-class lunch room. The author suggested a more appropriate name would be "dining car."

In making their image classier, lunch cars became dining cars, an allusion to the fine dining experience of the railway. And, as on the railway, "dining car" was quickly shortened to "diner."

This Jerry O'Mahony drawing demonstrates the compact, space-saving back-wall layout.

(George Mahoney)

Walking through the sliding door into the middle of any 1920s diner, the customer was struck instantly by the long marble counter. By now, all diners were configured with the counter running the length of the car. This came about because of the desire for more seating, which required more food-preparation room. Diners at this time had much more equipment, in addition to a lot more storage and work space. There were steam tables, burners, griddles, ice boxes, and sandwich boards. Now there were dishes, bowls, and mugs to store and wash, along with pots and pans and utensils. All this fit very well behind the ever lengthening counter. This "backbar" area became a model of efficiency and was integral to the success of the diner.

In the more elaborate models the patron saw a dazzling, almost dizzy combination of ceramic tile designs on the walls and floor. As natural light streamed through the skylights and etched and frosted windows, it was reflected off the shiny metal coffee urns and range hoods onto the ceiling of highly varnished wood or brightly painted metal. The stools were wholly constructed of white porcelain enamel, sometimes topped with wooden or leather seats.

Following World War I, the United States was riding high on a building boom. This age of prosperity was very good to the diner business. Returning soldiers and other entrepreneurs

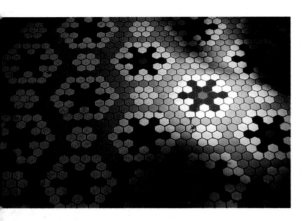

The floor in Phil's Diner in Los Angeles, built by Charles Amend, is an example of artistry in mosaic tile.

wanted to go into business for themselves . . . and the diner business, with its low overhead and installment purchasing plan, was a very attractive one.

The big three diner builders embarked on a massive media blitz, placing full-page articles in many newspapers and magazines. The purpose was not only to promote the industry, but also to show the great strides it had made. "The Social Progress of the Lunch Wagon" filled page 3 of the Sunday, December 28, 1924, issue of the New York *Herald Tribune*. This article was placed by P. J. Tierney Sons, Inc. After giving a brief history of the company, along with the usual mistakes (most prominently giving credit to the Women's Christian Temperance Union instead of the Church Temperance Society for introducing lunch wagons to New York City), the piece went on to extol the palatial features of the latest Tierney-designed dining cars. Standard cars sold for $7,000 to $9,500, completely equipped, though it was possible to spend much more on special sizes and appointments. (Worcester Lunch Cars were selling for $4,550 to $7,500 at this time.)

Other articles gently poked fun at the old wagons, implying that the new modern diner was a far cry from "that ludicrous vehicle that lumbered behind a bleary horse and bore such horrible colors and embellishments."

The diner of the 1920s had in fact made great advances over its predecessor. In size alone, it was impressive. The smallest diners were twice the length of a standard-size wagon. With customers thronging to diners, they had to increase in size. On Martha's Vineyard, longtime operator William Vinson Ripley always demanded a diner which the manufacturers claimed would be too large to construct safely. With the addition of steel into the framework in the twenties, the size of diners was almost unrestricted.

In interior appointments, innovation continued to be the rule. A new emphasis on cleanliness and ease of operation was touted: "There are no dark corners where the dirt can lurk." Tile floors

Steel frame of the Jerry O'Mahony Dining Car

Steel frameworks made for stronger and bigger diners. (George Mahoney)

Ted's Diner, in Milford, Massachusetts, was a big early diner.

and white tile walls were predominant. Countertops were often of white marble or white opalite, an opaque glass. Some diners built by Jerry O'Mahony even had white metal ceilings.

For behind the counter, all manufacturers offered a built-in refrigerator, steam table, gas stove, grill, dessert display cases, coffee urns, and exhaust hoods fabricated of gleaming German silver, an alloy that was the precursor to stainless steel. Through the 1920s, the back wall was finished in ceramic tile.

In 1922, if you purchased an O'Mahony diner, some equipment and supplies were included, but you still had to buy a cash register, menu boards, your dishes, silver, and pots and pans. By 1924, these were all included, which may have been a reflection on the stiff competition at the time.

The overwhelming whiteness of this O'Mahony diner emphasized its cleanliness. (George Mahoney)

The cover of the 1926 O'Mahony catalogue. (George Mahoney)

The O'Mahony sales literature began to include a number of derogatory remarks about other manufacturers' diners. The O'Mahony cars had roofs sheathed in the "best quality" No. 1 B white pine, not the "much cheaper and inferior" North Carolina pine that some of the competition used. They had ceilings of the "best" V-beaded quartered oak, which never warped or peeled off like the veneer ceilings used in inferior makes of cars. Now the less expensive option was an aluminum ceiling. The serving-counter top and other operating shelves were of the "finest" silver-gray marble, heavier than ordinarily used in dining car construction, and therefore less liable to crack or chip in service. No " 'bugs' or so-called seconds" in ceramic tile ever entered the O'Mahony plant.

Not to take criticism lying down, the Tierney sons took credit for being greatly responsible for the success of the diner business as diners grew from a novelty to an American institution: "Of the hundreds of lunch wagons scattered from coast to coast not a few of the finest will be found upon inspection to come from the Tierney New Rochelle factory."

P. J. Tierney Sons, Inc., also continuously operated diners, in addition to building them for others. In 1923 they set up a new organization, the Tierney Operating Company, turning over all cars run by them in New York City, Westchester County, and New Jersey. In a public offering of 250,000 shares of common stock, half of their holdings, the Tierneys embarked on a program to set up, on average, one new diner a week for the next four years, hoping to have two hundred diners eventually in place.

As the Tierneys worked toward this goal, they moved into expanded quarters, and celebrated with the liveliest dinner in dining car history. On July 10, 1925, they gave a gala dinner for close to a thousand people in the new plant. Many speeches were made praising the boys and their father and mother. The toastmaster, Edward Cordial, mentioned in his opening remarks that if

William V. Ripley continually traded in his old diners for bigger ones. Ripley operated in Oak Bluffs on Martha's Vineyard. He started out with a handout wagon, graduated to an "Owl," moved on to a Buckley, was converted by O'Mahony (below) and ended his career with this forty-five-foot-by-fifteen-foot diner (right). *(Norma N. Holmes)*

The Lackawanna Trail Diner, now known as Jerry's, is one of the few Tierneys still in operation.

he tried to talk about the Tierneys, he could go on for a year, and then only touch the surface.

It was an evening not to be missed. George Bayright, speaking on behalf of the Tierney employees, said they considered the reception to be one of the greatest events of their lives. Time and again the glorious accomplishments of P. J. Tierney and his sons were extolled. To illustrate how far they had come in the business, George Bayright reminisced:

We all remember when the lunch wagon business was not considered a business, when a horse was attached to the wagon and it was stealthily drawn to some advantageous spot to dole out meager rations to the wayfarer, to again be carted away to an obscure corner at the break of day. Tonight's reception is the most convincing evidence of the growth of this business.

The evening was a testimonial to the phenomenal success of the P. J. Tierney Sons Company, which had become (arguably) the largest manufacturer of diners in the world—at least that's what was painted on the side of the factory.

Their great new plant was turning out a diner a day, and this was only *half* of the production capacity! Under a roof supported by the longest span trusses to be found in Westchester County, 250 men could work on up to forty-six cars in various stages of construction at a time.

In the April 1926 issue of *Popular Science Monthly,* George Lee Dowd, Jr., reported on the progress made at the Tierney plant, in an article slanted to the editorial bias of the magazine: "Science Runs the Lunch Wagon." He claimed that the Tierneys were building at least two new cars a day and had close to a thousand of their diners operating across the country. When Dowd said that Tierney would be sending a hundred diners to Florida alone in 1926, his observations became suspect. It is inconceivable that there could be so many orders for diners from such a distant part of the country.

This interior view of the Tierney Training School shows the learning center for many would-be operators. *(Pat Fodero)*

This diner was being constructed on Cleveland Avenue in Worcester, at the house of Wilfred H. Barriere. *(Worcester Historical Museum)*

The *Popular Science Monthly* article detailed the workings of the Tierney Training School, "one of the strangest schools in the world—a lunch wagon training college where future proprietors are taught to wash dishes, scrub floors, cook, bake, order provisions economically, serve good meals without waste, and a hundred and one secrets of pleasing the eating public." In a diner set up next to the factory, the Tierneys taught their buyers the ropes during the two-week period in which their new diner was being constructed. After they set out on their own and opened for business, the company stayed in touch and offered advice in its trade publication, *Tierney Talks*.

Along with Worcester Lunch, Tierney, and O'Mahony, quite a few new companies arrived on the scene. Some were very short-lived (see the Directory), but the number of new builders was a good indication that the diner business was going great guns.

Wilfred H. Barriere (the original Worcester Lunch employee) came back to the Worcester, Massachusetts, company in December 1924 and stayed for a year and a half. Having been away from the business for sixteen years, he needed to relearn his trade. He left, again, on June 25, 1926, and started his own manufacturing concern, building diners in his backyard on Cleveland Avenue and on site. An untrained eye might have mistaken a Barriere diner for a Worcester Lunch Car, they were so similar.

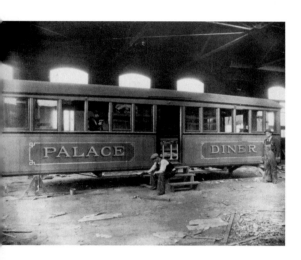

The Palace Diner is shown under construction by the Pollard Company in Lowell, Massachusetts. (George of Lowell)

Opposite

The Park Street Diner shows Barriere's unusual end-window configuration under the roofline. (Worcester Historical Museum)

The distinguishing feature of a Barriere was the use of three transom windows, as opposed to Worcester's two, in the end walls under the barrel roof. On the fancy Barriere models, the windows were elaborately leaded, with stained and etched glass.

In nearby Lowell, Massachusetts, Wilson H. Pollard, a former lunch cart operator, hooked up with Joseph E. Carroll, a sheet-metal worker, and the Pollard Company built several diners. In the western Massachusetts city of Springfield, Wason Manufacturing Company, a streetcar and rail-car builder owned by the J. G. Brill Company of Philadelphia, opened a dining-car division, Brill Steel Diners.

Another Brill subsidiary, the G. C. Kuhlman Car Company in Cleveland, Ohio, built Brill Steel Diners, concentrating on the central and Midwestern markets.

The Lake Erie region of western New York State became a diner manufacturing center. Charles Ward and Lee F. Dickinson formed the Ward & Dickinson Company in Silver Creek. The Mulholland Spring Company, a carriage and car-body builder in Dunkirk, introduced a line of diners. There were four other small concerns turning out diners in the Silver Creek area, one of which was Sorge Brothers.

In New Jersey, the Paterson Vehicle Company, in business since 1886, started building Silk City Diners. In Newark, Samuel Kullman left P. J. Tierney Sons to strike out on his own. In Camden, William H. Dodge ran the Dodge Dining Car Company.

This new crop of diner builders didn't only duplicate the current models available, although some did. It was still pretty hard to tell a Worcester from a Tierney from an O'Mahony. Throw in Pollard and Barriere, and you almost had to find a manufacturer's tag to absolutely determine who built what.

Ward & Dickinson's "Ward" Dining Car was most distinctive for its monitor roof, the low

Ward & Dickinson built a lot of look-alike diners in the Lake Erie region. (Brian Butko)

wheels cut into the body of the car, and the asymmetrical position of the front door, similar to the entrance on a trolley. The car was "practically fireproof," with its steel exterior skin and metal interior walls and ceiling. The standard color scheme was canary with black trim, making "a very pleasing combination that has a strong appeal to the public." In an unusual use of materials, the diner's floor was "Armstrong's half-inch thick Battleship Linoleum which will last a life-time." The six-door icebox, the display case, and the interior trim were built of hand-rubbed American walnut. The countertop was one-inch-thick opaque glass, known as Vitrolite.

Wason Manufacturing Company began building diners in November 1927. By April, the demand for quick deliveries was so great that production was stepped up to turn out one complete diner a week. Their Brill Steel Diners had a look of their own. Not surprisingly, the diners strongly resembled railroad cars in their exterior form and finish. Brills were boxy diners with monitor roofs and rather plain exteriors. The metal skins were finished in lacquer with modest sign-painting . . . but usually gussied up with a flower box or two. The interiors had ceilings and walls of porcelain enamel, plus tile floors and mahogany trim. One Brill innovation appearing in many diners was a glass countertop constructed as a refrigerated display case for salads, fruit, and pastry.

The Wason Manufacturing plant in Springfield sent diners to the "Maine woods," throughout the rest of New England, and to New York, New Jersey, and Pennsylvania. When going short distances, the cars were shipped in assembled form. Narrow diners were securely blocked onto railroad flatcars and shipped via the Boston & Maine Railroad, which had a siding on the property. In February 1929, Wason sent the Royal Diner all the way to Los Angeles. This car was "knocked down" after assembly, boxed for shipment by rail to New York, then sent by boat through the Panama Canal. A Brill representative supervised its erection in California.

Throughout the 1920s, most diners were still located within cities, near retail districts, traffic centers, theaters, and factories. But soon new diners started popping up along the highways as well. This was the beginning of the age of the roadside diner, which sprang up to feed the flood of auto drivers traveling the new motorways.

In 1928, the Hi-Way Diners Club of New England, Inc., was formed in Springfield, with the goal of creating a "chain system of the better kind of Dining Cars throughout the United States and located on the National Highways." They wanted to cash in on the ever-growing number of people traveling day and night. According to the club, nearly everything along the highway had been improved upon: wonderful new automobiles, long-distance trucks, and filling stations. Even the roads were now concrete. The exception was that there were no clean, convenient places to eat. Through the advisory services of William H. Dodge, now the New England sales representative for Brill Steel Diners, the "finest EXCLUSIVE locations" would soon be filled with new Brill diners under the chain's management.

From the back of the Blue Parrot Diner menu, a Brill located in Manchester, New Hampshire. (Henry Ford Museum & Greenfield Village)

Opposite

This unit of the Hi-Way Diners Club of New England was one of a chain. (Henry Ford Museum & Greenfield Village)

Their ambitious expansion program called for ten diners to be located in each of five New England states by the end of 1928. The first "luxuriously appointed" diner, complete with a soda fountain, opened May 1 at State and Main streets in Springfield, Massachusetts, with four more to come within two months. A commissary office and storeroom for the chain was located adjacent to this flagship diner. Five additional units were ordered by the Boston branch of the syndicate, the first, located on Stuart Street in the Back Bay district, being called Brown's No. 1 Dina Car, no doubt in a play on the Boston accent. It is not known how many diners were successfully launched as a part of the New England chain.

As the new diner builders gained a foothold in the ever-expanding market, one of the big three went under. In their desire to build the most diners *and* run the most diners, the Tierney sons ran into trouble. In October of 1926, Samuel Untermyer, of New York City, purchased a controlling interest in the company for $500,000. Under the terms of the agreement, the reorganized company would refrain from operating diners, and therefore would not compete with their buyers. Another aim was to increase production from the current level of 225 diners a year (roughly one per working day).

Within four months of losing control of their business, the Tierney sons and their uncle Daniel organized a new company, Tierney Brothers, Inc., to build diners. Capitalizing on the advertising of P. J. Tierney Sons, Inc., they fraudulently attempted to profit from the original company's reputation. They were immediately brought to court and restrained from using their own name.

While Tierney was struggling, O'Mahony picked up the slack. In 1928, the company's best year, Jerry O'Mahony, Inc., built 184 diners, which sold for $1.5 million.

P. J. Tierney Sons, Inc., continued making diners for a few years until the stock-market crash and ensuing depression forced them out of business.

DELICIOUS FOOD THAT SATISFIES

QUICK SERVICE

Hi-Way
DINERS CLUB of
NEW ENGLAND

QUICK SERVICE

DELICIOUS FOOD THAT SATISFIES

WASON MFG. CO.

The Wason Manufacturing Company in operation
building Brill Steel Diners. (*Henry Ford Museum*
& Greenfield Village)

The New York Times of September 14, 1927,
reported on the Tierney brothers' legal
struggles.

Opposite

This interior view of the Hi-Way shows Brill's
glass counters displaying food ready to eat.
(*Henry Ford Museum & Greenfield Village*)

RESTRAINS TIERNEYS FROM USING NAME

Court Grants an Injunction to Lunch Wagon Concern They Formerly Owned.

STARTED BUSINESS ANEW

Brothers Then Competed With Old Firm, "Misleading the Public," the Decision Holds.

A decision that a man may not use his name in his business under certain circumstances was made by Supreme Court Justice Frankenthaler yesterday, in granting an injunction to J. P. Tierney Sons, Inc., against Tierney Brothers, Inc., restraining the defendant from using the name "Tierney," in any way in the manufacture of dining cars and lunch wagons.

The opinion said that the plaintiff's business was originated in 1898 by Patrick J. Tierney. When he died in 1917 he was succeeded by his sons, Edward J. and Edgar T. Tierney, and his brother Daniel. They incorporated the business in 1922 and soon became the largest manufacturers of lunch wagons and dining cars in the country. Edgar T. Tierney sold his interest to Edward in February, 1926, and in September of that year the plaintiff's corporation became financially involved and Edward and Daniel then sold 51 per cent of the common stock and all the preferred to outsiders, and finally last July disposed of all their remaining interest.

The organization of the defendant corporation was begun last February by the three Tierneys, although Edward J. was still connected with the plaintiff. They are now directors and have opened a plant at Mount Vernon, although they have not completed any dining cars.

Frankenthaler finds that the defendant corporation sent out circulars to the plaintiff's customers giving the impression that they are "reunited" and that they are the plaintiff' manufacturing, whereas the defendant never manufactured any cars.

"There is abundant evidence that the Tierneys and the defendant are not only using the name Tierney in competition with the plaintiff, but that they are endeavoring by that project, unfair and fraudulent means to take advantage of that name for the purpose of profiting from the plaintiff's reputation and misleading the public into the belief that their products are those of the plaintiff," said Justice Frankenthaler.

For reasons stated in the opinion the Court finds ground to grant the relief asked by the plaintiff, in restraining the defendant from using the name "Tierney." The plaintiff's plant is at New Rochelle. William Rosenblatt is President.

In proceedings involving P. J. Tierney & Sons, Daniel ... and Ed... Spring...

Samu...

Winfield S. Daniels was the stableman in charge of moving the horse-drawn wagon for Fred Casey. *(Casey's Diner)*

The interior of Casey's shows the unusual all-oak construction.

The Story of a Diner: Casey's

As a youngster, Fred Casey worked in a horse-drawn lunch wagon that was pulled to the Natick, Massachusetts, common by a horse named Dolly. For seventeen years he did the three-P.M.-to-one-A.M. shift in the four-stool lunch wagon, which was built around 1885. The end of Fred's shift coincided with the last train that pulled into town every evening at one. When it pulled out, the street lights were turned off, and the wagon made its way home.

In 1921, Fred finally purchased the wagon from Ida Brooks, who had owned it with her late husband, George. In 1927, he acquired a secondhand Worcester Lunch Car, known as Mulligan's Diner, from next-door Framingham. He moved it to Natick and renamed it Casey's. At ten stools, this offered two and a half times the seating capacity of his old wagon. The original wagon was sold to the Stanley family, gypsies who lived for years in Natick.

For twenty-five years Fred ran the diner, which he *only* referred to as a lunch cart. He never served breakfast, but only lunch, dinner, and night-owl customers. Casey's reputation for an outstanding hot dog began in the original lunch wagon, where it was said that "millions of hot dogs and measureless oceans of coffee" were served.

Joe Casey, Fred's son, took over when his dad retired around 1952. For Joe Casey, this ten-stooler was more than adequate, and he felt no need to expand to larger quarters. He would just as soon let the take-out line grow longer. He did go back to the Worcester Lunch Car Company in 1958 to have them remove the old wooden ice chest and put in a sandwich board. At that time they also replaced the open burners with a flat-top grill so that hamburgs would no longer have to be fried in pans.

For fifty years the yellow-and-black diner was a fixture in the center of Natick, in the "Casey Block," a few paces off the common. In 1977 the land was sold to a bank, and Casey's moved around the corner and set up shop again. A local boy, Timmy Hopkins, had the last hot dog in

Casey's Diner in its original Natick location.

the old location and hot dog number one in the new. Years later, Tim became the middle counterman of the three-man shift that runs the diner.

Something of an anomaly, Casey's has survived, almost as new. It is still entered by sliding doors, one in the center and one on the left end. The right end features a take-out window to handle the crowds that can't fit on the ten stools. Behind the stools is a narrow shelf for stand-up customers. The interior, including the polished countertop, is wholly constructed of oak. The hexagonal-tile floor has withstood the countless customers. The gleaming Monel metal hood and backbar highlight the old five-gallon coffee urn, the copper hot-dog-bun steamer, and the hot-dog cooker. Several of the etched, frosted windows are still in place.

Fred Casey, grandson of Fred Casey, is now in charge of the diner, manning the take-out window and dishing out the dogs. Like his father and grandfather before him, he sees no reason to expand beyond ten seats. And his family now assists him in running the lunch cart.

The hours have been reduced gradually since the original Fred kept the place open past midnight. In those days, the theater brought people in; there were Friday night dances at the Knights of Columbus Hall; when the barrooms emptied, Casey's filled up. With the theaters gone and dances a thing of the past, Joe cut back, first to midnight, then to nine-thirty and eventually to eight o'clock. Fred keeps the diner open from eleven-thirty A.M. to eight P.M. and takes August off.

Business is good at Casey's these days, just as it always has been. As Fred says, "Some days it is just too much. You can't do any more; you can't go fast enough." Patrons clamor for "dogs all around," with mustard, onions, and relish. They stand two deep at the counter, hovering over anyone who looks as if he is almost finished. It is not the kind of place to enjoy a leisurely lunch. But that's not what the customers go for. They go for the camaraderie, the banter, the counter showmanship . . . and of course, for the hot dogs.

Diners on the Move

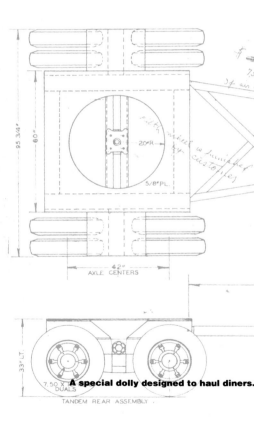

A special dolly designed to haul diners.

Contrary to popular belief, not all diners were built in factories. Certainly, nearly all were, but as early as 1926, some diner operators wanted to commission the building of new places that were too big to move through the streets. In that year, James J. and Joseph Crowe had Wilfred H. Barriere build them a new diner on site on the Boston Road in the White City section of Worcester. The end result, Warren's Diner, fifty feet long by fourteen feet wide, was big enough to accommodate the busloads of travelers who regularly stopped on the New York–to–Boston run. ¶ Previously, the size of a diner had been governed by the method of transport used to ship the diner to its site. In the early days, teams of horses were used to move diners around. Gradually, trucks replaced the horses. ¶ Up until the mid-twenties most diners going a long distance were put on flatcars and shipped by rail to their destinations. The diner's wheels were removed for that

POLLARD CO. INC.
DINING CAR BUILDERS
LOWELL, MASS.
BOB'S
DINER
17
P. COGGER, LOWELL MASS.

It took a large team of horses to move a big diner . . . but it wasn't much work for the help who went along for the ride.

Preceding page

P. Cogger used his chain-driven Mack to move Bob's Diner from the factory in Lowell. **(George of Lowell)**

part of the journey to cut down on the height, and the diner was bolted to a flatcar. The average diner at that time was thirty feet long and no more than ten and a half feet wide; anything over that ten foot six couldn't be accommodated by the railroad. So exact were the restrictions that exterior embellishments such as light fixtures and doorknobs had to be removed before shipping by rail. An apocryphal diner tale has it that a mistake in dimensioning by a manufacturer who built a car wider than the railroad could move brought dining car trucking into its own.

The manufacturer needed to prep the diner carefully for the move. Laurence LeBlanc of the Worcester Lunch Car Company revealed one of the tricks of the trade. The undercarriage of a diner utilized a pair of tie-rods with turnbuckles as part of the structure. Before the move, those turnbuckles were cranked tight, so the diner's floor had a crown in the middle. By the end of the move, it had settled so much that it was perfectly flat. Once the diner was on its foundation, the moving crew leveled it and made sure all windows and doors operated smoothly.

Trucks were being used to some extent in the early twenties for moving diners from the railroad tracks to the site, but for long-range moving, only P. J. Tierney Sons Company trucked the car all the way from factory to site. Most plants were built right next to the railroad tracks, but the Tierney plant was an exception. Located two or three miles from the nearest railroad, the Tierneys had their own in-house trucking operation. Unfortunately, their trucks always seemed to be breaking down, and invariably help was needed to get them back on the road. George and Frank Parker, identical twins from New Rochelle, New York, usually answered the call. They started in the garbage business, but were good mechanics and helped the Tierneys out of so many scrapes that in 1924 they gave up hauling garbage and started moving diners full-time.

Ten miles per hour was the limit during the move by road. Otherwise vibrations were set up that could seriously hurt the diner. Also, the truck's tires and wheels would heat up too much at

greater speeds. The Parker brothers told a story of moving a diner the short distance from New Rochelle to Bridgeport, Connecticut, a run that should have taken five hours or so. However, because of overloading they ended up burning out the hubs on twenty-seven wheels, and the move dragged on for four days.

More than once the unexpected would occur to make life miserable for the dining car truckers. Frank Parker once had to back a diner for four miles because someone told him that a bridge outside Little Falls, New York, had a safe clearance of sixteen feet; all it turned out to have was fourteen feet, six inches. When pneumatic tires came into use, a little air could always be let out in such a situation, or the wheels could be removed and the car could creep forward on six-inch rollers. If that proved to be of no avail, there always was the backing-up method; but that wasn't much fun with twenty tons blocking your view and being ornery every foot of the way.

The Bank Lunch, in midair, is guided onto a barge behind the Tierney plant. *(Pat Fodero)*

The other method of moving diners, especially good for long distances, was by water. The Tierney plant backed up onto the Long Island Sound, a convenient location for rigging diners directly onto barges—in addition to providing a mooring for the Tierney brothers' yacht. When Florida "discovered" the diner in the mid-1920s, Tierney was sending boatloads of as many as four diners at a time.

The Jerry O'Mahony Company had an arrangement with the marine salvage outfit of Merritt-Chapman & Scott Corporation in New York City to rig their diners and load them onto barges. The main line of the Jersey Central Railroad passed by the O'Mahony plant, with a nearby station at El Mora (which just happened to have an O'Mahony diner in operation). After the diners were loaded onto railroad cars right at the O'Mahony plant, the Jersey Central took them directly to the docks on the Hudson River in lower Manhattan. Even a diner going only as far as Brooklyn then took to the sea for smoother sailing to its destination.

A crew from the builders usually accompanied the diner to its site in order to see it safely installed on its foundation. According to Fred Crepeau, of the Worcester Lunch Car Company, the bigger diners always left the factory at night for truck transport. That way they'd be safely into the less populous countryside before morning traffic began. Fred recalled, "Up in New Hampshire you couldn't move a diner without a state trooper. We used to wait at the line until the trooper came. He used to get so mad. A lot of the diners were very heavy, and the old Mack was *very* slow. The troopers would be rippin' because they thought they could go along at twenty or twenty-five miles per hour and get the job over with. We'd go up hills and just barely be moving. The trooper would be waiting at the top of the hill, swearing."

When the diner rolled into town, it was quite an event. More than one proud owner was known to come along for the last leg, hop on the running boards of the truck, and wave enthusiastically to each and every future customer as the diner headed for its ultimate destination.

The method of moving diners has not changed much since the early days. The diners have just gotten bigger and more unwieldy. Opposite at bottom, Lamy's Diner, en route to Henry Ford Museum; above, Uncle Will's, on its way to become Le Galaxie in Montreal; lower right, unidentified diner, on the road in Pennsylvania; upper right, the Apple Tree Dining Car being moved inside a private residence.

CHAPTER 7

"Ladies Invited." Or Were They?

Diner owners were always looking for ways to make more money. After all, that was the point of the business. It took them until the mid-twenties to realize that there was still a large segment of the American population that had never even seen the inside of a diner: women. The reputation of the lunch carts—practically from the beginning, when they operated in the wee hours— seemed to be "men only," and the ladies did pretty much keep their distance. But all those women who weren't coming to diners meant good dollars that weren't making it to the till. So, here and there, signs began to appear, announcing "Ladies Invited." While these didn't exactly pack the cars, they were an indication of progress. Soon a number of operators started going out more actively after women, sending handbills to all the nearby offices. Then, gradually, small touches

From *Dining Car News*. (George Mahoney) began to appear, designed to attract the ladies. Flower boxes and shrubs added an appealing touch

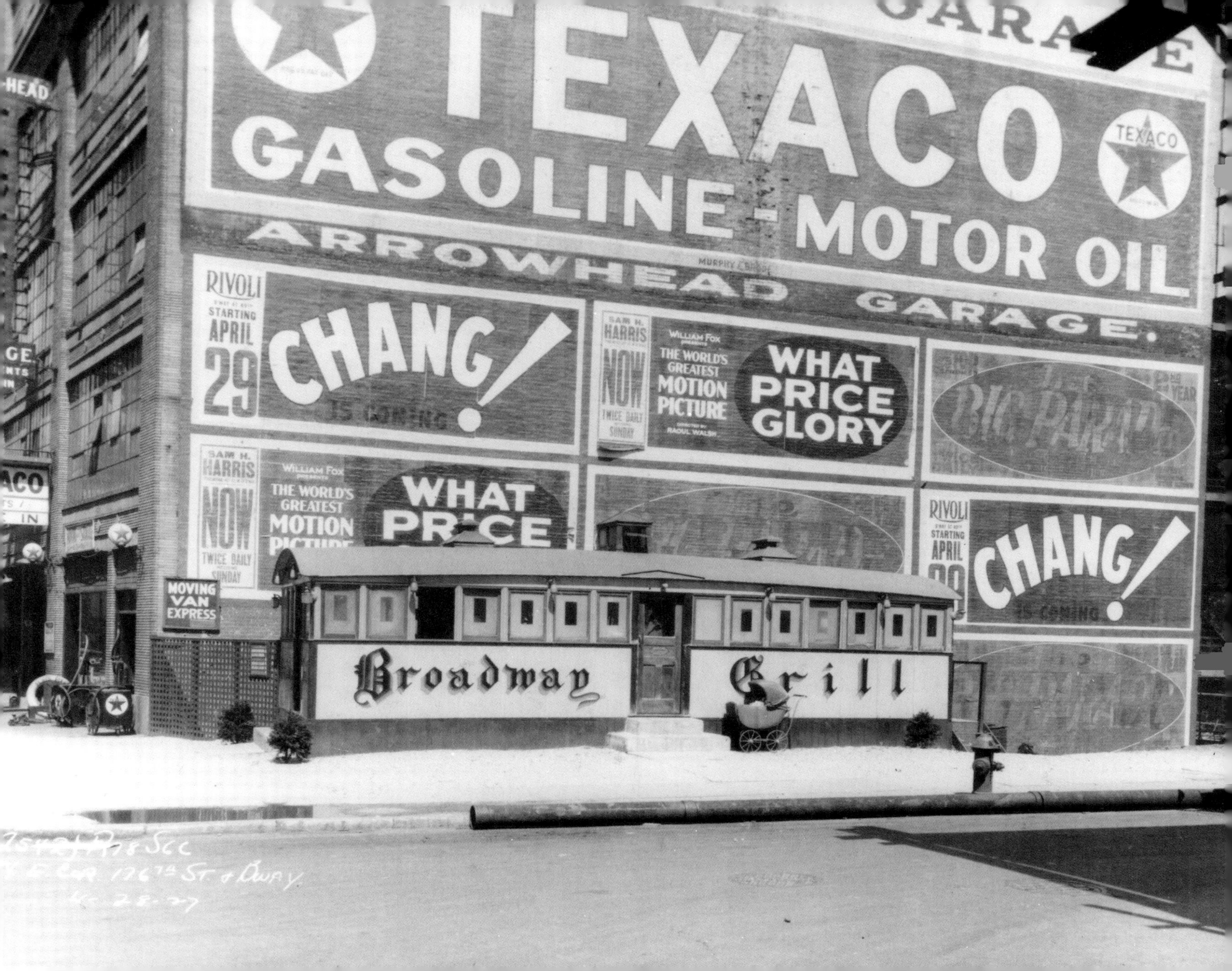

TEXACO
GASOLINE-MOTOR OIL
ARROWHEAD GARAGE.
RIVOLI
STARTING APRIL 29
CHANG!
IS COMING
SAM H. HARRIS
NOW
TWICE DAILY
SUNDAY
WILLIAM FOX
THE WORLD'S GREATEST MOTION PICTURE
WHAT PRICE GLORY
RAOUL WALSH
TEXACO
MOVING VAN EXPRESS
Broadway Grill

This late-1920s frosted window was in the Kitchenette Diner in Cambridge, Massachusetts.

Not many women would feel comfortable with this crowd in the Mayfair Diner in Philadelphia in 1932. *(Mayfair Diner)*

Preceding page

A baby carriage by the front door was an open invitation for women to come in. This diner was in New York City in 1927. *(The New-York Historical Society, New York City)*

on the exterior. Frosted-glass windows insured privacy from ogling passersby.

Making the diner more attractive was important to those promoting the business in general (i.e., the manufacturers). To this end, Jerry O'Mahony launched his own magazine, *Dining Car News,* in January 1927. The *News* was distributed free of charge to owners and prospective buyers of O'Mahony cars. While it did have a few articles of interest to owners, it was basically one big ad for O'Mahony.

The issue of April 1928 compared two diners within walking distance of each other. One had a lot of business, and the other was just getting by. The experts attributed this not to the food being served, but to the differences that went into maintaining the places. The popular one had concrete

The late supper menu from the Flying Yankee

Dining Car in Lynn, Massachusetts.

(Dave Waller)

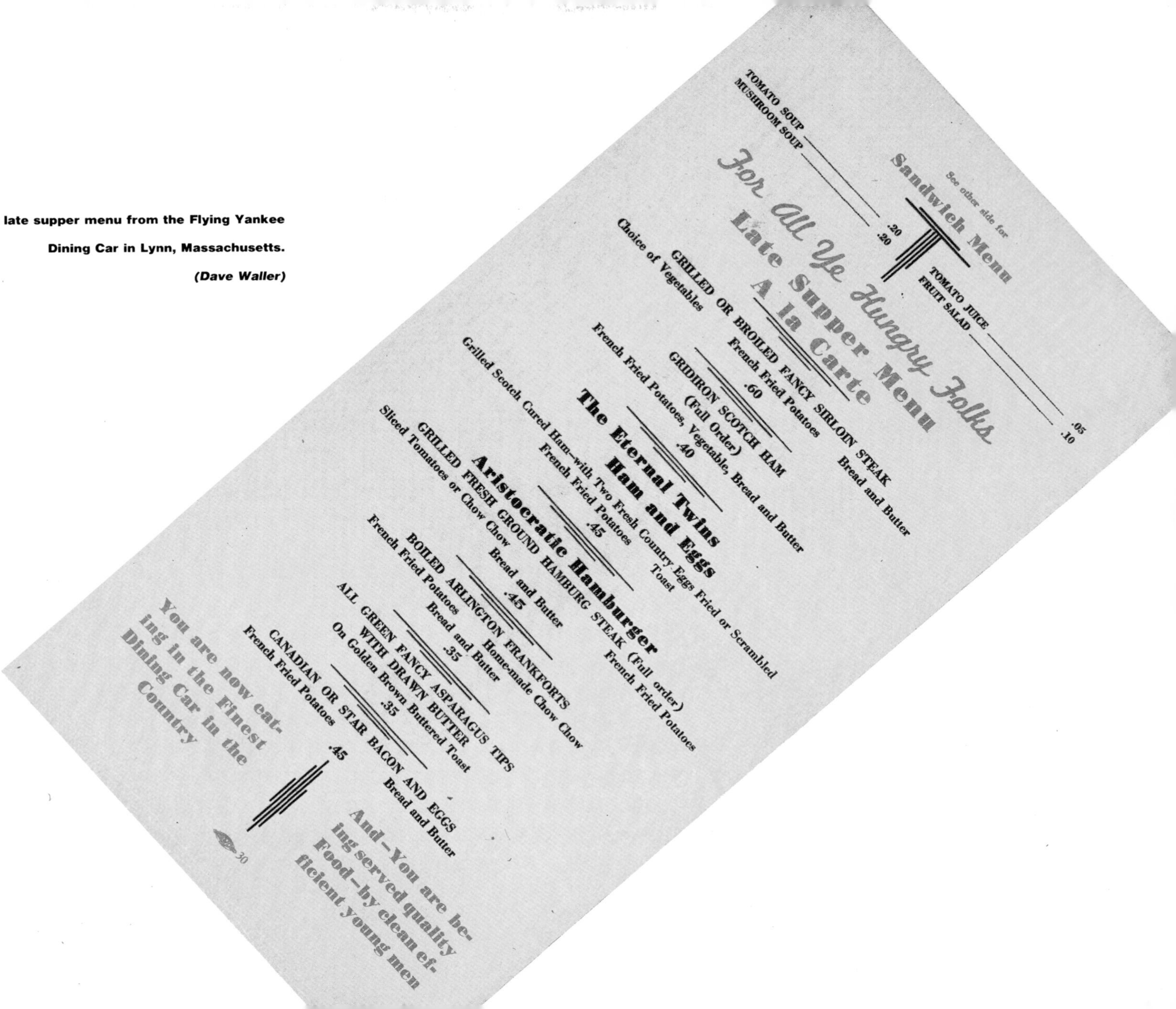

For All Ye Hungry Folks
Late Supper Menu
A la Carte

See other side for
Sandwich Menu

TOMATO SOUP ———— .20
MUSHROOM SOUP ———— .20

TOMATO JUICE ———— .05
FRUIT SALAD ———— .10

GRILLED OR BROILED FANCY SIRLOIN STEAK
Choice of Vegetables — French Fried Potatoes — Bread and Butter
.60

GRIDIRON SCOTCH HAM
(Full Order)
French Fried Potatoes, Vegetable, Bread and Butter
.40

The Eternal Twins
Ham and Eggs
Grilled Scotch Cured Ham—with Two Fresh Country Eggs Fried or Scrambled
French Fried Potatoes — Toast
.45

Aristocratic Hamburger
GRILLED FRESH GROUND HAMBURG STEAK (Full order)
Sliced Tomatoes or Chow Chow — French Fried Potatoes
Bread and Butter
.45

BOILED ARLINGTON FRANKFORTS
French Fried Potatoes — Homemade Chow Chow
Bread and Butter
.35

ALL GREEN FANCY ASPARAGUS TIPS
WITH DRAWN BUTTER
On Golden Brown Buttered Toast
.35

CANADIAN OR STAR BACON AND EGGS
French Fried Potatoes
Bread and Butter
.45

You are now eat-
ing in the Finest
Dining Car in the
Country

And — You are be-
ing served quality
Food — by clean ef-
ficient young men

30

This is the Monarch, a new type O'Mahony Diner, which is the talk of the dining car world.

May, 1928
Vol. 2   No. 5

In Our Line we Lead the World

sidewalks and steps, with a well-manicured lawn. The countermen were spotlessly dressed in white, and kept the interior in a similar condition.

The other diner had help in soiled aprons dishing out the food. To get into the diner, the patrons had to negotiate loose wooden planks, which on a wet day would flap on the ground and squirt mud onto their shoes. The editor of *Dining Car News* made it known that this kind of place was on the way out, and for good reason.

Most important, a wider variety of foods began to appear on the menu, to give the new customers a bit more of a choice. Some owners had colorful and attractive salads on display in the countertop cases. When the Rubyette, a new seedless red grape, was developed in California, it was immediately used to dress up plain cottage-cheese salads.

When the dining car owners discovered a surefire method to draw in women, they frequently shared their good-luck stories. An operator from Pennsylvania reported how on one occasion an O'Mahony serviceman dropped in with his family to see how things were going. The O'Mahony man sat his family (wife, mother, and three little girls) right by the front door, which he propped open. When the operator asked, "What's the big idea? Want to let in the flies?" the fellow replied that it was a trick to attract women. And sure enough, when two women passed by a few minutes later, they stopped to look. One said to the other, "Why, women do eat in there, Sarah. Look, there's some real nice ladies and three little girls, too. Let's go in." That was the start of that particular operator's "women business." Soon he didn't even have to seat his women customers by the door.

Increased patronage by women prompted one major design innovation. One of the reasons women had seldom gone into dining cars was that they just didn't feel comfortable perched up on stools. To remedy this, manufacturers started to offer diners with tables or booths. These were usually advertised by painting the news right on the diner.

The addition of table service caused a new headache for diner movers. Unless the extra seating was placed at the end of the diner, the car was too wide to be shipped by rail. However, the most logical way to accommodate a fair number of tables was to run them down the length of the entire car, yielding a diner fourteen feet wide or more.

While some operators were after the female clientele, others definitely were not. The question of women and dining cars was so hotly debated that it was made the subject of a monthly feature in early issues of *Dining Car News*. A letter in the issue of February 1927 clearly shows just how strongly some diner men felt about the subject:

TO THE EDITOR: What, No Women Department:
¶ I think you're all wet on the "What, No Women" question. Their money is as good as any man's, as you say, and there may be locations where women will bring in big jack, but not for me. ¶ I got a location, a good one too, down by the piers, and while a lady's safe enough in my car, she'll hear some cuss words that'll turn her ears pink. What do you think about that, Mr. Editor?

J. B., New York.

TWO EGGS 25

FRENCH TOAST 25

TWO DROPPED
SCOTCH H

WASON MFG. C
SPRINGFIELD
253-H

The owner of the Miss Roxbury Diner in Boston even added tablecloths and a waitress to draw in the sole woman in this photograph. *(Henry Ford Museum & Greenfield Village)*

The editor admitted that maybe J.B.'s was one case where women were "out."

Similarly in the Flying Yankee Dining Car, located by the General Electric plant in Lynn, Massachusetts, owners Jack Welsh and Jack Hines were not after the female trade. They felt that women took too long to order. "The women ate down in the cellar. Picture a couple of women coming in, and they say, 'Lookit. There's roast beef here. Did you ever have any roast beef here?' And you know, they would take ten minutes to make a decision. And the guy next to them would have eaten and gone. So we fixed up a place in the basement and I used to meet them in the doorway and say, 'Right this way!' and put all the women in the cellar. We only opened it for the [lunch] hour. We didn't get any turnover there at all."

Other diner owners would argue, saying that a woman's money was just as green as a man's. In the December 1927 article "Do Women Take Longer to Eat Than Men Do?" diner owner Henry Conture wrote that women were "as snappy as the men when it comes to eating in a Jerry O'Mahony Diner." If served promptly, the average man took from ten to thirteen minutes to eat a meal in a diner. Women did not spend any more time eating, according to the figures kept at the Burlington, Vermont, diner, where over two hundred of the 850 customers per day were women.

Despite the back-and-forth that went on among diner operators, the future of the business was clear: Feed people of both sexes.

Diners Survive the Crash

Diners were described as "depression-proof" businesses, because everyone still had to eat. The decade following the stock-market crash of October 29, 1929, was one of many changes in the diner industry. Only one major diner builder closed up shop, "orphaning" many cars; others laid off workers in order to stay afloat; incredibly, a handful of new companies began. ¶ Times were certainly rough during this period, but on the whole, if you owned a diner, you managed to stay in business. In the city of Worcester, Massachusetts, there were eleven lunch wagons or diners listed in the city directory in 1930. By 1936, four lunch wagons had disappeared, but ten new diners had made an appearance. At the end of the decade, another four had closed, but nine new ones opened. So, over the ten-year span, the number of establishments had doubled, from eleven to twenty-two.

B. G. Harley's patented diner.

All across the country, large numbers of restaurants were to be counted among the common business failures of the day. Jerry O'Mahony, Inc., pointed out this fact, along with the information that many famous hotels were replacing their fancy dining rooms with simpler lunch-counter operations. The restaurant industry was shifting gears, and the dining car was the perfect vehicle to benefit from this.

This was true because the size and functionalism of a diner were perfect for the inexpensive meal and low overhead required to make a profit. In 1932, it was estimated that more than half of restaurant patrons sought out cheaper meals, probably because they couldn't afford more expensive ones. Those people were coming into diners to eat.

As a result, people continued to go into the diner business. Diner manufacturers' sales literature from the early 1930s presented the business as a golden opportunity to become your own boss. The Kullman Dining Car Company related this chain of events: "First, your own business, then a home of your own, then a liberal education for your children, then a chance to enjoy the comforts and luxuries of life: these things seem to follow in an inevitable sequence."

In a 1932 article, Jerry O'Mahony asked the question, "Who Runs These Dining Cars?" In order to dispel the myth that all diners were owned by former restaurateurs, a survey was taken, showing that a "tremendous" number of diner operators switched directly from almost every imaginable profession or industry: bus drivers and bond brokers, clerks and college professors, bookkeepers and salesmen, housewives and businessmen, service station and garage workers . . . in addition to hoteliers, owners of other restaurants, stewards, and so on. (Later in the 1930s, it was estimated that seven out of every ten diner owners had not previously been associated with the restaurant business.)

By way of example—without mentioning the name, though this would be furnished to those

Newburyport, Ma.   June 1, 1932

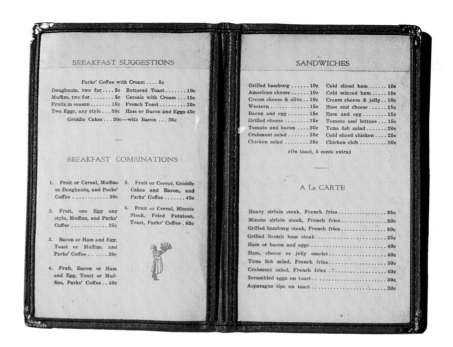

Donald W. Parks, along with his father, J. Edward, opened Parks' Diner in 1932 in Waterville, Maine. For the sixteen years they owned the diner, they never raised the prices. Don called it "the million-dollar diner," as the gross receipts nearly reached that figure: $940,058.60.

Opposite

Herman Rich opened his red-and-gold sixty-foot Worcester Lunch Car on June 1, 1932, in Newburyport, Massachusetts. He did so well that exactly one year later an annex of the same length, with booth seating only, was installed. According to Worcester Lunch Car factory workers, Rich paid for his diners with a suitcaseful of cash, allegedly from bootleg liquor. (*Donald A. LaPlante*)

inquiring by mail for more details—the story of a successful businessman in Virginia was related. This particular gentleman oversaw a roadside empire valued at over a half a million dollars: "a battery service station, filling station, tire shop, parking station, and a dozen other enterprises." Amazingly enough, his inventory of businesses did not include any food service, so, "being a man of action and means, he ordered an O'Mahony [diner] as smoothly as he would have ordered a dozen new tires for his shop." Before long, the diner became one of his best-paying investments—with a testimonial letter on file at the O'Mahony factory.

But of course, not every would-be diner owner was a person of means. Even the small down payment required on a new diner was often beyond reach. For those with limited capital, the "reconditioned" diner was often the answer. There was some confusion, though, as to how a reconditioned car differed from a secondhand one.

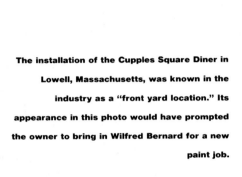

The installation of the Cupples Square Diner in Lowell, Massachusetts, was known in the industry as a "front yard location." Its appearance in this photo would have prompted the owner to bring in Wilfred Bernard for a new paint job.

When business was good, a diner owner often outgrew his car, sometimes as early as the second year of operation. And when the owner watched business walking away because of the crowds inside, he went right back to the factory to order a bigger and better diner.

All companies would take the older diner back, offering a fair trade-in value for it. If the owner had been particularly neat, another anxious buyer might take the diner "as is," moving it directly to his new location. In this instance, the diner was described as secondhand.

"Reconditioned" usually meant that the original owner "in his mad rush to make money has not cleaned his car as often as he should, grease may have run over, the urns may be dull, the car may need painting, a piece of tile may be broken, the ceiling may be smoked up from careless cooking." In this case, the diner was hauled back to the factory and gone over from top to bottom—polished, repainted, revarnished to such an extent that the patrons would never know it wasn't a new car.

The Boulevard Diner in Worcester is a 1936 Worcester Lunch Car. The diner retains its beautiful oak and gumwood interior.

Fred Crepeau, cabinetmaker at the Worcester Lunch Car Company, recalled that the vacant land across Quinsigamond Street from the plant was sometimes filled with as many as six diners awaiting reconditioning. As soon as a spot opened up inside, one would be brought in for a going-over. Worcester Lunch never gave up on a diner, no matter how bad it was. "We got one from somewhere and I'll bet you there were a million cockroaches. So they put it out in the lot and loaded it with insecticide. When it was all cleared out, they brought it in the shop. The diner was totally rotted. I said, 'Let's throw this away!' Charlie [Gemme] said, 'No, no, no. I know how to fix this.' He did too. That diner came out beautiful."

During the 1930s, reconditioned diners were extremely popular. Worcester couldn't keep any on the lot. Because they were such good buys, Jerry O'Mahony urged prospective owners to get their names on the "Reconditioned Waiting List." They would then be among the first to know

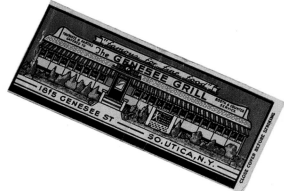

when the bargains became available. There was a "Used Car Coupon" on the back cover of *Dining Car News,* which made it easier for the buyer to get particulars on available cars.

This boom in reconditioned diners also meant work for the diner builders during tough times. When the Worcester Lunch Car Company didn't have enough work in the plant, they sent their men out on the road. Diner owners didn't have enough cash to upgrade to a new car . . . but could afford a new paint job.

Wilfred Bernard, who became the painting foreman at Worcester Lunch in 1930 at the age of twenty-one, spent a lot of time on the road during the depression, including an entire year when he was only home on weekends. In the years before porcelain enamel was widely used on diner exteriors, the paint job would only last three or four years, depending on the upkeep and exposure to the sun. On-site lettering jobs frequently attracted quite an audience. When he repainted the Miss Clinton—all freehand—there was such a crowd that he couldn't back up to assess the work. It was expected that the second "s" in "Miss" would perfectly match the first, so Bernard complained to the owner that he couldn't work with all those people watching him.

Fred Crepeau began work at Worcester Lunch at the age of sixteen, in 1928. "I got in at a bad time. The crash came and we were all out of work for a while till things picked up. We never got a backlog. We got a diner every now and then and were called back to work. We got other jobs in the meantime. It was very unsteady until 1932 or 1933, when it started to pick up."

That unsteadiness was enough to close down any company that was on a shaky footing. For example, the years following the crash were characterized by a rapid decline for new street-railway cars, and so the J. G. Brill Company and its subsidiaries put more resources into their line of Brill Steel Diners. They also diversified further, offering a line of mahogany motorboat hulls, another of automobile bodies, and a motor bus equipped with a separate smoking compartment.

For a time, they even constructed miniature golf courses. But all these efforts were to no avail, and the Wason plant in Springfield, Massachusetts, where most of the diners were built, officially closed in August 1932.

One company that bucked the depression and opened for business in 1931 was the Bixler Manufacturing Company. Louis C. Voelker started it in Norwalk, Ohio, constructing a line of sectional diners, which were shipped in pieces to their sites. According to John F. Rice, one of the company's two construction superintendents, Bixler's diners were the most modern available and were very desirable because of their ample width of sixteen feet. Only with "knocked-down" construction could diners this wide be shipped. "It came to me in sections, 4'-0" wide, shipped in one or two railroad cars. I would hire local help and erect or assemble the diner in two to three weeks. I erected many diners for Bixler all over the northeastern area and as far west as St. Louis, Missouri. Several were erected in Westchester County, New York—in fact, I erected one right across the street from the Tierney factory in New Rochelle, probably in 1932 or 1933."

In addition to their large size—any length in multiples of four feet—Bixlers were distinguished by a barrel roof with an unusual end trim and by their double-hung, modular, two-foot windows. Booths with tall partitions were standard. Like most of the competition, Bixler required a 10 percent deposit with the order, 15 percent before shipping, and the remainder in thirty-five equal payments.

In 1982, John Rice recalled that "$100 daily gross business would pay out the diner loan and provide an adequate profit." At Timothy J. Flood's Auburn Diner, a 1932 Bixler in Auburn, New York, that was a lot of ham-and-egg sandwiches at fifteen cents or pork-chop dinners at forty-five cents. In any event, Tim Flood's diner was paid off on time, by July 1, 1935.

But Bixler didn't last long. John Rice explained, "Unfortunately, the Great Depression finally

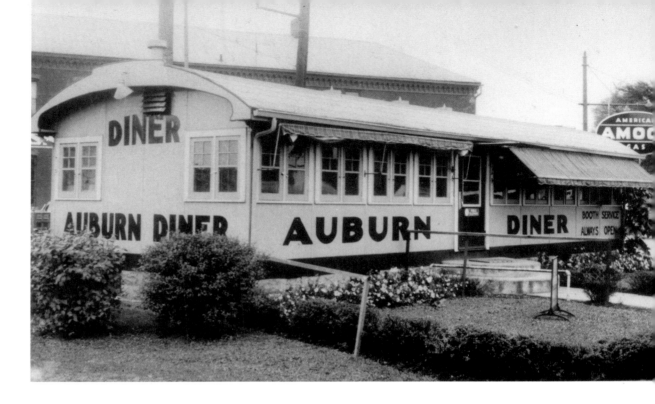

got us. The sales force just couldn't find buyers with the minimum $500 down payment, besides the funds needed for foundation, plot, permits, etc. There was no depression for me until about 1934, when the company couldn't keep me on salary. Sales really slowed. I needed steady employment and reluctantly resigned." By 1937 the Bixler Company was gone.

The depression couldn't beat everybody. Two firms that started in the early thirties are still in business in the 1990s. Arthur E. Sieber left Silk City to begin his own firm, Paramount Diners in Haledon, New Jersey. Angelo DeRaffele, a carpentry foreman with P. J. Tierney Sons, who started work there in 1921, began to build diners at the old Tierney plant in 1933 with his partner, Carl A. Johnson. They operated under the name of Johnson & DeRaffele.

Little Diners

Depression conditions brought about a return to the early days of the dining car; a one-man

operation with a limited menu made economic good sense in tough times. As a result, a new

demand for small units developed in the early thirties. ¶ These new "dinettes" were designed

especially for the short-order trade. The Kullman Dining Car Company offered a number of

crenellated and towered small diners to compete directly with the White Tower and White

Castle hamburger trade. In what had practically become the rule in diner design, the model

known as the "Castle Turret" copied not only design features, but also the name of the competi-

tion. ¶ After World War II, a new crop of small diners sprouted, for returning vets to invest in.

Kullman again led the way with the "Kullman Junior," stating in the sales brochure: "It brings

The deluxe double unit offered by Valentine. you all the tested features of a super diner . . . boiled down to everyday needs."

Preceding overleaf

Bone's Diner, in White Sulphur Springs, West Virginia, is a classic Valentine. (Don Hanlon)

Though most of the original, one-man lunch wagons had disappeared by the early thirties, they were still fixtures in a number of New England cities. Meals on wheels remained a tradition in Providence, Rhode Island; Portsmouth, New Hampshire; and Taunton, Massachusetts. Often when these wagons wore out, the operator went to the Worcester Lunch Car Company with a truck and had a diner built right on the back.

These dinermen enjoyed their modus operandi. They pulled into the center of town at dusk and set up in the very same spots for years. They didn't mind working the night-owl shift and were grateful for the nominal rent paid for only a parking space and utilities hookup. The cities looked upon these anachronisms with favor, and grandfathered each new model around any regulations that might have precluded its operation.

Taunton had the most unusual history, with four wagons, one on each side of the town common. A nineteenth-century city ordinance permitted the wagons to operate from four P.M. until two in the morning. Although the owners regularly upgraded their wagons, some were still horse-drawn as late as 1938.

The last remaining lunch wagon man was John F. Hickey, who shut down in 1986, having had the common to himself for the previous twenty years. Jack Hickey went to work in 1942 as a counterman for Galligan's, one of the night lunch wagons. Two years later he bought one, an eight-stool, horse-drawn unit that had been mounted on a 1938 White truck. After a couple of years, he grew dissatisfied with the sorry condition of his diner, so he went up to Worcester, sat down with Charlie Gemme, and designed a new ten-stool diner, which was built in 1947 on the same old truck. The truck wore out and was replaced with a '54 Chevy; the diner lives on in Taunton, having been purchased by the city to keep the tradition alive. It still operates on special occasions.

Hickey had trouble supporting his family of eight children working only the night shift, especially after the highways bypassed Taunton and the big bands stopped coming to play at the Roseland Ballroom. So in 1951, he leased a small plot of land on Court Street, a quarter mile from the center of town, and began operating a day shift. In later years, all of his sons worked at the diner at night while holding down their regular jobs. When it came time for Jack Hickey to retire, he offered to pass down the business, but asked his sons, "Who wants to work seventy-five hours a week today, with no benefits and no vacations?"

Despite the trend in diner building toward ever larger and more grandiose models, one Midwestern manufacturer built only small diners. Valentine diners, advertised as "Portable Steel Sandwich Shops," were built in Wichita, Kansas, by the Valentine Manufacturing Company, founded in 1938 by Arthur H. Valentine. These factory-built restaurants were highly influenced by the classic East Coast diner, but were really their own thing. First and foremost, they had a distinctive look: a brightly colored enamel exterior on a boxy little building with flying-buttress

corners and a pylon sign over the door . . . and ten stools. When Valentine *finally* offered a second model, fifteen years after the company began, the diners still had the same basic interior . . . and ten stools.

The Valentine diners were designed with two ideas in mind: that an operator could make a reasonable living from one unit, *and* that the diners would be ideal for chain operation. The most popular model was one known as the Little Chef, which sold in the post–World War II period for around $3,300.

Valentines were built with steel frames and were covered with either painted galvanized-steel panels or porcelain enamel. Part of the distinctive look of a Valentine diner was the bold use of stripes around the kitchen exterior. Most Valentines featured a take-out window.

Interior walls were finished in painted sheet metal or porcelain enamel, with the kitchen built entirely of stainless steel. The steel floor was covered with greaseproof asphalt tile or linoleum. The L-shaped counter began opposite the entrance and ended, at the back wall, with a round

If you wanted a big Valentine, you had to put several together, as did the proprietor of the U & R in New Mexico. *(Norma N. Holmes)*

mirror. The countertop was Formica and the apron was frequently stainless steel. The ten stools were perched on a raised platform one step high.

It has been estimated that 2,200 Valentines were built and shipped across the country to every state in the continental United States, with the possible exception of Washington.

Around 1950, the Valentine Manufacturing Company was hired by T. E. Saxe, president of White Tower (now Tombrock Corporation), to build fifteen White Towers. The buildings were all ten feet by twenty-five feet, with ten stools. Although their exteriors said "White Tower," the interior was unmistakably Valentine in layout, even including the signature round mirror at the short end of the L-shaped counter.

Valentine diners were certainly a departure from the norm. The fact that their basic design remained the same for nearly thirty years set the company further apart from the East Coast manufacturers. Although Valentines didn't change, demand for a new kind of diner did. As the country was lifted out of the depression, people wanted to be shown the way of the future. And diner builders, with the exception of Valentine, were eager to showcase their new products. This is when the industry really came into its own.

This view of White Tower's Richmond #5 unit was built by Valentine, with an interior exactly like every other Valentine. *(Tombrock Corporation)*

Jack Hickey's diner looked like any other barrel-roofed Worcester Lunch Car—except for its size and configuration.

The Golden Age of the Diner

During the 1930s, industrial designers gave a new look to virtually every product on the market: a new, futuristic, forward-looking styling. The streamlined look swept the nation, covering or housing thousands of everyday objects in smooth, teardrop-shaped packages. ¶ The diner was no exception to the trend. The hard-edged box design of the twenties diners slowly gave way to the newer look. By the end of the thirties, surfaces and textures were brushed, polished, rounded, or wrapped. In some cases the diners so thoroughly mimicked the sleek streamlined locomotives that symbolized the era that they actually brought about the immobilization of mobility. ¶ The most radical of these designs was the Sterling Streamliner, a diner with one or two bullet-shaped ends. These diners were built by the J. B. Judkins Company of Merrimac, Massachusetts, which started diner manufacturing in 1936. Judkins was a builder of custom automobile bodies, a specialty that

Drawing for a Worcester clock by the author.

The Sterling East Avenue Diner was a double-ended streamliner in Rochester, New York.

fizzled out during the depression. The company had all the crafts necessary for diner building within its shop, so the new line seemed like a natural.

Judkins acquired the patented designs of Bertron G. Harley, a boat builder from Saco, Maine, who had developed plans for a diner constructed in sections. The early Sterling diners were based on Harley's modular designs. They were boxy, with a monitor roof on the outside and a barrel-vaulted ceiling inside. They had an old-fashioned look, with orange leaded-glass transom windows, mahogany trim inside, and walls and ceiling of porcelain enamel.

In 1939, J. B. Judkins was assigned the patented "new, original, and ornamental Design for a Restaurant Building" by Roland L. Stickney, of New York City. This was the basis for the Sterling Streamliner, with its distinctive rounded nose sections. Whereas Stickney called for porthole windows in the nose, Judkins installed thin, rectangular windows in the ends. Most Sterling Streamliners had a roof-mounted fin on which the name of the diner was proclaimed. Depending on the siting of the diner, one or both of the ends were rounded.

Joey's Streamline Diner—the name says it all. This sleek O'Mahony diner has rounded corners and windows, and Broadway-style lettering baked into the porcelain enamel skin.

Not to be outdone by their nearby competitor, the Worcester Lunch Car Company introduced two streamlined models at the same time. These were sketched out on a sheet of kraft paper by Wilfred Bernard, the painting foreman, who showed them to Charlie Gemme, the plant superintendent. The whole crew then worked on making these complicated designs a reality. Worcester built only two double-ended bullet-shaped streamliners, called circular diners by the carpenters. One was the Mayflower Diner, built for Peter Calimaris in Quincy, Massachusetts, in 1940. The other was the Yankee Clipper, a postwar job sent to Providence in 1947. Neither has survived.

A less radical—and easier-to-build—streamlined design was offered by Worcester, and proved much more popular. Instead of being rounded, the ends were slanted, still giving that illusion of mobility. Several of these diners were given railroad names, such as the Pullman and the Streamliner.

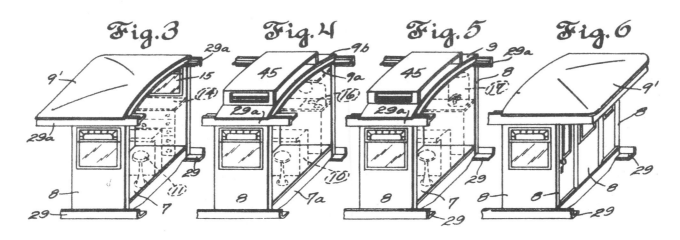

The more extreme applications of the new design ideas were not very widespread or long-lived, but the concept of streamlining persisted for more than twenty-five years. All diners were affected by it and—over the next decade especially—it came to be synonymous with modernization, as a more tempered version of streamlining dictated the character of diner design.

The decade of the 1930s saw the introduction into diners of many new materials, such as Formica, glass blocks, and stainless steel. Along with their contribution to the overall imagery, these materials helped to convey an idea of machine-age efficiency and cleanliness. Materials in diners have always been selected for longevity and good appearance.

Formica brand laminate was invented in 1913 by Herbert A. Faber and Daniel J. O'Conor, and was first used to insulate industrial products from oils, acids, and so on. Hence the name "for mica": "used in place of mica." In the late 1920s, decorative sheets were first produced in pearlized and marbleized patterns. Formica did not find its way into diners until the mid-1930s, when new production techniques made it less expensive to produce and more durable.

Paramount Diners, one of the first manufacturers to use Formica, pioneered its use as a ceiling surface, replacing wood, porcelain enamel, and metal. The sleekness of the surface, its relatively easy application, and the available combinations of colors introduced a new diner aesthetic. When a cigarette-proof grade was made available, it became the material of choice for countertops and tabletops.

By 1940 there were seventy colors to choose from, and the decorative possibilities were endless, with silk-screened designs and inlays of metal and other colors available. Companies such as Paramount and Kullman designed diners with an all-encompassing look. Tabletops featured Art Deco designs with stripes and circles of contrasting colors. The edges of the counter were inlaid with metal stripes. There were decorative panels above the windows and on the hood, employing a variety of geometric Art Deco themes.

Standish F. Hansell patented his radical design for the Penguin Diner (below), which was installed outside Philadelphia in 1942. His single-ended Sterling Streamliner (right) was the perfect vehicle to mimic a train emerging from a tunnel . . . the kitchen.

Opposite

Peter Calimaris had his initials in enamel between the two doors to his diner, shown on Southbridge Street in Worcester, alongside the plant. The interior view (inset) shows the mahogany woodwork that was such a challenge for the cabinetmakers because of the curves.

Stainless steel, a tough, durable metal from which a variety of equipment could be made, gained especially prominent use in diners, also beginning in the mid-thirties. According to a story told by Erwin Fedkenheuer, Jr., about his father, the first use of stainless steel—other than for equipment—in a diner came about this way. Erwin Senior, a German immigrant sheet-metal worker, was employed by S. Blickman, Inc., food service equipment manufacturers in Weehawken, New Jersey, in the early 1930s. One weekend he was asked to come to Paramount Diners by the owner, Art Sieber, to fabricate some stainless steel coffee urns on their equipment. While there, he remarked casually to Sieber that a little stainless would look nice in the diner that was currently under construction. Sieber concurred, and had Fedkenheuer bend some pieces for window trim.

When the diner was installed, the story goes, other diner builders dropped in for coffee and left with sketches they had made on napkins of Fedkenheuer's innovation. Stainless soon spread to the backbar and replaced tile as *the* wall surface. Erwin Fedkenheuer left Blickman's and became the lead sheet-metal man at Paramount, a position he held for many years, turning out some of the most incredible stainless steel diners ever made.

It wasn't long before stainless was used on the outside of diners, and it was the combination of stainless steel with porcelain enamel that produced the most eye-catching, colorful diners of all time. The various manufacturers were known for their own exterior styles. Worcester and Sterling stayed with polychrome flat porcelain enamel panels with integral graphics. Although Worcester turned out diners in many colors, the most popular was a medium-blue field with cream or yellow lettering. Sterling made cream diners, with green or red trim and lettering, almost exclusively.

Joe Fodero's company, variously called National or Fodero, built diners in a number of

Opposite

Topp's Diner was a Paramount located in Coopersburg, Pennsylvania. The interior combines color and panache with its brilliant use of materials.

Paramount always used materials to their best advantage. Glass blocks, decorative Formica, and outstanding tilework combined to make the company's diners among the most stylish available. (Pat Fodero)

streamlined styles with the same body shape: the "terra cotta" design was a skin of flat porcelain panels, usually in two colors, with rounded corners, rounded corner windows with stainless trim, and Broadway-style Art Deco lettering; the "fluted porcelain" design employed vertical semicircular flutes of colored porcelain with thin strips of stainless trim in between; the "streamlined" design used alternating horizontal strips of stainless and one color of porcelain, banding the entire diner; and the "modernistic" design, to split hairs, was identical with the "streamlined," except that it used two colors of porcelain.

Using this system of nomenclature, as advertised by Fodero in *The Diner* magazine in August 1947, one can categorize the models made by other manufacturers before and after the war.

Essentially, O'Mahony offered the terra cotta, the streamlined, and the modernistic. Kullman and DeRaffele specialized in the fluted porcelain. Mountain View advertised the terra cotta before the war and the fluted porcelain after the war. Silk City built its very own version of the terra cotta. Paramount offered the terra cotta and the fluted porcelain.

But Paramount crafted all-stainless steel exteriors that were never copied. These came in flat panels below the windows with a variety of patterns worked into them—vertical creases, quilted patterns, and the penultimate: a double row of burnished circles between horizontal bands.

All these various designs were advertised at one time or another in a new trade publication, *The Diner,* which began with the June 1940 issue. The man behind the magazine was Arthur F. (Bud) Neumann, who wrote most of the articles, several under pseudonyms. Over the years, the magazine (through several name changes) promoted the dining car business by profiling successful operators; running a series on the diner builders, entitled "Meet the Manufacturer"; featuring a chef of the month, with recipes; announcing new diners in "Openings of the Month"; and editorializing *continually* on keeping a neat, clean, well-run establishment, using the word "diner" in the name.

Polychrome graphics in porcelain enamel looked great and lasted a long time.

Opposite

This National diner, under construction in 1939, has the stainless steel and tilework complete, but still needs a countertop and other surfaces. Stool columns sit on the footrest, awaiting installation.

The Mack Diner was a Fodero of the "terra cotta" design.

Opposite

The Mayflower Diner was O'Mahony's version of the modernistic design. The Hightstown Diner was the DeRaffele combination using porcelain enamel and stainless in broad stripes.

Opposite, bottom

The Kullman "Challenger" was introduced in 1941. Built to ship by rail, it had fifteen stools and four booths at one end.

World War II brought one important change to the diner business. For the first time, on a large scale, women were to be found working the counters of diners. Just as women were needed in industry to help replace lost manpower, they were also recruited into diners. Now that the diner waitress has become an institution, it's hard to imagine a time when women were rarely seen on the working side of the counter.

One of the first proponents of women working in diners was Sam Yellin, who owned the Stratford Diner in Stratford, New Jersey. In 1941 *The Diner* published his article entitled "W-O-M-E-N Spells Success!" He made the radical move of having an all-women staff operate his diner. Here are the reasons he gave (remember, this is 1941): Women will work for less pay; women don't stay out late drinking and then call in sick the next day; women belong around food; women

MAYFLOWER DINER WASHINGTON, D. C.

5TH & RHODE ISLAND AVENUE. N. E. (U. S. ROUTE 1)

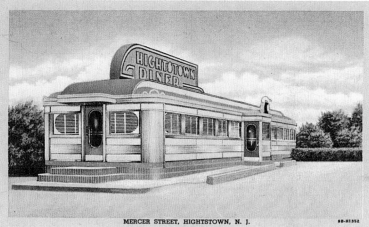

MERCER STREET, HIGHTSTOWN, N. J.

9B-H1352

The New **KULLMAN** *"Challenger"*

AMERICA'S SMARTEST DINING CAR

The crowning triumph of modern dining car construction

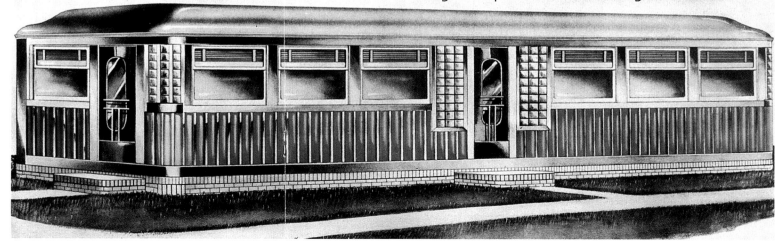

The Aetna Diner in Hartford, Connecticut, was totally clad in stainless steel with burnished circles.

The Highway Diner had at least two waitresses working in 1945. *(Pat Fodero)*

Opposite

This monthly feature in *The Diner* kept the industry up-to-date on new installations.

Openings of the Month

The purpose of this column is to acquaint the operator with new arrivals in the field, changes that are being made in modern Dining Car construction and the pace at which the Dining Car business is expanding. Perhaps you'll see here something new, something different, a name of a friend you have been trying to locate, the selling of a location you have had your eye on, or a dozen other interesting little things that are so vitally tied up with openings of Dining Cars.

The column contains data on owner, location, make of car, size of car and any unusual features which the manufacturer cares to release. If there is anything you want to know about special construction features, costs, terms, write direct to the manufacturer. He will be glad to supply you with this information.

KULLMAN DINING CAR CO.

THE AIRPORT DINER, INC., was installed over on Astoria Boulevard at 94th St., Astoria, Long Island, on July 9th. Its owner is Emanuel Veremakis who has been in the restaurant business before. The Car is on the Castle Turret plan, being 20' x 30', seating 18 at the counter, no tables, no booths.

JOE FORLENZA opened up a reconditioned Car at 236 Bay St., Tompkinsville, Staten Island. The Car is 10'6" x 36' and is unusual in that it has no booths and tables but devotes itself entirely to counter service and 16 stools.

J. B. JUDKINS CO.
Manufacturers of
STERLING DINERS

On July 10th MR. EMMETT A. SIMPSON, former steward on the Missouri & Pacific Line, opened up a Diner on the corner of Bell and Main Streets, Houston, Texas. The Car, complete and up-to-date in every respect, including air-conditioning, heating plant, full cellar, is 54'8" x 14'8". Finished in Ivory and Green, and boasts 14 booths and 14 stools. The name? Simpson's Dining Car.

PATERSON VEHICLE CO.
Manufacturers of
SILK CITY DINERS

THE BARTONSVILLE DINER was opened up on the Lackawanna Trail in Bartonsville, Pa., by Allen Besecker on July 3. The Car, 14 x 34, with 5 booths and 14 stools, is reconditioned.

THE PRINCETON GRILL, we are informed, was delivered to John F. Will on July 17th. The Car is 40' x 14'6", has 21 stools and 6 booths and will be located at Penns Neck on the Brunswick Pike traffic circle.

Jersey City, N. J., is a bit more decorated by the addition of Harold Mertz's new diner MERTZ'S DINER, over at 233 Communipaw Avenue. This Car, reconditioned, is 12'2" x 34', and has 5 tables and 16 stools. This is Mr. Mertz's first try at the Dining Car field, his former business being railroads.

JOE SMITH opened up the Colonial Diner, 215 North Avenue, New Rochelle, New York, on or about July 25. A new job, the Car is 40' x 14'6", seats 19 at the counter and has room for many more at 6 booths.

Just under the wire for a July opening, goes PERRIMAN'S GRILL, 890 Lexington Ave., Clifton, N. J. 40'2" x 14'8". Finished in Blue and Cream, having 5 booths and 15 stools, the Car is the property of S. W. Perriman.

JERRY O'MAHONY, INC.

MORRIS & SEIGAL, former gas station and parking lot owners (largest in N. Y., it is claimed), are trying their hand at the Dining Car business over on 10th Ave. at 33rd St., New York City. The boys have formed an incorporation, the Morris Diner, Inc., to run the Red Ball Diner, a 15' x 40' job, with 18 stools and 6 tables.

FRED TAYLOR has opened a Diner at 502 Rhode Island Ave., Washington, D. C. What his previous Dining Car experience had to do with his selecting a 16' x 45' Car, 22 stools and 8 booths, we don't know, but there it is.

GEORGE LE BLEU has opened a reconditioned Car on the corner of Hillman and Purchase Streets, New Bedford, Mass. The Car is 16'6" x 40'.

TOM SPRAGUE has replaced his old Car on Route #4, Manahawkin, N. J. with a factory-reconditioned Car, 12' 6" x 36'. The Car, which has 5 tables and 18 stools, is to be known as the "Manahawkin Diner," a fact surprising no one.

ROUTE #6, PARSIPPANY, N. J. is further enhanced by the installation of Bill Reher's new Car, the Troy Hills Grill. This Diner, which is 15' x 45' and has 8 booths and 20 stools, is not Bill's first.

SIMPSON'S DINER
Houston, Texas

TROY HILLS GRILL
Parsippany, N. J.

Women nearly outnumbered men at the Mayfair Diner in Philadelphia in 1944. Owner Henry Struhm and his wife Loretta are flanked by one of the shifts. *(Mayfair Diner)*

will work harder than men; women are always happy; women are more honest than men; women clean diners better than men; women are cleaner than men; the customers like women better; customers don't swear in front of women; more women patronize the diner. All this added up to a unique environment . . . with more profit for the owner.

The wage issue was foremost. "What man will work for as little as a woman will? We pay a woman 15 to 20 dollars a week (plus tips) for a 9 hour day. This is a fairly good wage for a woman. Tips amount to about $7.00 a week per girl here at my Diner. Each girl gets two meals a day free. That all adds up to about 25 to 35 dollars a week counting meals and my help is satisfied. Where could we operators get a good counterman for $20.00 a week? We couldn't do it."

Yellin felt his "girls" were way more efficient than countermen: "Girls don't let work pile up on them. They don't waste half the time bulling that men do. They can talk and work at the same time. They're always happy and ahead of themselves and that keeps things going at the right pace."

In fact, if *The Diner* is any guide, the problem of good help plagued the business perpetually. Operators were always writing in to complain that their staff was lazy, irresponsible and clipping them, to boot. Jimmy Foley recounted the various means a dishonest worker would use to clip him in his Kenmore Diner in Worcester. Often the man who wanted to do the dishes had a good reason for it: He'd already swept the customer's change off the counter into the water-filled sink below, where it silently fell to the bottom. The jargon popular in diners of the time had a term for this practice: "pearl diving."

In older diners the floor behind the counter was kept covered with sawdust to absorb spills and allow the countermen to slide effortlessly from position to position. The sawdust provided a soundproof cover for change to be "accidentally" dropped on the floor all day long. The man who swept up got to fill his pockets. Another sawdust trick was to put some in pants pockets; that way change could be slipped in all day and it wouldn't jingle.

Taking money directly from the register was known as "playing the piano" in the trade. With the low wages and twelve-hour days typical in the business, it was hard to get honest, hardworking men during peace time. With the threat of war, better-paying jobs in the factories exacerbated the situation. Eventually, the armed services took away the able-bodied men who remained.

When the United States went to war, production of diners came to a near standstill. For some companies, it was the end of the line: Sterling Diners and Ward & Dickinson closed their doors around 1942, never to reopen. Worcester Lunch stretched the construction of a handful of new diners over a period of three years to get the company through the lean war years. Jerry O'Mahony was awarded a contract to build truck bodies for the war effort. Fodero ceased

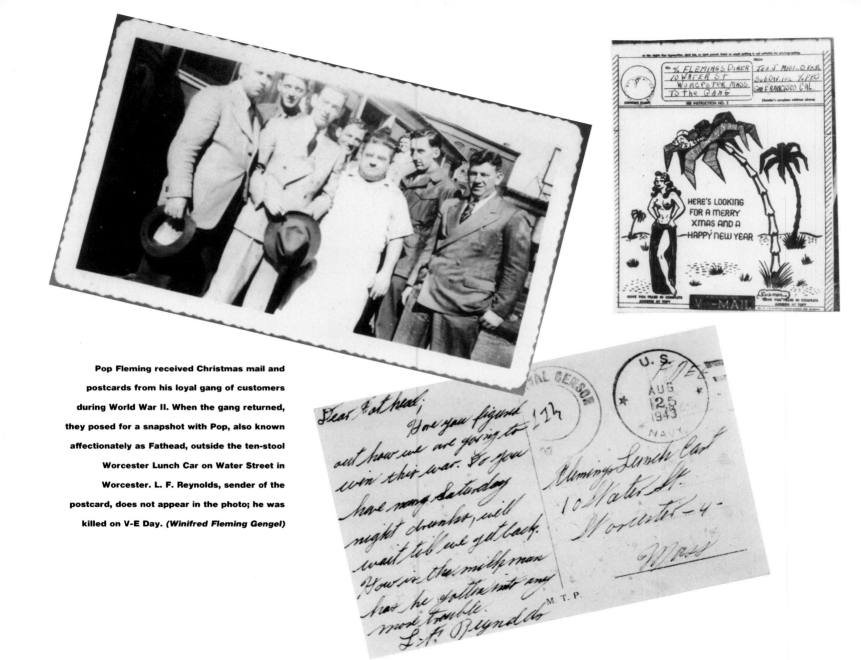

Pop Fleming received Christmas mail and postcards from his loyal gang of customers during World War II. When the gang returned, they posed for a snapshot with Pop, also known affectionately as Fathead, outside the ten-stool Worcester Lunch Car on Water Street in Worcester. L. F. Reynolds, sender of the postcard, does not appear in the photo; he was killed on V-E Day. *(Winifred Fleming Gengel)*

The same matchbook salesman made the rounds at both Kullman and O'Mahony, producing very similar messages. *(Don and Newly Preziosi)*

production and then started up again afterward. It was nearly impossible to build diners with depleted manpower and the government confiscating steel, copper, and other essentials.

But when the war ended, the demand for diners was greater than ever. When O'Mahony resumed diner building, they claimed a back order of more than fifty units. There were still materials shortages, so the waiting period was even longer.

Shortages were a way of life for the diner operators, as well. Jimmy Foley told of his experiences supplying his Kenmore Diner in Worcester. Sugar was rationed to such an extent that he could not get nearly enough needed to run the diner. Using his veteran's status, he went to the ration board, complained, and managed to get so much sugar that he was selling it to other businesses. He claimed that this was the best thing the service ever did for him.

The Diner was full of tips on how to make rations go further, as well as how to cook less-desirable cuts of meat and still have them turn out well. *The Diner* had ceased publication in December 1941 and resumed in July 1946. When one operator wrote in asking for back issues from before the war to complete his collection, he was informed that the magazine had donated all back issues to the paper drive for the war effort.

Gradually, life got back to normal. Prices came down; more people ate out and diners proliferated. The next generation of diner builders returned from the service and entered the ranks. Phil DeRaffele joined his father, Angelo. Pat and Ted Fodero started working with their father, Joe. Harold Kullman began work with his father, Sam.

Other companies splintered off from the established businesses, as many a shop foreman decided to go into business for himself. John Costello and Tom McGeary left Jerry O'Mahony and started Comac. Ralph Manno and Vincent Giannotti left Kullman and started Manno Dining Car Company. Master, Supreme, and Superior all appeared out of the woodwork. And in a blast

from the past, Edward J. (Ned) Tierney advertised he was back in business as Tierney Diners Inc., with offices on Broadway in New York City. (But his advertisements never showed more than a rendering.)

The new postwar models were fluid-looking structures with no hard edges; all corners were rounded, including, in some cars, the corner windows. In many cases, these diners were similar to the prewar designs. Ninety percent of the cars had table or booth service as well as a counter. Expensive materials such as marble, mahogany, and leather were rarely used. Such tilework as there was, was subdued. The new interiors made generous use of Formica, and the booths were framed in chrome tubing and upholstered with Naugahyde.

One Golden Age innovation can be attributed to Paramount Diners, who invented the "split

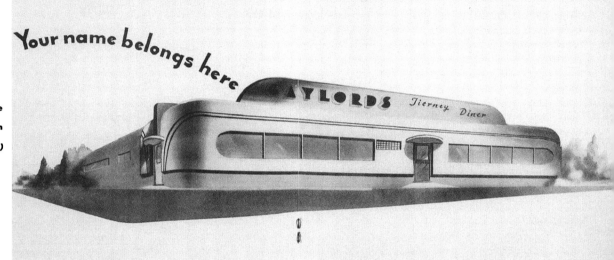

KNOW WHY IT'S *EASY* TO OWN YOUR OWN TIERNEY DINER

Your name belongs here

diner," which was protected by their patent, number 2,247,893, received July 1, 1941. Using this construction method, Paramount was able to build diners in two or more sections, which could be easily moved by truck or by rail. For example, all diners shipped to Florida went by rail. Before split construction, Florida-bound diners could have booths only if these were placed at the end of the diner. With split construction, a sixteen-foot diner could be built of two eight-foot pieces, shipped separately by rail, and still contain a full row of booths opposite the counter. When it reached its destination, the diner would be assembled into one unit on the foundation.

No one had successfully designed a diner that could be split lengthwise and shipped separately, because of rigidity problems during transport. Each piece of Paramount's split diner had one open

Here are two of Fritz Plassmeyer's five O'Mahony diners. The 1940 model (above right) had been outgrown by 1947. The cost of the blue-plate special went up fifteen cents to help defray the costs of the new double unit with its factory-built kitchen.

wall, yet the structural integrity was maintained. Paramount solved the problem by making the edges at which both halves joined continuous structurally without any vertical supports. Central floor support was provided by a combination channel and truss plate under the floor of each half at the joined edge. The rest of the structural frame was standard steel construction.

Other manufacturers quickly followed suit and began building diners in more than one section, as needed. A common configuration was a two-piece diner, each section sixteen feet wide, with one being the traditional diner layout and the back half serving as a full kitchen. A variation on this was to utilize part of the back half for a separate dining room and rest rooms. It may not have been clear at the time, but the breakthrough of split construction would lead the way to the giant diners of the postwar period.

Homemade Diners

Granted, most diners were built in factories. This has been true from the early wagon days right up through the present. But there have also been exceptions to the factory-built rule that definitely qualify for the sobriquet of "diner." ¶ The original Worcester Lunch Car Company employee, Wilfred H. Barriere, built diners on site in Worcester that were indistinguishable from factory-built diners. There is also a good chance that Barriere traveled to Montreal and there built the Mount Royal Diner into the first floor of an existing two-story building. ¶ And what about all those turn-of-the-century trolley lunches? These were reconditioned vehicles pressed into service and called diners. Converting trolley cars has continued (with the occasional actual railroad-car conversion) to this day. There were certain heydays to this phenomenon, most notably when cities discontinued their electric streetcar service, just as they had done with the

Moody's Diner in 1946, drawn by Rod McCormick. (What's Cooking at Moody's Diner, West Rockport, Maine: Dancing Bear Books, 1989)

Toto's Diner was a fantasy place that combined dining and dancing in a zeppelin rooted to the ground. (Paul Gray)

Preceding page

Bing's Diner, in Castroville, California, the artichoke capital of the world, is a beautiful diner converted from a streetcar. (Jim Heimann)

horse trolleys years before. Thus, Sisson's Diner in South Middleboro, Massachusetts, was a car retired from the Middleboro, Wareham & Buzzards Bay Street Railway Company in 1926 and converted on its very rails (or so they say) by Elmer Sisson. In another twist, the streetcar that became Sisson's Diner was built by Wason Manufacturing in Springfield years before they started building Brill Steel Diners.

Edward E. Mullens got his way around the postwar construction material shortage by converting two streetcars from the old Los Angeles Yellow Line. In the restaurant business since 1916, Mullens wanted to capitalize on the increased summer tourist trade along Route 101 in Buellton, California (the birthplace of split-pea soup, according to local lore). He installed the two cars with space in the center for a kitchen and a U-shaped counter, covering the complex with a hip roof. Each car was outfitted with seating at tables. Mullens used the vehicle motif, operating under the name Mullens Dining Cars, leaving the old streetcar signs ("PASSENGERS WILL HAVE FARES READY"), and designing special uniforms with conductor's caps for the waitresses.

Railroad rolling stock, with an average length of sixty to eighty feet, provided more room for seating, though the cars were much heavier and more costly to move. Southern California was the site of a number of homemade diners, converted into fantasies of immobilized streamlined locomotives. The actress Alice Faye was a partner in the Club Car on Wilshire Boulevard in Los Angeles, where tourists went for a square meal and an autograph.

Going after a different market, Herbert L. and Raymond E. Boggs operated in San Diego near three large aircraft plants: Consolidated-Vultee, Solar, and Ryan. The Boggs Brothers Airway Diner, two railroad cars end-to-end with a streamlined locomotive nose, was located on Highway 101 across from Lindbergh Field. One car was set up as a "coffee shop," with a counter and stools, while the other had table and booth service. The Boggs brothers took over the 1935 diner in July

From the street, only the unbroken row of windows gives the appearance of a diner, but on the inside, this Montreal establishment looks more like a real American diner. *(Worcester Historical Museum)*

1942 and subsequently added a drive-in and an "ultra-modern, high class restaurant" to the complex.

Just because a diner wasn't hauled to its site from a factory didn't mean it wasn't a diner. The voice of the dining car industry, *The Diner* magazine, did not discriminate against diner operations that were built from scratch. Ed Mullens and the Boggs brothers were both the subject of feature stories in postwar issues of *The Diner*.

In many cases, these homemade diners replaced factory-built units that the business had outgrown. The owners knew exactly what they wanted in a newer, bigger diner, and they hired local craftsmen to construct it for them. Two Boston-area diners, the Town Diner and the Blue Diner, fit this mold. In the mid-1940s, George Kontos and his father turned their old Worcester Lunch Car into the kitchen for their new Town Diner in Watertown. They built a combination "Worcester Lunch Car/Paramount Diner," with round glass-block corners and glistening two-

tone porcelain enamel skin. In downtown Boston, the Blue Diner, with its opaque blue-glass exterior, replaced an old barrel-roofed diner. These owners had a diner, needed a new one, and copied current diner designs.

Up in Waldoboro, Maine, Alvah and Percy B. Moody built themselves a roadside food stand in 1935 that was for all practical purposes an immobile lunch wagon. They expanded this original building twenty-two times, finishing in 1949. Moody's Diner was (and is) a diner in concept, shape, atmosphere, name, and menu. Though it may not use the flashy materials for which diner builders in New Jersey were known, its look is just right for down-home Maine.

Especially in parts of the country distant from the diner manufacturers, people took it upon themselves to construct their own diners. Some of these are more successful than others in capturing the true diner look. Some so closely resemble factory-built models that it is impossible to determine if a manufacturer was responsible for its construction.

But regardless of who built it, there is more to a diner than its architecture.

Opposite

The Town and the Blue are both diners built on site in the 1940s that could pass for factory-built diners to the untrained eye.

The superb sign of Moody's Diner beckons customers from far and near.

A Place to Take the Kids

When I was six years old, in 1924, my father did a shameful thing. He took me out to eat at Pete's Diner.

Mother couldn't have been more shocked if he'd taken me to the local speak-easy. Last month, however,

mother came home from an automobile trip a veritable Duncan Hines of the roadside-diner world. We heard

more about a certain de luxe diner in Virginia than we did about the Natural Bridge. Mother hasn't changed;

diners have. ¶ Pete's Diner was one of those surplus trolley cars sold after buses took over in our

neighborhood, and no motorman's glove was ever less appetizing than the counter there. The old converted

trolley car had deteriorated to the point where nobody would go into it in bad weather. No amount of

patching and propping seemed to keep the wind and rain from coming in the split seams and warped window

frames. Later, Pete got one of the new factory-made dining cars and put up a TABLES FOR LADIES sign. Soon

the girls from the bank and the stenographers from our two-story Lawyers' Building began to eat their

A Worcester Lunch Car booth service panel,

drawn by the author.

Up in the Berkshire town of Adams, Massachusetts, Joseph J. Wilusz was ready for a new place to supplant his old Worcester Lunch Car. The new Miss Adams was delivered on December 7, 1949, and is shown on its foundation, but not yet ready for business. The Miss Adams was not a great deal bigger . . . but it was newer. *(Adams Historical Society)*

Preceding page

Ford's Diner, an early 1950s Fodero in Amityville, Long Island, was an L-shaped double unit with the right half being a dining room.

(Pat Fodero)

lunches there. Last year Pete replaced his twenty-eight-seat car with a new chrome-and-neon job. It's now one of those sanitary juke joints which can be identified as a diner only by the sign out front. With a landscaped terrace and a blue-plate special retailing for two dollars, Pete's air-conditioned lunch wagon is the leading restaurant for family Sunday dinners out.

So wrote Blake Ehrlich in the June 19, 1948, issue of the *Saturday Evening Post* in an article entitled "The Diner Puts on Airs." Yes, the diner had come a long way. Ehrlich certainly knew his lunch wagons. It's interesting that he felt the latest models were so modern that it was hard to call them diners. When Pete's Diner became the place to go in town, the diner had shifted gears once again.

As time progressed, diners became more and more "respectable." The standard of comparison for the newest places was always something more old-fashioned. The big, new deluxe diners were a far cry from the streamlined and Art Deco models of the prewar era. In Pete's case, trading in an early-thirties dining car with a couple dozen seats for some postwar razzle-dazzle was enough to cause more than one customer to scratch his head and wonder what the diner business was coming to.

The families of the 1950s were eating out more often, and diners had to grow a little to handle the crowds. The changes in size also brought about changes in details. In 1946 the O'Mahony Company had introduced a new model that featured enlarged windows, curved glass corners, and taller trim above the windows, all tending to deemphasize the roof. The railroad-style monitor roof, a diner element for twenty-five years, was on the way out. It wasn't needed to provide light and ventilation anymore, and not only that, it just didn't fit in with the diner's new image.

This model was sheathed in cream-colored porcelain enamel with two horizontal porcelain

The Golden Arrow, on the Lincoln Highway in Trevose, Pennsylvania, was a new postwar O'Mahony model.

stripes, in either turquoise or red, meeting by the door to form two arrows. These diners were almost always made up of multiple sections. Uncle Bob's went to Flint, Michigan, by rail in 1947, split into four eight-foot-wide sections. Its purchase price was $51,000. Smitty's went to Massillon, Ohio, the same way in the same year. The Owl Diner went to Clearwater, Florida, in 1948. This model had as standard features both air-conditioning and radiant heat.

In November 1946, the O'Mahony Company announced the installation of the Deluxe Diner in Union, New Jersey, an immense diner of this style. With an L-shaped plan, eighty feet facing the street and 53½ feet to the rear, the diner sat 153 patrons. It was touted as the world's largest diner. It was also one of the first places to remove the short-order range and the sandwich board from behind the counter; all cooking was done in the kitchen. The only things in the diner proper were bread and butter, beverages, water stations, and salads and desserts, which were kept in display cases.

If you sat at the counter, things were no longer quite the same. The short-order cook had moved behind closed doors to a big kitchen annex in the back, and the customer was no longer

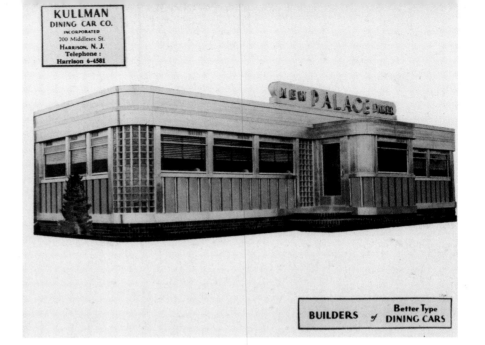

The monitor roof completely disappeared from view on the outside of Kullman diners by 1950.

where the action was. Counter showmanship—good, inexpensive entertainment—was a thing of the past, now to be found only in older cars.

Inside, the monitor design remained, but now indirect lighting washed the ceiling in fluorescent light. Sometimes a strip of mirrors ran down the center of the ceiling, adding an illusion of spaciousness. Tile floors were a thing of the past. Terrazzo, an aggregate of small chips of marble, set in colored cement and polished, added new decorative possibilities to diners, as contrasting colors, geometric designs, and logos could all be worked into the floor pattern.

Interior color schemes were based on a pastel palette rather than on the primary colors of earlier years. The Formica Company regularly updated its lines with whimsical patterns and the ever popular wood grain. In 1950, the Skylark pattern, designed by Brooks Stevens, was introduced by Formica. It was better known as Boomerang, because of its characteristic shape. The Skylark pattern flourished on every conceivable diner surface. Among Brooks Stevens's other

These vintage slides of the Kless Diner, in Irvington, New Jersey, were stereo views used by the Fodero Dining Car Company to market their 1950s diners. The predominantly salmon-colored interior was typical of its period. *(Pat Fodero)*

design accomplishments were ten complete railroad trains for the Chicago, Milwaukee and St. Paul Railroad, automobile designs spanning forty years (including the classic Excalibur), and the 1958 version of the Oscar Mayer Wienermobile.

Stevens is credited with coining the term "planned obsolescence," which he described as "the desire to own something a little newer and a little better, a little sooner than necessary." He wasn't talking about diners . . . but he could have been. The fact that an operator down the street could bring in a new diner and instantly make yours out-of-date was a constant worry for diner owners.

The industry made good use of this paranoia, so many owners traded in old diners for new ones, rather than adding on to an existing place.

In fact, new diner designs appeared so fast and furiously during the fifties that they can't be categorized. *The Diner & Counter Restaurant* (successor to *The Diner*) reported annually on changes in diner design in a feature entitled "Trends in Diners." After every company had changed its roofline, enlarged the windows, and switched to Thermopane, it attempted to develop its own unique look or detail. In many cases, the corner of the diner became the signature for the company.

Paramount offered the Zenith in 1950, with a distinctive skyscraper corner design: a wedding cake of stainless steel surmounted by a gleaming silver ball.

Mountain View offered a Streamliner, which toned down their characteristic postwar corner design, the cowcatcher, by replacing the large-radius glass-block corner with a curved glass window. Underneath that, they left a shrunken cowcatcher, a sheet of stainless steel that squares off the rounded corner to a point.

DeRaffele kept a vertical, fluted, porcelain enamel corner, offset by flared stainless steel pilasters, while having the body of the diner covered in horizontal porcelain-and-stainless stripes.

Master Diners, a new company in the postwar era, sliced off the corner of their diner and placed a double door there. This was no doubt a distinctive feature, but it also cut valuable floor space out of the diner.

Silk City's early 1950s designs involved little more than a change to the exterior finish. The diners were covered in concave horizontal flutes of stainless steel, with a strip of porcelain enamel in the middle for signage. The corner was remarkable for its lack of window; vertical stainless steel was topped with a curved flat panel that gave off the look of a torchère floor lamp.

Paramount's unique corner featured a stainless steel wedding cake. Mountain View had the cowcatcher.

Fodero did not have a unique corner, but the company was renowned for the excellence of its work in stainless steel. The Ingleside Diner is in Thorndale, Pennsylvania.

Opposite

A series of Silk City diners shows the evolution of their designs from the late 1940s to the late 1950s. Sam's (upper left) is still in East Rutherford, New Jersey, but it is unrecognizable, having been covered with wood. The Village Diner (upper right), in Red Hook, New York, is listed on the National Register of Historic Places, and thus its exterior, at least, will remain intact. The B & G (lower left) in Allentown, Pennsylvania, has been bricked over. Omar's Diner (lower right) in Meriden, Connecticut, has been converted to a Chinese restaurant. Note the old O'Mahony turned around and used as a kitchen behind Omar's.

The flexglas still looked good in the late 1980s when this photograph was taken of the New Royal Diner in Branchburg, New Jersey.

Opposite, upper left

Emmett Simpson (left) visited Jerry O'Mahony at the plant to check on the progress of the new stainless steel and flexglas diner he had ordered for his location in Houston. This unit replaced a Sterling Streamliner, which had replaced a Ward & Dickinson.

Opposite

Al McDermott of Fall River, Massachusetts, entered the diner business in 1910 and had so many diners they cannot all be accounted for. Continually upgrading, in 1954 he replaced the late-forties Fodero (below) with the big DeRaffele shown above.

This era was not without its setbacks. A new material called Mirroflex glass (generic name: flexglas) was used on diner exteriors, along with stainless. Flexglas was a small colored glass tile with a smooth front and a mottled silvered back. Mounted in strips, it added a sparkling, reflective, colorful touch to the façade—until it started to fall off. This was one of the least successful new materials put to use in diners.

In August 1950, the Fodero Dining Car Company announced, "The company is convinced it has devised a system that ensures the satisfactory installation of glass stripping on exteriors." This was no doubt in response to vociferous complaints about problems with flexglas.

Six years after her 1949 Jerry O'Mahony diner, the Emma Liner, was installed in Cleveland, Ohio, Mary Etta Cook wrote the company: "Gentlemen, The red glass flexi-blocks around the outside of our Diner continue to fall out. We purchased new ones from your company along with the cement you recommended and replaced them a year or so ago. Now, the old ones put in before you improved your methods continue to fall out. Do you feel that we are due any adjustment by your company for this trouble?"

It's doubtful that the O'Mahony company in 1955 would be concerned about a few pieces of flexglas falling off a diner. The company had much bigger problems to contend with. After Jerry O'Mahony sold the company on October 4, 1950, and retired to Florida, things slowly went downhill.

The new owners had big plans to expand the diner into the Midwestern and Western markets. In August 1952, they purchased the Herman Body Company, a truck-body manufacturer with a seven-acre plant in St. Louis. A number of diners were built there. However, Jerry O'Mahony, Inc., was mortgaged to the hilt and struggled to stay in business. The last diner under the Jerry O'Mahony name was built in Elizabeth and went out to South River, New Jersey, in 1956.

Bill Howard

Mountain View was turning out many diners of this style when the company went out of business in the late 1950s. This diner has been moved to Louisville, Kentucky.

At the same time, plant manager Joseph Montano, sales manager John Cronk, and treasurer Joseph Cavallo bought the company, incorporating it as Mahony Diners, Inc., in South Kearny, New Jersey. Using O'Mahony sales literature, with the name crudely changed only sometimes to read "Mahony," they embarked on a major public-relations campaign by installing a showcase diner and motel unit at the 1956 National Hotel Exposition in New York City. It was not unusual to see a diner at the big restaurant shows, but it was a coup for such a new company to steal the limelight. After the show, the diner traveled to Rahway, New Jersey, where it was installed as the LauraLyn Diner.

Undercapitalized from the start, the Mahony company built only four diners and then was forced to give it up within two years.

Along with the Jerry O'Mahony Company, several other leading manufacturers went out of business around this time. Mountain View outsold the competition in the early 1950s but did not

Stella's, now the Main Street in Woburn, Massachusetts, was one of the first Worcester diners to have stainless steel on the outside.

lead the world for long. In 1956 they attempted to go public, probably because of cash-flow problems, but this must have been unsuccessful because by 1958 they were gone.

Up in Worcester, Massachusetts, potential buyers had been complaining for years that the Worcester Lunch Car Company wasn't building anything up-to-date. It wasn't until 1952 that the company finally added some stainless steel to the porcelain enamel on the outside of its diners. By this late date, Philip Duprey, still the owner (as he had been since 1906), refused to put any money into the company to retool. Worcester Lunch Car Company continued to turn out their conservative New England model, which nobody wanted. Although they sold four diners in 1955, they didn't sell their next one, which was their last, until May of 1957. Worcester Lunch Car #850, Lloyd's Diner, went to Johnston, Rhode Island.

One half of Twaddell's Diner, Swingle's very first, is ready for shipment (above). The interior view (opposite, below) shows a typical early Swingle diner.

The dining car industry was populated with men who moved from company to company with the hope of starting their own outfit. One success story from this era was Joseph W. Swingle.

Joe Swingle married into the business by taking as his wife Kay Bruns, whose mother was Jerry O'Mahony's sister. When Joe returned from World War II, Uncle Jerry asked him to come by the plant after learning he was making thirty dollars a week as a schoolteacher. Although Joe had no experience whatsoever, Jerry offered him sixty dollars a week to be a manufacturer's representative. He gave Joe a car and told him to go eat in diners, learn what was going on, and spread the name of Jerry O'Mahony.

Joe liked the business. He left when O'Mahony started to slide, and landed the job of sales manager for Fodero Dining Car Company. He was so taken by diners that he and his brother, Dallas, opened their own diner on Route 22 in Springfield, New Jersey, in 1953. They invested $100,000 into the sixty-eight-seat diner, which was built by Fodero.

By 1957 he had learned enough about manufacturing to strike out on his own. With a pair of orders, he set up shop in Middlesex, New Jersey. The first Swingle diner was Twaddell's, delivered to Paoli, Pennsylvania, in November of that year. The next month, Spurlock's was sent to St. Petersburg, Florida.

Swingle began building diners during yet another period of great change in the business. The decade of the 1950s produced so many giant diners (nearly every company built "the world's largest" during this time) that most of the places were more dining room than diner. Kullman announced that their 1955 model was a "diner-restaurant," signifying the start of the ominous trend of getting away from the name diner.

The interiors of these new behemoths reinforced that shift. Walls were decorated with murals; planters abounded as decorative elements, and fish tanks were known to have been built into walls.

The Mari-Nay, in Rosemont, Pennsylvania, was a mid-fifties Kullman that was definitely getting away from the "diner" feel, with its interior appointments. The murals depicted local college life. In this opening-day view, all the bouquets of flowers still have the cards attached.

(Mrs. Joseph W. Swingle)

Catering to the small fry became big business: One owner ordered six hobbyhorses in lieu of counter stools.

Kenny King, who operated several drive-ins and a diner in Cleveland in 1956, included a toy giveaway at his places. As soon as kids walked in the door, they'd ask, "Where is the toy chest? Where is the toy chest?" As part of the "Clean Your Plate Club," children were given a card to exchange for a free ten- to fifteen-cent toy. King reported on this promotion as part of a diner

It was mainly fish on Friday at Fitzpatrick's Diner in West Roxbury, Massachusetts, during the week of February 3, 1952. *(Daniel J. Fitzpatrick)*

Opposite, upper left

The art director showed his sense of humor when placing these two ads side by side in the January 1954 issue of *Diner ● Drive-In and Restaurant* magazine.

Opposite, upper right

No question about it—diners got real big in the fifties.

FRIDAY'S LUNCHEON SPECIAL

TOMATO JUICE OR CUP OF FISH CHOWDER
FISH CAKE & BAKED BEANS WITH SWEET RELISH
ROLLS & BUTTER
JELLO OR PUDDING WITH WHIPPED CREAM
TEA OR COFFEE...............65

Please do not ask us to change our special.

****

FISH CHOWDER.....30   CLAM CHOWDER.....35
OYSTER STEW.....50

BAKED STUFFED HADDOCK,POT.,VEG.,ROLLS.......60
BROILED SWORDFISH,POT.,VEG.,ROLLS...........75
BROILED HALIBUT,POT.,VEG.,ROLLS.............75
BROILED MACKEREL,POT.,VEG.,ROLLS............60
CREAMED FINNAN HADDIE,POT.,VEG.,ROLLS.......60
CREAMED SALMON ON TOAST,POT.,VEG............60
FRIED SCALLOPS,FR.FR.POT.,COLE SLAW,ROLLS...75
FRIED CLAMS,FR.FR.POT.,COLE SLAW,ROLLS......75
FRIED FILET OF SOLE,FR.FR.POT.,COLE SLAW...65
FISH CAKES & BAKED BEANS,RELISH,ROLLS.......45
BAKED MACARONI & CHEESE,ROLLS...............30
SPANISH OR CHEESE OMELET,FR.FR.POT.,VEG.....65
HOT TURKEY SANDWICH,POT.,VEG.,GRAVY.........75
GRILLED MINUTE SIRLOIN STEAK,FR.FR.POTATO
          TOMATO & LETTUCE,ROLLS............1.15
HAMBURG STEAK & ONIONS,POT.,VEG.,ROLLS......65
GRILLED LIVER & BACON,POT.,VEG.,ROLLS.......75
GRILLED PORK CHOPS,POT.,VEG.,ROLLS..........85

****

SALADS

****

DESSERTS

JELLO OR PUDDING WITH WHIPPED CREAM.........15
FUDGE CAKE WITH ICE CREAM...................20
CHOICE OF PIES OR PASTRIES   WITH ICE CREAM
FRAPPES   SUNDAES   BANANA SPLITS

****

26   DINER ● DRIVE-IN AND RESTAURANT, JANUARY, 1954

Elkton Diner
"The World's Longest Diner"
U.S. Route 40
ELKTON, MARYLAND

operators' meeting: "We are thinking about putting on the card, 'Please do not force your children to eat it all because we portion pretty heavy,' as sometimes the parents want them to eat everything on the plate. They think they can't get a toy unless they do, but they can have a toy anyway."

Bigger families must have been one reason for building bigger diners. The 1957 Windmill Diner, on Route 1 in Providence, Rhode Island, was DeRaffele's entrant into the continual "world's largest diner" competition. At 150 feet long and thirty-five feet deep, it was pretty big. The central section could seat one hundred. It was flanked by symmetrical dining rooms, each seating 138 guests. Joseph D'Antuono, the proprietor, offered a smorgasbord every Sunday night, with thirty-eight different dishes for $1.95.

The manufacturers were still turning out small diners on demand, but with cover stories in *Diner Drive-In* featuring the likes of the Windmill, it's no wonder that diner operators saw this as the wave of the future.

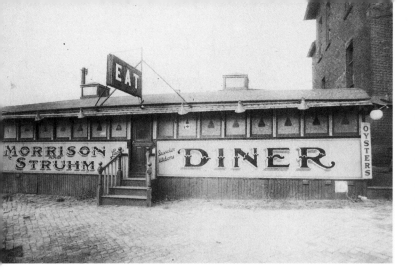

The Story of a Diner: The Mayfair

Morrison and Struhm's is shown before it was renamed the Mayfair. (Mayfair Diner)

Though it hardly looks like the same diner, the Mayfair was spruced up for its relocation to northeast Philadelphia. (Mayfair Diner)

The present Mayfair Diner in northeast Philadelphia was described by Joe Montano, plant manager for Jerry O'Mahony, Inc., as "the diner that made Jerry O'Mahony retire." This may have been an exaggeration, but a period of nearly ten years elapsed between the time the diner was ordered, after World War II, and the day it finally opened for business, after Thanksgiving in 1956. But more on that later.

As a youngster, Henry Struhm lived with two aunts who operated a horse-drawn lunch wagon at Fourth and Susquehanna streets. When he was not much more than a boy, Struhm joined forces with Ed Mulholland and Tom Morrison in a hot-dog stand. Their success led them to purchase a twenty-stool Jerry O'Mahony diner in 1928, which they operated, under the name of the Morrison and Struhm Diner, at Forty-first and Chestnut streets in Philadelphia.

In 1932, they gave the diner a new paint job, picked it up, and moved it to a rural area known as Mayfair in northeast Philadelphia. They had a hunch that the region was about to boom. They renamed their diner the Mayfair and went after prospective customers in the sparsely populated area, blanketing the neighborhood with flyers advertising their specials, along with their take-out orders and home delivery. Ads for their forty-cent daily supper and Sunday special came with the following announcement: "TO THE HOUSEWIVES OF MAYFAIR: We invite you and yours to try the above mentioned Special. Make it a habit to dine with us at least once a week. It will be both a treat and rest for you. Your husband will enjoy a nice Oyster Supper which we carry at all times. COME IN AND LET US GET ACQUAINTED."

By 1938, the Mayfair Diner had not only survived the depression, it had beaten it, and a larger Jerry O'Mahony diner (painted in the exact same style as the previous one) was brought in to handle the expanded business. It was longer, wider, and had booth service. So as not to interrupt business, the old barrel-roofed diner was set on the side of the lot, and continued to operate until the new one was installed. A mere three years later even this was too small, and the Mayfair moved a few blocks north, where a dining-room addition as long as the diner itself was constructed of cinder block.

It was with an eye to the future that Henry Struhm went back to the O'Mahony company after the war to discuss his needs for a replacement. Having twenty years in the diner business under his belt, Struhm knew *exactly* what he wanted. Everything was custom in the diner. According to his nephew, Jack Mulholland, one of the current owners, Struhm drove the company crazy. "He went over every square inch as they were building it. He'd make changes. There'd be fifty different drawings of the same plan. I have twenty-seven revisions of the hostess stand alone. I probably have twenty-five drawings of refuse cans."

Each time Struhm made a change, Ray Inisko, the draftsman for Jerry O'Mahony, would draw it up. When they finally got to building the diner, the change orders continued. Although the diner

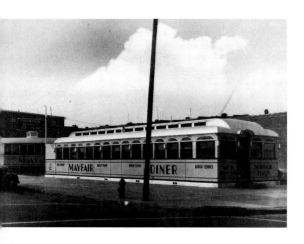

The old diner had yet another paint job when it was set aside to make way for the bigger O'Mahony model. (Mayfair Diner)

was delivered by Parker Brothers in the fall of 1954, it took two years for the O'Mahony company to complete the job to Struhm's specifications. The cinder-block dining room was remodeled at that time, inside and out, to match the new stainless steel and green flexglas diner. The final result is an incredibly long diner—118½ feet.

In November 1956, the extended Mulholland family had Thanksgiving dinner in the yet unopened new diner.

All that attention to detail has ensured the longevity of the present Mayfair Diner. By the mid-1970s, when many diner operators had renovated their stainless steel buildings with stucco, stone and brick, the Mayfair, now operated by the three Mulholland children, Jack, Ed Junior, and Claire, bucked the trend.

Jack explained his reasoning: "I thought, gee, we've got a pretty nice diner here, still in good shape. The species is going to become rare, so if we can see our way through this period, we'll end up with something that's unusual. It's accepted in the community; they don't look at it as being peculiar."

The Mulholland family has consciously kept the diner true to its 1950s origins, while renovating it every eight years or so, as surfaces get worn. The booths, lighting, countertops, tabletops, and ceiling have all been updated. Even the terrazzo floor needed repair—and that is the sign of a *successful* diner.

Of course, the food is the real key to the success of a restaurant, and the Mayfair's home-style cooking has emphasized quality since day one. As advertised on the 1930s handbill, "Quality comes first with us always." That's what keeps the three thousand or so customers who eat there on an average day coming back. In a typical twenty-four-hour period, the chefs might cook two hundred chickens, ninety dozen eggs and six hundred asparagus spears. Fresh vegetables are one

The present-day Mayfair gleams in the sunlight.

of the highlights of Mayfair fare. Soups and desserts are made from scratch.

The approach to the menu is similar to the idea of keeping the architecture true to form. Jack says, "We haven't just forever served croquettes. We have them, though. We've tried to stay with trends and keep up-to-date. With this neighborhood you can't get too far out, because they won't let you. You try to stay on the edge without calling it anything that will scare them. This is basically a neighborhood place. But people come and admire the fact that we're still a fifties-style diner—an original one."

When Stainless Steel Lost Its Shine

The five thousand or so roadside diners still operating in the 1960s had come to signify something

unique in the twentieth century. Through their unusual form and distinctive appearance, they

had earned a special place in the hearts of the public. When you drove up to a diner, you knew

what to expect: good, home-cooked food, and plenty of it, at a good price. Though a stranger, you

immediately felt at home when seated at the counter alongside one of the regulars. ¶ Diners

could bear a strong resemblance to each other and at the same time possess personalities all their

own. The families that operated them, either individually or in small chains, invariably put their

own imprints on the food, the decor, and the conversation. ¶ All this was to change with the

muscling in of the fast-food chains on a national scale. The roadside became more homogenized

A wide-open Erfed diner design.

with the growing nationwide restaurant chains erecting copycat outlets from coast to coast. On

The All American Diner in Allentown, Pennsylvania, was built in 1960 by DeRaffele. The stainless and porcelain façade is downplayed by the large windows and flared overhang.

Preceding page

The Country Diner in Windsor, New Jersey, is a 1960s Kullman with a boxy, picture-window façade.

October 5, 1962, the first national advertisement for McDonald's appeared in *Life* magazine. The red-and-white-tiled hamburger stands, still take-out only, were having a large impact on the way the American public ate on the run. By the end of 1962, the seven hundred millionth hamburger had been sold.

What the fast-food chains offered, of course, was predictability. This was in contrast with the local diners. When you went into a fast-food place, you knew beforehand what you would order, and you knew it would be exactly the same as the last time you had it, no matter where in the country that might have been. What the diners offered was regional cooking and atmosphere.

With the rising popularity of fast food in the 1950s, tastes changed and diners changed with them. Occasionally, a radical design would give a new look to one company's model. In the mid-1950s, Kullman introduced an oversize (six-foot) projecting canopy running around the

PUBLIC DEMAND CREATED THIS CHARCO-GRILL

Above left

The Kullman Charcolette featured garage-style overhead doors that opened up the building during the fair-weather months.

Above right

The Trio was sent to the Miami area by DeRaffele around 1960. The flared corner entrance with recessed lighting was its most prominent feature.

roofline. With recessed lights illuminating the diner, these top-heavy units looked as if they were going to tip over.

Many manufacturers experimented with combination diner/drive-ins. This was pioneered by Paramount's "Roadking" design as early as 1948 . . . but not very successfully. In 1956, in another twist, DeRaffele Dining Car Company combined the overhanging canopy with a self-serve walk-up custard stand in an attempt to diversify the diner. This unique diner, the O-Ma-Ha, was located at the entrance to the Long Island Expressway in Queens, New York.

After experiencing a period of growing pains, during which the old look no longer seemed to fit—custard stand, drive-in, or whatever—diner designers turned to new sources of inspriation for their designs. The incredible futuristic diners of the early sixties were clearly the offspring of the space age. Great juggernauts of glass, tile, and stainless steel, they had an undeniably new look.

The P & B, built by Swingle in 1963, for a Glassboro, New Jersey, location, had a new exterior look with ceramic tile.

Opposite

The April 9, 1963, menu for Swingle's Colonial Diner, on Route 22 in Springfield, New Jersey, featured their char-broiled hearth specialties, which accounted for five of their six "unretouched" dinner photographs.

(Mrs. Joseph W. Swingle)

Their identifying feature was the now ubiquitous overhanging roofline—a bizarre zigzag canopy that looked as if it had been cut out with a gigantic pair of pinking shears. The vigor of the space age, as seen in diners, was akin to the public's keen interest in the race to the moon.

The zigzag roof, technically known as a "folded plate," was a common feature of countless coffee shops across the nation, and the diner builders were borrowing the design in an effort to stay up-to-date.

As always, new materials were showcased in the diners, and builders rarely failed to point out that they were innovators in the same tradition as the aerospace industry. Not precisely the stuff of rocket flights, the new diner materials of this period included beach-pebble marble imported from Italy, bamboo draw curtains, and handsome light fixtures that looked like little flying saucers.

On the opposite side of the spectrum, far from the futuristic, some builders were looking to

Char-Broiled Sirloin Strip Steak 1.59

Char-broiled Virginia Ham Steak, (Hawaiian) 1.50

Char-broiled Half Chicken 1.35
Actual Unretouched Photographs of our Dishes

Sea Food Suggestions

SERVED WITH FRENCH FRIED POTATOES AND COLE SLAW

Broiled Lobster Tail, Drawn Butter 2.45

Fried Deep Sea Scallops, Tartar Sauce 1.25

Fried Jumbo Fantail Shrimps, Cocktail Sauce 1.35

Fried Filet of Haddock, Tartar Sauce ...... .95

Combination Sea Food Platter 1.45

Char Broiled Specialties

CHAR-BROILED OVER A BED OF LIVE GLOWING COALS

Boneless Sirloin Steak, Onion Rings 2.70

Swingle's Open Steak Sandwich, Onion Rings 1.55

Ham Steak Hawaiian 1.50

Loin Pork Chops, Apple Sauce 1.45

Chopped Prime Steak, Grilled Onions 1.25

above orders served with
Cole Slaw and French Fried Potatoes

Sandwiches — Sandwiches

All Sandwiches Royal Style .40 extra (French Fries, Cole Slaw, Lettuce and Tomato)

Fried Egg	.25
Taylor Ham and Egg	.50
Ham or Bacon and Egg	.50
Egg Salad	.35
Western Egg	.50
Canadian Bacon	.65
Liverwurst	.35
American Cheese	.30
Swiss Cheese	.35
Lettuce and Tomato	.30
Individual Bumble Bee Salmon, Bermuda Onion	.70
Grilled Cheese	.35
with Ham or Bacon	.55
Hamburger	.40
Cheeseburger	.50
Taylor Pork Roll	.35
Tuna Fish Salad	.50
Shrimp Salad	.50
Pastrami	.75

Corned Beef	.75
Grilled or Boiled Ham	.45
Ham and Cheese	.55
Ham and Swiss	.60
Filet of Haddock	.55
Bacon, Lettuce, Tomato	.50
Frankfurter (Char-Broiled)	.25
Chicken Salad	.55
Cream Cheese .30 w. Jelly	.40
Cream Cheese with Lox	.75
Peanut Butter	.30
Roast Beef	.60
Sliced Turkey (Breast Meat)	.80
Sliced Turkey (white and dark meat)	.70

SIDE DISHES

Side Order of French Fries	.25
Vegetable, Side Dish	.20
French Fried Onion Rings	.35
Lettuce and Tomatoes	.25
Tossed Salad Bowl (Large)	.75
(Small)	.25

ON ALL SANDWICHES: TOMATO .10 EXTRA   (Small)
BUTTER by REQUEST

ALL ITEMS ON MENU WILL BE CAREFULLY WRAPPED AND PACKAGED TO TAKE OUT

Char-broiled Prime Chopped Steak 1.25

Char-broiled Loin Pork Chops 1.45

Fried Shrimp 1.35

The Penn Queen, an immense DeRaffele of the space-age style, was in Pennsauken, New Jersey.

the past for new ideas. And the colonial diner hit the roadside.

Colonial imagery has been in fashion, out of fashion, and strongly revived a number of times over the history of the United States. Considered old-fashioned twenty-five years after the American Revolution, it was first revived in the mid–nineteenth century with the preservation of George Washington's headquarters in Newburgh, New York, and his home at Mount Vernon. The Centennial Exposition of 1876 and the reconstruction of colonial Williamsburg begun by John D. Rockefeller II in 1927 were other influential events.

Occasionally, colonial style was applied to roadside architecture, but in the early twentieth century, this was the exception rather than the rule. It is true that many diners had been named "The Colonial," but they didn't look like colonial buildings.

Basically, diner designers thought they had pretty much exhausted the possibilities with the

This shows the shift from heavily worked stainless steel and porcelain enamel, through ceramic mosaic tile, to the conglomeration of stone surfacing that began to be used on diner exteriors.

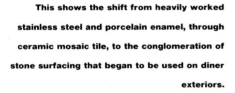

The Tamarack Diner, built by Swingle, was one of the very first diners to use colonial styling on the inside.

usual materials. After manipulating stainless steel into every conceivable configuration and profile for exterior use, diner builders began to experiment. As the amount of glass expanded, the body of the diner shrank. What stainless there was, was replaced by mosaic tile—not only on the outside, but on the backbar surfaces as well.

The colonial diner design was a bold step, and it was first taken only on the inside.

It was Joseph W. Swingle, of Swingle Diners, Inc., who was the first to turn to a variety of Americana images for his newly built diners. These included colonial, Old West, and nautical motifs, all sprinkled together in varying amounts over the years.

The Tamarack Diner in Somerville, New Jersey, built by Swingle in 1959, had a traditional stainless steel exterior, but a colonial-styled interior, which included knee bracing actually made of tamarack, the wood used to brace the hulls of whaling ships. The ceiling featured a wooden ship's wheel suspended by wrought-iron sea horses. An oil painting with a nautical theme complemented the motif. The diner also had what Joe Swingle later called "a very colonial dining room," with wooden booths and benches reminiscent of an early-American inn. The backbar and hood were now built of brick, hammered copper and small mosaic tile. As diner designers looked for new ideas, these Americana diners were seen as a breakthrough.

The Swingle family had been running their own Fodero-built diner since 1953 on Route 22 in Springfield, New Jersey. By 1960, they replaced it with Swingle's Colonial Diner, a diner with a stainless steel exterior. A pair of coach lamps on the vestibule was the only hint of early Americana. At night though, the wagon-wheel lamps inside were plainly visible through the large picture windows. The back wall was paneled in wood, and a hand-painted sign with a portrait of a bull was displayed, reading, "1801. Colonial Eatery. Towne of Springfield."

Not to be outdone, the Kullman Dining Car Company of Newark, New Jersey, started using bricks, salvaged from old colonial houses, on the exterior of their new diners as a reaction to the fast-food restaurants, which were very flashy and colorful. Diners wanted to get away from the fast-food image, so the trend was toward more conservative designs, and, on the interior, more dining room and less diner.

With the widespread urban-renewal projects that ushered in the 1960s came scores of city planning boards, which began to legislate taste in buildings. This was an ominous sign for diners, as the old flashy look was often no longer tolerated. In some regions, all new diners had to conform to stringent regulations, which often banned not only stainless steel buildings, but even the word "diner." Several of the diner builders even dropped "diner" from their names: Paramount Diners became Paramount Modular Concepts; DeRaffele Dining Car Company became DeRaffele

Kullman became well known for its finely detailed colonial diners, which fit into any suburban neighborhood. The Candlewyck is in East Rutherford, New Jersey.

Manufacturing; Kullman Dining Car Company became Kullman Industries.

The first colonial diner with an all-brick exterior was built by Kullman in 1962 in Ocean City, New Jersey. Harold Kullman reminisces, "We made it more like a restaurant . . . no real architectural design. It had its own particular design. We went to Americana for the look. The township didn't like the jazzy look, so we designed a brick diner that wasn't a diner, but a restaurant." Kullman later admitted in a newspaper interview that when he advocated the colonial look, "my father thought I was ready for a mental institution."

The Kullman colonial diner had a decidedly Georgian feel to it. It had a brick exterior with a center entrance adorned with coach lamps. Its symmetrical bay windows imitated divided lights in stainless steel. A row of dentils—small cubes—in stainless ran along the roofline, which was often surmounted by an ornamental balustrade used to hide the air-conditioning ducts.

The inside featured a plethora of plastic-laminate wood-grain panelings. Nearly all stainless steel had disappeared: The wall of the backbar, formerly shimmering sunburst panels, was now covered in ceramic tile; the stainless hood was now constructed of copper. If the wagon wheel was not employed for mounting overhead early-American light fixtures, it was used merely as a

decorative element, dividing the counter area from the booth seating. Exposed beams were another standard feature, covered in wood-grain and sometimes "held up" with ornamental cast-iron brackets.

The public response to the colonial diner was very positive, and many old-style-diner owners wanted to redo their places or replace them with new colonial designs. These new roadside showplaces were really unlike anything else . . . and were thus in keeping with the diner tradition of unique architecture. Ironically, patrons did not necessarily think of the new places as "diners," which is exactly what the diner builders wanted.

The colonial diner pointed the way for diner design for nearly twenty-five years. (Even in the 1990s, there are still cities in New Jersey whose ordinances won't allow the installation of any diner not of colonial design.) As the public was enticed with more fast-food choices, the diner was striving to be more than a roadside restaurant. The image was that of a conservative, family-oriented place to eat, with an ever larger menu and a less flashy look. The diner menu offered hundreds of choices of food from several nationalities. It was difficult to open more than two of the gigantic menus simultaneously at a table for four. The dining rooms stretched on forever, and

The Brooklawn Diner, in Brooklawn, New Jersey, was built in 1977 by the king of the Mediterranean-diner builders, DeRaffele.

featured tables more often than booths, while the number of stools at the counter continually shrank to an all-time low of eight or even six. (And this in a two-hundred-seat restaurant.)

Although the old stainless steel diners began to dwindle in numbers, the diner business did not really decline. Those who predicted that *all* old diners would disappear were a bit premature. In fact, the diner manufacturers continued to thrive, building their colonial restaurants. But by the decade of the seventies, even the colonial was not enough of a departure from the old diners.

In search of something "flashy" that was not necessarily shiny, with at least a little push or shove from the ever growing number of Greek diner owners, manufacturers gave birth to the Mediterranean style, which signified the diner look of the 1970s.

The typical Mediterranean diner was a palazzo of stone with a row of repetitive arches, surmounted by a Spanish quarry-tile mansard roof. The arches encased windows, with in-fill panels of brick, stucco, or a coarse stone aggregate. The flash took over on the inside, where the design and multitude of materials might be called excessive: wall-to-wall carpeting, smoked mirrors, flocked wallpaper, imported tile backbars, scalloped countertops, Tiffany-style lamps, crystal chandeliers, Grecian statuary, nailhead-studded chairs.

In a 1979 interview, John Baldares, touted as Long Island's foremost diner architect of the 1970s because of his prolific involvement with the diner manufacturers, explained the decade's diner aesthetic. First of all, he admitted he was Greek. He gave most of the credit for the Mediterranean design to the builders and owners. "The architect essentially does the planning and technical work. He's not the main influence." The latest diner designs were merely modifications and elaborations on existing places. (This was nothing new in diner design.)

Sitting in one of his own creations, the Sweet Hollow Diner in Melville, New York, a stuccoed and paneled, beamed and carpeted, Italian-tiled, scalloped-countered place, he remarked, "No, it's not what I would do. It's what my client wants. And I don't think it's all that bad if it succeeds as a business venture. The public really likes it. As social engineering, I think it's high art."

This was the state of the art, especially on Long Island, also known as Diner Island in the trade. At the end of the 1970s, the Diner and Restaurants Associations from the boroughs of Nassau, Suffolk, and Queens counted 230 diners within their districts. With so many big, new flashy diners appearing, the little stainless steel ones were really feeling the crunch. It was literally the crunch—of the bulldozer—that did away with many of the diners that were traded in for new models.

The Old Colony survived intact until the 1980s, and is shown here at its last location in Dracut, Massachusetts. At the time of its construction, it was the largest Worcester Lunch Car ever built.

The Story of a Diner: Victoria Dining

The Victoria is the only colonial diner in Boston. And it's not even called a diner anymore—not since May 1971. Owners Nicholas and Charles Georgenes wanted to attract more family trade. The name was changed from "Victoria Diner Restaurant" to "Victoria Restaurant" (after the owners' mother, Victoria). In the early 1980s, it was changed again, to "Victoria Dining."

The Georgenes family has always been following trends and adapting to them. This was the case when their uncle James purchased his first diner from the Worcester Lunch Car Company in the 1920s. By 1936, James and his brothers George and Peter, along with some friends and cousins, had a chain of five Worcester diners in the greater Boston area.

The hub of this chain was the Old Colony Diner in South Boston, owned by James. The United Diner, on Mystic Avenue in Somerville, had a bake shop that supplied the other diners. Charles

George Georgenes poses outside the new diner.

remarked about working there as a youngster, "It's funny, you never minded going to the bake shop even though you had to do some work. There was always a fig square or a turnover." One of his jobs was to pump the jelly into the jelly doughnuts. Part of his reward was a small supply to take home; he would always double-pump those.

In describing some of the food trends over time, Charles looked back at some of their old menus. They were quite sophisticated. Some of the chefs who worked for the family had come out of Boston hotels and other tablecloth restaurants and brought with them the recipes they'd learned there. These showed the influence of all the people who had settled in New England. From the Irish came corned beef and cabbage; fancy brisket with spinach; and Irish lamb stew. There were Greek dishes and Italian dishes; there was a Mediterranean fish stew. It was not just a hamburger, meat loaf, and liver-and-onions bill of fare.

Following the deaths of James and Peter in 1938 and 1941, the chain splintered. Charles and Nicholas's father, George, ended up with two diners. One he ran and the other he leased. But he sold both in 1947 and spent a year planning for a new diner. Charles recalled that all their other diners looked alike. "We wanted to be different so we could be identified. We wanted a place that didn't look like any other place."

They bought a fifty-two-seat stainless steel Jerry O'Mahony diner from New Jersey and opened it on January 3, 1949. It was located on Massachusetts Avenue near the intersection of four communities: Dorchester, South Boston, Roxbury, and the South End. Massachusetts Avenue was also one of three major roads from Boston to the southeastern part of the state. There was plenty of traffic, and business was good.

Over time the area changed. The tourist traffic, which had been a constant, diminished when an expressway bypassed the area. But business in the diner didn't really suffer because new industries moved in. Meat cutters, union officials, tradesmen, and truckers continued to fill the diner.

By 1965, Charles and Nicholas, owners since their father's death in 1956, decided to replace their diner with a new one. This was the height of the colonial period, and the brothers thought this new look was just what they needed. They were lobbied hard by Fodero, but purchased a Swingle, which came in two sixty-eight-foot-by-seventeen-foot sections, along with a vestibule.

The Victoria is alive and well, and has gone through periodic remodelings. A dining room, the Cafe George, named for their father and styled after an English pub, was added in 1975. This was a conscious effort to attract more of the family market. They did not change the diner part of the restaurant at this time, so as not to discourage the workers from coming in. Five years later a complete overhaul took place. Half of the counter was removed, more booths were added, and the old wagon-wheel lamps were replaced.

Today the food follows the latest trends: more fish and chicken than beef; more fresh vegeta-

The exterior of Victoria Dining still is very similar to its look when new in 1965.

bles. "We still sell our share of steaks and chops, but the market is changing. What was true fifteen years ago is not the same today."

The Victoria has always supported the local community. One example is a new tradition the owners have started. The graduating fifth-grade class from the local inner-city elementary school is invited, with their teachers and principal, to a four-course luncheon in celebration of their achievement. They take over the banquet room, which is set formally with tablecloths, cloth napkins, and water goblets. Part of the presentation includes an etiquette class on how to attend a function. The kids are taught how to fold napkins, how to set a table, and which silverware to use. The whole event is topped off with hot-fudge sundaes.

Although the name "diner" was removed from the Victoria, it has continued to offer the quality, the service, and the friendliness that have been the hallmark of the Georgenes family since the 1920s. A third generation of family members is now in place at the Victoria.

New Faces on Old Places

When a diner got run-down, there were a few choices: If you had no money, you lived with it; if you had a lot of money, you traded it in on a new model; if you were somewhere in the middle, you renovated. There was certainly pressure to do something. ¶ Diner owners and builders alike wanted to see better-looking diners on the roadside. A stronger, more positive presence was good for the business. In a letter to the editor of *The Diner* in January 1947, E. A. Simpson wrote: "Upon my recent trip to New Jersey I drove practically all over the State—anywhere I could find a Diner in operation. I saw some of the worst looking, dingy traps. I think it would be wise for the Dining Car manufacturers, in the future, when they sell a new Car and the operator trades in the old one, to take the old one immediately to the junk yard and blast it to pieces." The editor concurred:

A new vestibule designed by Erfed.

"We were particularly pleased to get your opinion on what should be done with old junky Diners.

Diner renovator Erwin Fedkenheuer, Jr., was constantly on the lookout for diners to remodel. He snapped this picture during his travels, but it did not translate into work for the company.

Erfed Corporation also got work by using direct mail.

Preceding page

The Wurtsboro Diner, in Wurtsboro, New York, was an old Silk City spruced up by Erfed in 1963.

While many replacement Diners still have years of service in them, it would be well, as a matter of policy, if any Car over a certain age was destroyed before it blights our industry."

This radical solution did not, however, solve the problem of what to do with older diners that weren't traded in. Often, when a diner shifted location, it was the perfect time for a facelift. When Tom Morrison, Henry Struhm, and Ed Mulholland moved their O'Mahony car, the Morrison and Struhm Diner, from Forty-first and Chestnut streets in Philadelphia to the new Mayfair section of town in northeast Philly, they decided it was time for a new paint job. The result hardly looked like the same diner. They renamed their diner the Mayfair, based upon the supposition that this new area of the city "may fare well." They also replaced most of the frosted and etched windows with clear glass.

Henry Struhm did periodically go back to Jerry O'Mahony for a brand-new diner, but when he required work in the meantime, or when he needed assistance installing the new diner, he went to a local diner renovator, George E. Skirdlant, who had a company in Philadelphia called Modern Diner Builders.

Modern Diner Builders was one of the earliest diner-reconditioning outfits that was separate from the manufacturers. The company would refinish your woodwork, apply a canvas roof, or install a porcelain ceiling or exterior—all without interference to your business.

Perhaps the most prolific diner renovator was the Erfed Corporation, started in 1956 by the father-and-son team of Erwin Fedkenheuer, Sr., and Erwin Junior in Rutherford, New Jersey. Erwin Senior left Paramount Diners with two other sheet-metal men in 1956. He had been with Paramount as the sheet-metal foreman for over twenty years.

The Erfed Corporation, in its first press release, announced that it would be designing and building high-quality food-service equipment, as well as making modern diners. In addition, they would *"specialize in the repair, modernization and renovation of existing Diners on location*—a service that is definitely needed in the Diner Industry." New diners could be shipped anywhere, but the repair-and-modernization trade was confined to the metropolitan New York, New Jersey, and Philadelphia areas.

They set up shop on a former dairy farm. They only built five new diners, but over the subsequent twenty years renovated and modernized between fifty and sixty old ones. Their first job was fabricating a stainless steel parapet to hide the railroad-style monitor roof on the Hollis Diner, a 1939 Paramount set up in Queens near the New York World's Fair.

The usual modernization included both outside and inside work. On the exterior, it meant modifying the roofline to get rid of the old-fashioned look, enlarging the windows by removing every other vertical support, and installing a new outside skin. This was the forte of Erfed. With their unequaled craftsmanship in stainless steel, they worked up some beautiful profiles and

Following pages

The old Cadillac in Westwood, New Jersey, comprised two diners in an L shape: an old unit and one from the fifties. Erfed remodeled the old diner to complement the newer one.

details. The stainless was combined with Mirawal, a porcelain enamel product that came in thirty-two different colors.

On the inside, new Formica was usually installed, along with new snap moldings. Because work had been done on the windows, new sills and other trim were required. Counters and tabletops were resurfaced if necessary. A local tile man was brought in to redo the floor.

Most of Erfed's jobs were accomplished while the diner remained open for business. The renovators would work on one end of the diner while patrons were eating away in the other half during most of the day, but they would always take time off from eleven-thirty till one so as not to interrupt the lunch rush. It usually took three months or so to do a diner.

Besides working on the jobs, Erwin Junior was the salesman, who visited countless diners trying to hustle work. He carried with him a sample wall segment, which he would put up in front of the diner, sliding in various porcelain colors until one hit the mark with the proprietor. The owner of the Cadillac Diner in Westwood, New Jersey, fancied bright orange. When the Grant-

wood in Cliffside Park, New Jersey, was redone as Russell's, that owner wanted a brilliant yellow to attract customers on dreary, rainy days.

Erfed was occasionally called upon to convert an ordinary restaurant into something that looked like a modern diner. The Rail Diner, on Railway Avenue in Paterson, New Jersey, was a nondescript stucco building before Erfed tuned it up in 1962 by encasing it in stainless steel and bright orange porcelain enamel. Evidently business was good, because the renovators were called back two years later to add more seating. The 1964 addition consisted of a flagstone-faced dining room with picture windows. It was tied into the original building by extending the Erfed-installed

The Bel Air was one of only five new diners built by the Erfed Corporation.

parapet of stainless and porcelain along the roofline and adding foundation planters of flagstone along the length of the old and new buildings.

Usually an increase in business was what was desired. That was not the case with the Fort Lee Diner, an old Silk City in Fort Lee, New Jersey. After the Erfed renovation, Erwin Junior recalled, "The guy hollered at us! He was doing about three thousand a week in there. We remodeled it and he was doing about four thousand. 'Now I have to have another chef and I have to get so many of this and so many of that. All I wanted to do was make it look better!' "

Although Erfed only built a handful of new diners, they were ones of distinction. Shirley's, in

West New York, New Jersey, was a classic 1960 design with an overhang with recessed lights and a corner of curved glass, fluted stainless, and slanted pilasters topped by a pair of projecting stainless elements. In this era when the diner corner was such a statement, Erfed had a version of this design as a showpiece at their plant. When a customer came for a consultation, the curtains would be drawn back, revealing this incredible corner structure, inside and out.

Another distinctive feature of Shirley's, probably unnoticed by most customers, was the fact that one wall was built at 87 degrees, because the owner insisted it follow the street. Erwin Junior exclaimed, "You couldn't take a square to it, because it was out of square. It had to be! It drove us insane!"

The Bel Air Diner, completed in the spring of 1964 and installed in East Rutherford, New Jersey, was a most unusual new Erfed creation. It had gigantic picture windows framed by thin, rectangular, intersecting vertical supports of porcelain and stainless. These supports cut right through the narrow-depth roof canopy. The body of the diner was covered in small, light-blue mosaic tiles.

Erfed Corporation moved on from the diner business in the mid-1970s, when there was little call for the expert stainless work for which they were known.

The trend in both new diners and renovations during the seventies was to make the place look less like a diner to passersby. This was the era when countless old diners were converted to "restaurants" by pulling down the stainless steel façades, altering the windows, refacing with brick or stone, and capping the whole thing off with a mansard roof.

By this time, diners were way too big to haul back to the factory and recondition. All diner manufacturers did (and still do) renovations on site. Nowadays, the colonial and Mediterranean places are showing their age, and consequently are being redone into today's latest styles.

Yes, There Are Still Diner Builders

Despite the proliferation of colonial and Mediterranean diner-restaurants, thankfully there were

a few diner owners who wanted something else. And the diner builders always aimed to please.

These requests for a new kind of diner always resulted in a one-of-a-kind unit. ¶ Two Kullman

diners built during the 1980s stand out from the crowds. The Silver Star, in Norwalk, Connecti-

cut, was one of the early high-tech diners. The indescribable glass, brick, metal, and stainless

exterior is more reminiscent of an office-park building than a diner. Without the sign, the function

of the building would be unknown. ¶ At six thousand square feet, the Silver Star is typical of the

period, with more restaurant and less diner. There is still a counter (with jukeboxes), some very

plush stools, a vast number of booths, and a dining room that seems to go on forever. The

A recent Kullman floor plan.   elaborate horseshoe-shaped bar is much more prominent than the counter. Stainless steel trim is

used throughout, but in an updated mirror finish, which became Kullman's new trademark.

The interior color scheme is beige, mauve, and ivory. Abundant live plants decorate the diner. In a new variation on an old theme, a wall panel above a heavily tufted booth was rendered in a sunburst design . . . but instead of being made from stainless steel, it is Naugahyde.

In 1985, Kullman delivered The Ritz of Philadelphia to its site on Route 1. This Darth Vader of a diner is a box of black mirror glass with bay windows and an octagonal vestibule along the front. It sits on a plinth of stone, an allusion to the regional residential architecture of northeast Philadelphia. The inside features a fair amount of granite, which has become one of the new diner-interior materials.

In the meantime, Kullman, DeRaffele, Paramount, Musi, and Swingle were progressing into a new "modern" style. Often these buildings were stone, with a row of vertically rectangular windows, each individually capped with a small bronze mansard roof. The greenhouse phase hit

The Metro, in Iselin, New Jersey, features a large, carpeted greenhouse dining room with chandeliers. It was built by Kullman in 1987.

The Silver Star is a 1980 high-tech diner built by Kullman.

the diner business as well, and many bronzed-glass dining rooms were appended to the designs. DeRaffele has brought back the use of skylights, which now flood the dining areas with daylight. This is a totally different look from the heavy, dark interiors of the colonial phase. The new diners are light and airy, and people feel more comfortable in them.

The diner builders, when left on their own, continued to rework the formula into contemporary designs. The latest trends have been to use more glass and mirrors, less stone and brick, more polished granite and marble, and, believe it or not, more stainless steel. Today's diners also defy categorization. Builders simply refer to them as ultra-modern.

One other significant trend has been the recreation of old-style diners, that is, new versions of forties and fifties classics. Swingle Diners went back even further, when Joseph and Joyce Morozin contracted for a new 1930s-style Jerry O'Mahony diner. From the outside, the result did bear a resemblance: windows trimmed in mahogany, stainless steel monitor roof, and 1930s

graphics. The six-section diner, The Dining Car, was installed in northeast Philadelphia in August 1981 and proved to be a big hit.

When Jeffrey Gildenhorn went to Kullman to recreate a classic diner for him to install in Washington, D.C., he opened the first edition of *American Diner* to page 49, pointed to the 1940 Kullman diner illustrated there, and said, "Make this in blue." The resulting diner, named the American City Diner, was Kullman's first attempt at recapturing their old look. The exterior is beautifully done in royal-blue porcelain enamel flutes with floor-to-ceiling glass-block corners and a metal roof. The doors are updated and clad in mirror-finish stainless, with oval windows. The inside features a stainless backbar and shrunken hood, with cooking behind the counter. A prime icon of the interior is a flaming-red Coke machine, which supplies the diner with 6½-ounce bottles.

Joe Swingle went back to his O'Mahony archives to base a new diner on the Monarch model of the 1930s.

Within a year after this diner arrived on Connecticut Avenue in 1988, another Washington restaurateur, Robert T. Giaimo, brought in the prototype for his chain, the Silver Diner. Giaimo, in partnership with master chef Ype Hengst, had assembled a team of professionals to help him formulate a new diner concept for the 1990s. The group included Charles Morris Mount, an award-winning New York City–based restaurant designer; Cini-Little International, Inc., food-service consultants; Mike Collier of Uniwest Construction; Kullman Industries; and myself, Richard J. S. Gutman, as design development consultant.

It was the stated aim of the Silver Diner to fill the niche for a new family restaurant in an old diner atmosphere. After nearly two years of research and development, the first Silver Diner opened in February 1989, on the Rockville Pike in Rockville, Maryland. This five-thousand-square-foot, seven-section, 197-seat diner was an instant success. It commands a strong presence

along the road with its twenty-six-foot glass-block entrance tower, surmounted by a clock announcing "It's time to dine." The exterior is sheathed in horizontal strips of red porcelain enamel and brushed stainless steel, with glass-block corners.

The interior is focused on an open kitchen. The materials were chosen to reflect the best of the old: marble counter, ceramic tile floors and walls, Formica ceiling and tabletops, stainless steel backbar, and mahogany trim.

The success of the first unit was followed by the on-site construction of two more free-standing Silver Diners in the Washington, D.C., area, and a fourth built into an existing shopping mall in Towson, Maryland. The Silver Diner group has plans to franchise its concept.

All of the new old-style diners have come about because of the incredible interest in diners. If one takes Kullman Industries as an indicator, the diner revival is going strong. In 1990, diners represented only 5 percent of Kullman's modular buildings; in 1991, the proportion grew to 10 percent; the forecast for 1992 was 20 percent.

Of the original diner builders—with ties to the old days—four are still in business: Kullman, DeRaffele, Paramount and Musi. From all accounts, business is good.

The 1990 DeRaffele specially designed by Lyndon Quinn.

The Story of a Diner: The Lyndon

After more than forty years in the diner business, Bill Quinn stepped aside and let his son, Lyndon, take over. Lyndon had been working as short-order cook for his dad, and had built quite a name for himself. And thus Bill's Diner, a 1960 Silk City, became the Lyndon Diner.

In 1989, with the fervor of a missionary, Lyndon Quinn went off to the diner manufacturers in search of a new place. After checking out the competition, Lyndon settled on DeRaffele and contracted with that company to build the "diner of the future" for him.

In 1990, the five-section, 180-seat diner was delivered to the site of the old Silk City in

A large skylight washes the diner with light. A granite counter and a marble backbar complement the color scheme.

Manheim, Pennsylvania. The body of the diner is dark mirror glass top and bottom with a band of large windows in between. The vertical structure at the corners is clad in white stone. Bill Quinn remarked, "On the outside it doesn't look like a diner, but on the inside it does."

The large vestibule features the Quinn family coat of arms in gold on a mirror. Inside the Lyndon is a granite counter with eight stools facing a green marble backbar. The well-designed interior features an attractive color scheme based on ivory, cranberry, gray, green, and beige. Lyndon specified two large skylights, which haven't been used in diners since the Tierney days, to flood the diner with daylight. According to Bill, "Everything has to go back to the old days, but it has to go back nicely."

Lyndon took his father up to New Rochelle to inspect the diner right before it was completed.

"This diner was built and they didn't have any stainless steel around the windows. Dad walked right in and said, 'Hey, you haven't put the stainless steel in here yet.' " As a result of that visit, the Lyndon does have that glint of stainless steel that for Bill Quinn really makes it a diner.

The Lyndon Diner is so modern that people came in and told them they shouldn't call it a diner. But for Lyndon, this is what a diner is: It's clean; it's modern; it's new. This is the future. When people think of diners, he wants them to think of the Lyndon Diner.

Lyndon acknowledges that the diner business got off to a great start with the old models. He explained, "If old diners are refurbished, just like that one in the Henry Ford Museum, it's wonderful. It ought to be sitting right next to an old Model T. That's where it belongs . . . in a museum." He continued, gesturing around the Lyndon Diner, "These are the things here that have got to make history as diners for the *next* forty years. I'm trying to push it now to get all new diners in, to keep it going, because if you keep going backwards, this is going to die. These new diners will try to overcome the bad rap that old diners give everybody."

With multigenerational diner owners like the Quinns, the future of the business is assured. Lyndon strives to be on the cutting edge of diner design. He's proud of his accomplishments. Now that his father has retired, he's carrying on the diner tradition. As Bill says, "I'll tell you, I like every bit about diners. I like every stage I came through, and I wouldn't trade it for anything. And this boy of mine, seems like he fell in the same way. He's a dyed-in-the-wool diner guy."

The Diner Is Rediscovered

It's doubtful that Mr. Average Diner Owner in the 1940s, working long hours to earn a living, would have thought that his diner might someday be considered a historic structure. When Joseph Zuromski and Arnold Wood brought the Modern Diner to Pawtucket, Rhode Island, in 1941, they were proud of their brand-new, maroon and cream, single-ended Sterling Streamliner. To their minds, this was the last word in diner design. ¶ Nearly forty years later, the Modern Diner, Sterling Diner #4140, became the first diner nominated to the National Register of Historic Places, and this nomination proved a watershed in the recognition of the place of diners in American culture. Normally, a building must be at least fifty years old before it is even eligible to be considered for the register. But the fast-changing pace of roadside architecture forced historians to take an earlier look at what had come and was already disappearing.

An early design sketch by Charles Morris Mount for the Silver Diner.

Over the next fourteen years, four other diners were individually listed on the National Register of Historic Places, with a number of others included within historic districts or listed on state registers. The individual listings represent a good range of locations and manufacturers, but they are not necessarily the most significant diners in the country. These nominations represent the hard work of historians, enthusiasts, and diner owners who feel strongly about the diner's place in history.

The other diners on the register include the Miss Bellows Falls, Worcester Lunch Car #771, dating from 1941, and located in Bellows Falls, Vermont; Mickey's Diner, a Jerry O'Mahony diner delivered to St. Paul, Minnesota, in 1939; the Village Diner, originally known as the Halfway, an early 1950s Silk City located in Red Hook, New York; and the Tastee 29 Diner, a 1947 Mountain View in Fairfax, Virginia.

While these diners were being placed on the register, another interesting phenomenon was taking place. Individuals all around the country began to reclaim old diners. Usually they were moved to new sites. They almost always required restoration. The menu concepts ranged as far and wide as the diverse locations.

One of the first in this new wave of old diners, and the one that undoubtedly has received the most attention (H. J. Heinz Company recently used its image in a *Time* magazine ad campaign for its ketchup) is the Empire Diner, located at 210 Tenth Avenue in Manhattan. In 1976, Jack Doenias and his partners took a 1946 Fodero diner and subtly modified it for the emerging upscale crowd. The diner previously had undergone a minor facelift, wherein the windows were changed and the monitor roof hidden from the outside. Otherwise the diner remained intact. The 1976 changeover included painting a gigantic "EAT" on the wall behind the diner; installing a miniature stainless steel Empire State Building on the diner's roof at the corner; and replacing

Preceding page

Manhattan's Empire Diner, where new diner chic

really began.

Preceding page, inset

Miniature Empire Diner knockoffs began

to make an appearance in Japan in the 1980s

as temporary buildings set up on idle land

before new construction projects started.

(Don Levy)

The Miss Bellows Falls is the only Worcester Lunch Car individually listed on the National Register of Historic Places.

The Modern Diner made history when it was placed on the National Register of Historic Places.

the Formica countertops and tabletops with black glass. The rest of the diner is vintage Fodero, including the company's signature winged clock, popularized after World War II.

The Empire was an instant success and was given the *New York* magazine stamp of approval: periodic coverage, including a cover story, "The New Great-Looking Dining Places: Is the Food as Good as the Design?" This appeared the same year that the Empire opened. The Empire pioneered the concept of the diner being something other than *just* a diner. With candlelight, live piano music, and an untraditional menu somewhat on the pricey side, this was a new tangent for diners.

Diner purists bristled at this use of a diner. In hindsight, the Empire Diner has become an icon, not only as immortalized in John Baeder's 1976 oil painting, but also because it was the first of

Gordon Tindall's diner before an automobile nearly demolished the right side, causing him to rebuild the diner and replace the vestibule.
(Gordon C. Tindall)

the upscale diners. Its image as an art director's locale has done a great deal to further the popularity of diners.

John C. Chapin was probably inspired by the Empire when he purchased Phillips' Diner, a 1946 Worcester semi-streamliner, and dismantled it, shortened it by eight feet, and reassembled it inside Bushnell Plaza in Hartford, Connecticut. Renamed Shenanigans, the diner became the focus of Chapin's upscale restaurant in the early 1980s. He converted the backbar to a bar, removed the windows and doors, and allowed customers to sit at booths inside the diner or tables outside . . . all indoors. Unfortunately, the diner was a victim of the very bad times that hit the insurance industry and Hartford in the late 1980s, and the diner was closed, though it remains in place.

The Diner on Sycamore was Philip R. Adelman's contribution to the diner renaissance in the Midwest. In 1984, he moved a 1954 Mountain View diner from Massillon to Cincinnati, Ohio, added a glitzy dining room to bring the seating up to 140, and installed a menu of some traditional diner food with a twist, along with the likes of wild rice and chicken piccata.

Adelman had enough success with his first place to build from scratch in 1987. The Diner on 86th was built into a shopping center in Indianapolis. This was followed by The Diner on St. Clair, another old Mountain View, in Cincinnati in 1988.

It is often a transplanted Easterner who promotes diners in areas of the country where they are not well known. When Gordon C. Tindall traveled from Iowa back to New Jersey, where he grew up, the idea of opening a diner gnawed away at him. He was fortunate to acquire a local haunt, the Clarksville Diner, which was slated for demolition because of road work. He took the 1940 Silk City diner to Decorah in 1988 and spent four years restoring it to its former beauty. Only weeks before the opening, a drunk driver careened into it and heavily damaged a great deal of Tindall's hard work. Undeterred, he set out on a three-thousand-mile journey to procure original parts from other Silk City diner owners. Getting pieces of booths here, a door there, stainless steel trim from yet another place, and even a unique custom-made vestibule, Tindall reassembled his diner, straightening steel wall members, matching old ceramic tile, and refabricating some exterior porcelain enamel.

For many owners, Gordon Tindall included, a diner is a vehicle for traditional diner food only. Many people who reopen old diners revel in serving breakfast anytime, meat loaf every day, and daily specials from chicken croquettes to liver and onions.

For others, the *image* of the diner was the ticket; it was the architecture first and the menu second. That was the case with Susan and Jack Seltz, creators of the Ediner chain of shopping-mall restaurants. They were planning to open an American café in the Galleria Mall in Edina, Minnesota, when, according to a newspaper article, Susan was looking in a bookstore and came across a copy of *American Diner*. As journalist Dick Youngblood described it: *"Voila!* All that was

Ed Debevic's Beverly Hills outlet has a re-created Paramount-style diner appended to it.

Johnny Rockets is a Los Angeles–based chain of hamburger stands with very dinerlike interiors, based on White Towers.

left was to find a name. That came from their designer, a perfectly logical fellow who suggested that a diner in Edina could be called nothing else but Ediner." The first one opened in September of 1982.

What the Seltzes pioneered in the Midwest, building diners on site in shopping malls, has since been copied by other entrepreneurs and diner builders alike. One of Kullman Industries' latest projects has been the on-site replication of a 1930s-era diner. John Daskalis contracted with the company in 1992 to build a new version of its old Weequahic Diner, which was located in Newark, New Jersey. The new diner, named Jack and Jill's, is in a shopping mall in Middletown, New York. Like the old lunch wagons that traveled to where the customers were, many of today's diners gravitate to where people are spending their time . . . at the malls.

This is not to say that the diner is not still a destination in its own right. Across the country, restaurants are opening under the name "diner" because the word is a drawing card. Beyond the name, imaginations have run wild. At one end of the spectrum is Ed Debevic's, a caricature of a diner based upon a mythical diner owner. Ed's was founded in 1984 by Chicago restaurateur Richard Melman of the group Lettuce Entertain You Enterprises. By 1990, the company had added six restaurants in the United States and one in Japan.

Ed Debevic's is an experience in addition to being a restaurant. The places are cluttered with memorabilia from the 1950s and memorable quotations from mythical Ed, who's mysteriously never at the restaurant, but always out bowling. Waitresses are auditioned before they are hired. They must be able to smack their chewing gum and properly say, "Hi ya, hon!" to the customers. The Debevic's menu has been described as "burgers, fries, milkshakes, and laughter."

Entrepreneur magazine described Rich Melman as "widely recognized as the founder of the modern diner concept." But some would argue whether Ed Debevic's three-hundred-seat restau-

The Fog City Diner in San Francisco is as much of an icon on the West Coast as is the Empire Diner on the East.

rants deserve the name "diners" at all. A *New York Times* article reporting on the enormous success of the first Ed's operation in Chicago quotes patron Wally Heatherly's opinion on the diner: "It's just a big bar with funny signs. I've never seen a diner this large. A diner is a room with a row of booths on the side and a counter up front. But my daughter thinks it's a diner, so I won't disillusion her."

As Ed's is middlebrow, the Fog City Diner in San Francisco is highbrow. Also the result of a restaurant group, Real Restaurants, the Fog City is a one-of-a-kind institution. Its flashy black-and-white checkerboard tile exterior was instantly copied by Fog City wannabes across the country. Opened in 1985, the Fog City was designed as a nouvelle California cuisine diner. It refers to classic diner design in its materials and layout, but the concept and feel are much more expensive. The high prices have not scared away the patrons. People come for the experience, on the basis of its good reputation, and return because of the outstanding food, such as grilled

The 5 & Diner is an Arizona factory-built, old-style diner, built in 1987. (Reznik Cutter)

eggplant and onions, jalapeño corn muffins, cold rare sirloin, tapenade, onions, asiago and anchovies salad, and crab cakes with sherry-cayenne mayonnaise.

The idea, notion, image of a diner has successfully provided many jumping-off points for restaurant concepts in the eighties and nineties. All this attention and publicity has been good for traditional diners, as well. They have helped keep diners in the media and full of customers. It's safe to say that fewer diners have been demolished because there is simply a greater awareness of them today.

Sculptor Jerry Berta rescued one of Michigan's few remaining diners, Uncle Bob's, a 1947 O'Mahony that was sitting vacant in the city of Flint. Berta's specialty is small ceramic sculptures of diners, and he purchased Uncle Bob's in 1987, moved it to Rockford, Michigan, and converted it to a studio and showroom. He meticulously restored it, opening The Diner Store and advertising "No Food, Just Art." So many people came looking for food that he eventually purchased a second diner to install next door to feed his hungry patrons.

The second diner in Berta's diner village is one well known to any person who has turned on a television. In 1990, Berta bought Rosie's Diner, home of "the quicker picker upper," Bounty paper towels, and backdrop to more than one hundred other TV advertisements. Rosie's is a 1946 Paramount that spent most of its life in Little Ferry, New Jersey. Berta, ever the craftsman, took it upon himself to learn to bend replacement stainless steel panels for the restoration of the diner.

Another diner moved to Michigan in 1984. The Henry Ford Museum in Dearborn wanted to add a classic diner to its collection of twentieth-century artifacts. They bought the Hudson Diner (originally Lamy's), a 1946 Worcester semi-streamliner (#789), and trucked it 850 miles from Hudson, Massachusetts, to Dearborn. A three-year restoration ensued, which included bringing the diner back to its factory-built condition after it was altered by the Worcester Lunch Car

The addition of Rosie's Diner (right) to Uncle Bob's (left) completed Jerry Berta's diner village by serving food and art in the same location. *(Fred Tiensivu)*

Lamy's Diner is a permanent fixture in the Henry Ford Museum's exhibition "The Automobile in American Life." The quality of the restoration makes the visitor feel as if he is present in 1946, when the diner left the Worcester Lunch Car Company plant. *(Henry Ford Museum & Greenfield Village)*

The Owl Night Lunch is shown in a dilapidated condition in 1934 and in its fully reconstructed glory in 1988. (Henry Ford Museum & Greenfield Village, left)

Company in 1950. A second diner was located in a field in central New Hampshire, where it had sat abandoned for nearly twenty years, and purchased for salvage. This provided original fixtures, furnishings, and other parts for Lamy's.

While the diner was being restored, the museum developed a major new permanent exhibition, "The Automobile in American Life," covering sixty thousand square feet of the vast museum's space. Lamy's Diner became an integral fixture in a section devoted to the automotive landscape. The diner sits inside the museum building, and visitors can walk through it, perch at the counter, occupy a booth, talk to the counterman, and listen to 1946 music through the vintage Seeburg wall-box system. In fact, museumgoers can do nearly everything except order some food and eat it.

Previously, the museum had reconstructed another important artifact in its collection: the only remaining horse-drawn lunch wagon. This wagon survived only because it had been acquired by Henry Ford in 1927, when he was amassing items for his indoor and outdoor museum complex, then in the planning stages. In fact, as a young man working for the Edison Electric Illuminating

Company in the 1890s, Ford had eaten at this very wagon, John M. Colquhoun's Owl Night Lunch, located near city hall in Detroit.

When Colquhoun died on October 31, 1927, Jerry O'Mahony's *Dining Car News* reprinted the Associated Press death notice. In the 1930s, the lunch wagon was restored and provided the only food service in Greenfield Village, the outdoor portion of the Henry Ford museum complex. It was subsequently rebuilt several times, but by the early 1980s was relegated to use only as a popcorn and soda wagon. When the museum learned of the importance of this unique artifact, a decision was made to bring it back to its former glory.

Although the Owl was built by a local Detroit wagon manufacturer, it was rebuilt in the style of Thomas H. Buckley's designs. The five-stool interior features handcrafted woodwork of cherry, oak, and ash. The body of the car is elaborately painted in block lettering and scrolling, and is ringed with flash glass and frosted windows etched with an owl-moon-and-star motif. For a number of seasons, the Owl served a limited menu of frankfurters, pie, coffee, and soda in Greenfield Village, until it was moved inside the museum.

This photograph captures two trends of the 1990s. The owner of the Peter Pan Diner in Kuhnsville, Pennsylvania, replaced his classic 1950s Mountain View with the five-piece Swingle on the right. A Massachusetts man then purchased the vintage diner to move to Cape Cod and set up in Falmouth as Betsy's Diner . . . without the mansard roof.

With its foundation removed, Reggie's Diner is ready to be trucked to the docks for shipping to its new home in Barcelona, Spain. This original 1948 Fodero spent all its former life by the ocean in Beach Haven, New Jersey.

Since the Henry Ford Museum paved the way, museums and other groups have acquired or are planning to acquire diners and diner parts for their collections. This is happening from California to Georgia to Maine. In 1984, Henry Ciborowski donated Worcester Lunch Car #705 to the Worcester Heritage Preservation Society. The diner was restored and put into use as an information booth on the Worcester Common.

In 1987, the Orange Empire Railway Museum in Perris, California, acquired the Liberty Bell Cafe, a Pullman passenger car that was converted to a Streamlined Moderne diner in the 1930s. It awaits funding for restoration.

Also in 1987, the Kansas Museum of History opened an exhibition, "Our Recent Past," which includes a reconstruction of the interior of a Valentine Diner. It was specially fabricated by a former employee of the company.

The Savannah College of Art and Design has bought two diners as part of its ongoing program of building restoration in Savannah, Georgia. Both diners, the Streamliner, a 1938 Worcester, and Bobbie's, an early-fifties Mountain View, are working restaurants in the college town.

The Adirondack Museum in Blue Mountain Lake, New York, received the Bill Gates Diner

There is an ever-growing trend of salvaging old diners and bringing them back to life. Palooka's, in Wilkes-Barre, Pennsylvania, is named in honor of the cartoon artist Ham Fisher, who was from the region and created the character Joe Palooka. The 1952 diner was restored in 1986.

as a gift in 1989 from I. Robert Wolgin. Wolgin had purchased the diner but never operated it. He replaced it with the Service Diner, Worcester #791, moved from North Attleboro, Massachusetts. Because the Bill Gates Diner, a converted trolley, was such a fixture in the region, it was added as an exhibit at the museum.

These nationwide projects have proven that diners are alive and well, and it's too soon to count one out, even when it's closed and forlorn. This is not to say that diners don't still get demolished. But it happens less often than it used to.

Twenty years ago, if you asked a diner owner if you could take a picture of his place, he'd think there was something the matter with you. If you ask nowadays, he'll not only give you the okay, but also tell you how many other people have been around photographing the place recently. This new sensibility has made diner owners prouder of the fact that they own diners, not just ordinary restaurants.

Diners have been around now, in one form or another, for longer than anyone can remember. The way things are going they'll be around for a long time to come.

A Directory of Dining Car Manufacturers

The following directory is intended to list the various companies that either engaged in lunch wagon or diner building, or specialized in the remodeling of diners. It is not a complete history of each company or a thorough description of all of their products. In some cases, little is known about the enterprise. By and large, these were private companies, family businesses whose records, such as they were, are long gone.

There are other companies whose names have popped up, but the location of the business remains unknown. For example, the Lake Erie region near Buffalo, New York, had no fewer than six diner builders between the world wars, but only three names, included below, have been identified. Other companies that remain elusive are the Galion Dining Car Company and the Monitor Car Company.

Although the major builders are all represented here, the research for this section did turn up many obscure and short-lived companies. Undoubtedly, there were many more. Many wagon builders were contracted on a onetime basis to construct a lunch wagon. Likewise, it appears certain that many automobile-body makers went into the diner business for a short time. There were also many individuals who built their own diners or built them for others . . . and thus were diner builders. This last category accounts for the large number of diners for which it is impossible to identify a manufacturer.

The identification of diners by builder is difficult for a number of reasons. Not all builders used a manufacturer's tag to credit their work. Many tags have not survived. Renovators would usually remove the original tag and replace it with one of their own. This was done by the major manufacturers as well as the renovators. For example, the Short Stop in Bloomfield, New Jersey, was built by Kullman, but now sports a Manno tag because Manno brought the unit to its factory and did some work on it.

The copying of another manufacturer's details or style further confuses the issue. In the case of the Colonial Diner, a late-forties Paramount in Stroudsburg, Pennsylvania, Fodero received the contract to build a dining-room addition only after agreeing to replicate all design features of the original Paramount design. No one would know this work was not done by Paramount.

The colonial and Mediterranean era has baffled diner spotters since its heyday. These diners were such a conglomeration of styles, materials, and images that it is impossible to pin down a manufacturer without a tag. And when there is a tag, the diner still might be a renovation or redo of someone else's old diner.

The issue of who built the diner remains a hot one for many enthusiasts. Part of the reason for this is the rarity of some manufacturers' products and certain unusual diner styles. In a perfect world, there would have been no diner renovations and every place would have a tag. But that would make life too easy and the hunt not as enjoyable.

Photographs appear before manufacturers.

Charley's Diner, late 1920s, Los Angeles.

Purple Diner, Worcester. (Worcester Historical Museum)

Charles Amend   *Los Angeles, CA, 1927–?*

Charlie Amend was a transplanted Easterner who went to California, probably from the P. J. Tierney Sons Company. Phil's Diner, the only remaining unit from J. F. (Phil) Phillips's chain of diners, and still extant in 1992 in North Hollywood, is most likely an Amend diner. It is very reminiscent of the Tierney product of the time.

Americana Diner Consultants   *45 South California Street, Ventura, CA, 1992–1996*

Pat Fodero retired from Fodero Dining Car Company but kept a hand in the business. In this latest venture he joined forces with Ed Warren, a successful California restaurateur, to provide diner design, site analysis, menu consultation, and more for diner-type operations.

Wilfred H. Barriere   *1 Cleveland Avenue, Worcester, MA, 1905–1906, 1926–1936?*

Wilfred H. Barriere was a carpenter for Thomas H. Buckley from 1899 to 1905. He then joined a blacksmith, Stearns A. Haynes, and built lunch wagons at 69 Franklin Street under his own name. The Haynes and Barriere company was acquired by Philip H. Duprey in December of 1906, and renamed the Worcester Lunch Car and Carriage Manufacturing Company. Barriere continued there for nine months. He then left the dining car business and went into the hardware business. In December 1924, he returned to Worcester Lunch for a year and a half and polished up his old skills in diner building. In 1926, he set out on his own again, building diners in his backyard on Cleveland Avenue. He may have also built a diner on site in Montreal.

Barriere's early wagons were very similar to Buckley's later models. His 1920s models were also very similar to Worcester Lunch Car's offerings of the time. They featured unusual leaded-glass windows and a very high barrel roof, usually with three windows on the ends. In 1935, he also ran one of his own diners, the Perfect Diner, at 622 Park Avenue in Worcester. He died on February 6, 1943.

Unidentified Bixler diner.

Bixler Manufacturing Company 50–70 Newton Street, Norwalk, OH; Sales Office: 270 Madison Avenue, New York, NY, 1931–1937?

Owned by Louis C. Voelker, the company specialized in sectionalized construction. Diners were built in four-foot-wide sec-

tions and shipped "knocked down" by rail. Distinctive features included extreme width for the time period; two-foot double-hung windows; and a barrel roof with a fancy profile on the ends. Bixler was not a prolific builder.

BRAMSON DINERS HAVE IT

DESIGNED TO PRODUCE PROFITS	SERVICE WITH MINIMUM EFFORT
ENGINEERED FOR EFFICIENCY	PLEASANT SURROUNDINGS
CONSTRUCTED WITH BEST MATERIALS	PLANNED SEATING
BUILT LIKE A BATTLESHIP	CUSTOM BUILT AT
LAID OUT BY EXPERTS	MASS PRODUCTION PRICES

Bramson advertisement. (From Adhocism, *by Charles Jencks and Nathan Silver)*

Bramson Engineering Company Box 337, Oyster Bay, NY, mid-1950s

Bramson was a father-and-son operation whose main business was manufacturing large sterilizers for hospitals. They got into diners as a sideline, and advertised one-, two-, three-, and four-section stainless steel diners for delivery anywhere in the U.S. According to James Cucci, who had a business nearby, Bramson came to Oyster Bay in the late 1940s. Only two diners were actually built, and they sat on the lot unsold for quite a while. One diner may have been sold, but the other was donated to a "local nonprofit organization."

Royal Diner, 1929, Los Angeles. (Henry Ford Museum & Greenfield Village)

J. G. Brill Company *Dining Car Division, Philadelphia, PA; Subsidiary: G. C. Kuhlman Car Co., Cleveland, OH; Subsidiary: Wason Mfg. Co., Springfield, MA, 1927–1932*

The J. G. Brill Company of Philadelphia, a noted manufacturer of street-railway vehicles, introduced a line of all-steel diners in 1927. These were constructed at two of their subsidiary plants, G. C. Kuhlman Car Company in Cleveland, Ohio, and Wason Manufacturing Company in Springfield, Massachusetts.

Their standard model was forty feet in length and furnished with either counter service only or tables/booths also. The "Universal" was a twenty-foot-six-inch model with ten stools only. Brill Steel Diners were built almost exclusively with a monitor-style roof. The most distinctive feature was their use of two doors at both ends on the façade of the diners. This gave the diners a real streetcar look.

White House Café, 1890s. (Worcester Historical Museum)

T. H. Buckley Lunch Wagon Manufacturing and Catering Company *281 Grafton Street, Worcester, MA, 1891–1908*

Thomas H. Buckley built his first wagon in 1888, but didn't list himself as a lunch wagon builder in the Worcester City Directory until the 1892 edition. His firm operated under several different names. Buckley was the most prolific of the early lunch wagon manufacturers and popularized the name "White House Café," which was that of his best-known model.

Builders and Renovators Unlimited   345 Passaic Avenue, Fairfield, NJ, 1978–1996

Joseph Giannotti, a third-generation diner builder, began a diner-renovating operation called Modular Designs in 1978. In September 1991, the business was renamed Builders and Renovators Unlimited and relocated in the old Manno factory. They specialized in Art Deco–revival alterations to existing restaurants.

Campora Diner, 1957. (Mrs. Joseph W. Swingle)

Campora Dining Car Company   24 Johnston Avenue, Kearny, NJ, 1957

Jerry Campora was the owner of this short-lived company. An advertisement for Campora, "destined to set the trend for Mod-ern Diners," appeared in *Diner Drive-In* in March 1957. The company may have built only one diner. Jerry Campora became shop superintendent of Swingle Diners when the latter opened later in 1957.

Papa Cantella's Diner, 1986, Industry, California.

Thomas Cantella & Company   910 South Santa Fe Avenue, Los Angeles, CA 90021, 1984–1987

Thomas Cantella built two 1920s-style "fancy commercial coach diners" at a factory in Los Angeles as outlets to market his Papa Cantella's sausage. These barrel-roofed diners had gaily painted exteriors rendered by a sign painter whose work had been featured at Disneyland.

Ann's Wagon, Bordentown, New Jersey, 1950 advertisement.

Albert H. Closson *Glens Falls, NY, 1904–1905*

Albert Closson was a lunch wagon builder who patented his unique design for a low-wheeled lunch wagon in 1905. A number of these wagons were built and operated in New York State.

1950s advertisement.

Colonial Fixture Manufacturing Company *2133 South Boulevard, Charlotte, NC, early 1950s*

Colonial advertised in trade magazines their "Club Diner." This unit was a conglomeration of many diner styles including flying buttresses; rounded windows; industrial sash; glass blocks; stainless steel, and more, all in a very small, flat-roofed diner.

Comac, Inc. *160 Shaw Avenue, Irvington, NJ, 1947–1951?*

Thomas J. McGeary, formerly general manager at Jerry O'Mahony, Inc., and John J. Costello, formerly steel-construction foreman at O'Mahony, set up their own company in 1947. They delivered their first diner to John Kontos in Fairview, New Jersey, later that year. Comac's diners were banded in horizontal stainless steel and porcelain enamel strips.

Cottrell & Cottrell *Lincoln Park, NJ, 1954*

This company advertised diner repair and modernizing with specialties in stainless steel and Formica. They targeted North Jersey diner owners.

West Side Diner & Bar, mid-1950s. (Mrs. Joseph W. Swingle)

DeRaffele Manufacturing Company, Inc. *2525 Palmer Avenue, New Rochelle, NY 10801, 1933–present*

Angelo DeRaffele began as a carpenter with the Tierney sons in 1921. In 1927 he advanced to the position of foreman, which he held until the company was "liquidated in 1933." At the Tierney plant, with Carl A. Johnson, past president of P. J. Tierney Sons, Inc., he began to manufacture diners under the name of Johnson & DeRaffele. In October 1947, it was announced that DeRaffele had become the sole owner, and the name was changed to DeRaffele Diners. "The plant will be easily recognized by old time diner men as being the home of the original Tierney Diners." The firm subsequently moved several times. Philip DeRaffele joined his father after World War II, and a third generation is currently working at the plant.

DeRaffele diners have followed diner trends through the decades. The company was particularly well known for building large diners, beginning in the 1950s, and it popularized the folded plate roof. It is currently the largest manufacturer.

Destiny Industries *Moultrie, GA, 1989*

Destiny is a mobile-home builder that constructed one diner, the Silver Dollar Diner, which was installed in Albany, Georgia. Pat Fodero consulted on this project.

Rendering of Happy Days Diner. (Diner Group, Ltd.)

Diner Group Ltd. *One Capital City Plaza, 3550 Peachtree Road, Suite 1170, Atlanta, GA 30326, 1971–present*

Originally known as Module Mobile, Inc., the company was formed in 1971 to manufacture modular food-service units. Later in the 1970s, they expanded their business to include a variety of modular structures. In 1987, they introduced a line of reproduction diners, the Happy Days Stainless Steel Diners. The company was reorganized as the Diner Group Ltd., offering diners and drive-throughs. The latest models are constructed without any wood whatsoever within the structure. The diners range in size from a fourteen-foot-by-forty-foot self-contained unit seating twenty to a twenty-eight-foot-by-seventy-six-foot double unit with seating for 108. The diners have an exterior skin of mirror-finish stainless steel.

Dodge Dining Car Company   307 Market Street, Camden, NJ, 1927

William H. Dodge, Jr., a former newspaperman and advertising man, started this small dining car company. In 1928, he became the Boston sales representative for Wason Manufacturing Company's line of Brill Steel Diners.

Frank Dracont   Providence, RI, 1883–?

Dracont was a wagon builder who constructed lunch carts for Ruel B. Jones.

Shirley's Diner, 1960, West New York, New Jersey.

Erfed Corporation   231 Route 17, Rutherford, NJ, 1956–mid-1970s

Erwin Fedkenheuer, Sr., lead sheet-metal man with Paramount Diners for twenty years, started this company with his son, Erwin Junior, and several other sheet-metal workers from Paramount. The company specialized in the repair, modernization, and renovation of existing diners on location. They renovated fifty or sixty diners and built five new ones. Their work was characterized by superb stainless steel detailing.

Fancamp Diner Service, Inc.   Barrington, NJ, late 1950s

George J. Fannin, Sam A. Campagna, and Joseph A. Montano

joined forces briefly in this organization, which specialized in new diners, remodeling and relocating. Joe Montano was associated previously with Jerry O'Mahony, Inc., and Mahony Diners, Inc.

5 & Diner, Inc.   *1146 North Mesa Drive #102, Mesa, AZ 85201, 1989–present*

A new company was set up by Kenneth Higginbotham to build and franchise new old-style diners based upon the 5 & Diner prototype built by Pedco. (See Pedco.) The steel diners seat an average of a hundred people, and are built of two units and a vestibule. The company plans to expand across the United States.

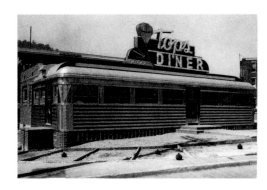

Tops Diner, 1948, Johnstown, Pennsylvania

Fodero Dining Car Company   *136 Arlington Avenue, Bloomfield, NJ 07001, 1933–1981*

Joseph Fodero was foreman of the metal shop at P. J. Tierney Sons, where he began at the age of twenty-five in 1922. He left Tierney with Samuel Kullman in 1927 and served as a foreman for Kullman Dining Car Company until 1933. He then started Fodero Dining Car Company, building diners at the side of his house in Bloomfield. Short of capital, he went into partnership in 1939 with Milton Glick, renaming the company National Dining Car Company, at 55 Delancy Street, Newark, New Jersey. National closed down because of World War II. Scotty's, in Pittsburgh, is possibly the only National Diner extant. After the war, production resumed under the name of Fodero again. The outfit moved to Bloomfield around 1953. Joe's sons, Pat and Ted, joined the company after the war.

Fodero built an excellent diner with great attention to detail. Their diners were highly decorative, with outstanding stainless steel work. Their signature clock of the 1940s was encased in stainless steel wings. In the 1950s they built some very notable large diners.

Wilson Goodrich   *53 Wilcox Street, Springfield, MA, 1892–1897*

Wilson Goodrich built night lunch wagons at his home on Wilcox Street. In 1895, he also had four wagons running in Springfield, with other operations in Massachusetts, New York State, and Montreal. He was the pioneer in this line of business in Canada. He sold out in 1897 to Camille R. Remillard.

Ephraim L. Hamel   *49 Wheeler Street, Lynn, MA, 1891–1910*

Thomas H. Buckley assigned half of his first lunch wagon patent to Ephraim Hamel in 1892. Hamel was a leatherworker before he got into the lunch wagon business. He built White House Café Lunch Wagons in Lynn, Massachusetts, under an arrangement with Buckley. Hamel also operated the first night lunch wagon in Lynn.

Hayes Equipment Manufacturing Company   *Wichita, KS, 1940s*

Hayes built a small, boxy, Valentine-type diner, of which none are known to exist.

John J. E. Hennigan   *22½ Cutler Street, Worcester, MA, 1907–1917*

Hennigan first operated a night lunch in 1899 in Worcester. He started manufacturing in 1907, building a model known as the Franklin Lunch Wagon. He operated his own lunch car at 3 Lincoln Square, Worcester, from 1907 to 1916; he also had wagons at Washington Square, Salem Square, and Vernon Square. He retired in 1933. His wagons were distinguished by the initials "F.C." in the flash glass windows—these stood for "Franklin Café."

Johnson & DeRaffele

See DeRaffele Manufacturing Company, Inc.

Franklin Café, Worcester. (E. B. Luce, photographer)

Nonotuck, 1889, Springfield.

New Palace Diner, c. 1950.

Samuel Messer Jones   Union Street, Springfield, MA, 1884–1898

Samuel M. Jones introduced the night lunch wagon business to Worcester, MA, in 1884. He manufactured wagons and operated them there until 1889. In the fall of 1887, he built the first wagon a customer could enter. Before moving to Springfield in 1889, he sold all his wagons but one to Charles H. Palmer. In Springfield, Jones built and sold a line called the Pioneer Lunch until 1898.

J. B. Judkins Company

See Sterling Diners.

G. C. Kuhlman Car Company

See J. G. Brill Company.

Kullman Industries, Inc.   One Kullman Corporate Campus Drive, Lebanon, NJ 08833, 1927–present

The Kullman Dining Car Company, located at 390 Frelinghuysen Avenue, Newark, New Jersey, was founded in 1927 by Samuel Kullman, accountant for P. J. Tierney Sons. When he left Tierney, he took Joseph Fodero with him. The firm was subsequently located in Harrison, New Jersey, before moving to Avenel. Harold Kullman joined his father after World War II. Harold's wife, Betty, began consulting on interior design with the company in 1955. Robert Kullman, the third generation, is now president.

Kullman always built a high-quality diner. Their 1930s models were among the most stylish Art Deco diners built. Kullman regularly offered a small dinette model. The company has the dubious distinction of building the first all-brick-exterior colonial diner. In the 1980s, it was the first to build real "old-style" new diners, the American City Diner and the Silver Diner prototype, both in the Washington, D.C., area.

In 1969, Kullman branched out widely into other types of modular construction, and these enterprises account for a greater percentage of their business than do diners.

LK Builders Inc. *212 Carson Place, Bergenfield, NJ 07621, 1959–1979?*

Leo Kassalias was the owner of this firm, whose services included building custom-designed diners and restaurants, as well as commercial buildings and homes. Their advertising stressed that they worked on the job site . . . *not prefabricated.* Their diners were typical of the North Jersey style of the late 1970s: stone or brick with repetitive arches and quarry-tile mansard roofs.

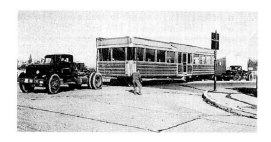

LauraLyn Diner, 1956. (Mrs. Joseph W. Swingle)

Mahony Diners, Inc. *60 Jacobus Avenue, South Kearny, NJ, 1956–1957*

Joseph A. Montano, plant manager for Jerry O'Mahony, Inc., John L. Cronk, sales manager there, and Joseph Cavallo, treasurer, purchased the inventory of Jerry O'Mahony, Inc., and set up a new enterprise, Mahony Diners, Inc., in South Kearny. They were undercapitalized and only built four diners, the first of which was the LauraLyn Diner in Rahway, New Jersey.

White Circle, 1957, Bloomfield, New Jersey.

Manno Dining Car Company *345 Passaic Avenue, Fairfield, NJ, 1949–1978*

The company was founded in 1949 by Ralph Manno, who had previously spent twenty-two years with Kullman, and Vincent Giannotti, previously with Kullman for four years. Giannotti's father, Joseph, was a foreman with the Tierney sons in the 1920s and then worked for Kullman. Manno started out as a diner-renovating company, located at 24 Florence Avenue in Belleville, New Jersey. In the 1960s, Manno built some very unusual diners with nearly all-glass façades and interesting stainless work.

De Luxe MASTER DINERS

Each Master Diner is truly a masterpiece of sound diner construction, built to the exacting standards of the modern craftsman. Let us

MASTER DINERS
Newark–Pompton Turnpike, Pequannock, N. J.

Master advertisement, 1947.

Master Diners   *Newark–Pompton Turnpike, Pequannock, NJ, 1947–mid-1950s*

Master was a small company that built diners with an old-fashioned feel. Their diners had stained-glass transom windows, a unique detail for post–World War II diners. Inlaid Formica tabletops were a standard feature, as well.

Modern Diner Builders   *6541 North Sixteenth Street, Philadelphia, PA, 1940?–1954?*

George E. Skirdlant was the owner of the Modern Diner Builders, who advertised to recondition diners: porcelain ceilings and exteriors installed, canvas roofs applied, natural wood refinished. They also built vestibules and dining-room additions. Work was done while the diners remained in operation.

Modular Designs

See Builders and Renovators Unlimited.

Module Mobile, Inc.

See Diner Group Ltd.

Ayers Diner, c. 1952, North Salisbury, Maryland. (Mrs. Joseph W. Swingle)

Mountain View Diners   *Route 23, No. 20 Newark–Pompton Turnpike, Singac, NJ, 1939–1957*

Mountain View was founded by Henry Strys and Les Daniel. Daniel was a foreman for another diner builder, and Strys was a building contractor. They built some very stylish and unusual diners before and after World War II. Their unique postwar corner detail, the "cowcatcher," was one of their trademarks. In the 1950s, Mountain View was the most aggressive marketer of diners, sending their units all over the country and outselling the other manufacturers. The company attempted to go public in June 1956, and was out of business shortly thereafter.

Mulholland Company *208–220 Buffalo Street, Dunkirk, NY, 1920–1930?*

The Mulholland Spring Company was founded in 1881 by Richard and P. J. Mulholland and George P. Isham, following the patent on Richard Mulholland's design for a vehicle spring. In addition to fabricating springs and gears, they made a full line of buggies, carriages, and road wagons, and then automobile, truck, and ambulance bodies. At some point around 1920, they branched out into diner manufacturing. Mulholland was one of several companies that appeared in the Lake Erie region.

Musi Dining Car Company, Inc. *377 Roosevelt Avenue, Carteret, NJ 07008, 1966–present*

Company founder Ralph Musi emigrated from Italy in 1947 and began working at Kullman. In 1966, he formed his own company building new diners in the colonial and Mediterranean style. More recently, they have done a lot of remodeling work, but have also continued to build new diners in the ultramodern style of chrome, mirrors, and glass.

National Diner Sales
See Valentine Manufacturing Company.

National Dining Car Company
See Fodero Dining Car Company.

New England Night Lunch Wagon Company
See T. H. Buckley Lunch Wagon Manufacturing and Catering Company.

Lehigh Diner, c. 1950. (Mrs. Joseph W. Swingle)

Jerry O'Mahony, Inc. *977–991 West Grand Street, Elizabeth, NJ, 1913–1956*

Jerry O'Mahony began the manufacture of lunch cars in Bayonne, New Jersey, with his partner, John J. Hanf. The company moved to larger quarters four times, ending up in Elizabeth in 1925. Jerry O'Mahony, Inc., was one of the leading manufacturers for decades. Like the Tierney outfit, O'Mahony gave many dining car builders their start. Through its long history, Jerry

O'Mahony, Inc., produced hundreds of diners in numerous styles too diverse to recap. In the late 1920s, the company introduced Jerry O'Mahony's *Dining Car News,* a magazine devoted to the interests of the dining-car owner. It was distributed free of charge to any past or prospective client.

Orange Dining Car Company   *294 Central Avenue, Orange, NJ, late 1940s*

This company was a diner reconditioner. Nothing is known about it, other than a single small classified advertisement in *The Diner* in February 1948.

Dauphin's Superior Diner (now Highland Park), 1948, Rochester, New York.

Orleans Manufacturing Company   *Albion, NY, 1947–1948*

Orleans Manufacturing is thought to have built only two diners. One is extant. Originally called Dauphin's Superior Diner, in Rochester, New York, it was recently restored and reopened as the Highland Park Diner on its original site.

Palmer wagon, 1890s.

Charles H. Palmer   *51 Salem Street, Worcester, MA, 1889–1901*

Palmer was the first to receive a patent for his design of a night lunch wagon. He got into the business by buying Samuel M. Jones's fleet of wagons before he began to build his own. Palmer was one of the first early successful wagon builders. His enterprise was ended in 1901 when fire struck his factory in Sterling Junction, Massachusetts.

Godfrey Diner, c. 1950.

Paramount Diners   *56 Spruce Street, Oakland, NJ 07436, 1932–present*

Arthur E. Sieber, who previously worked for Silk City, founded Paramount in Haledon, New Jersey, on the outskirts of Paterson. After Erwin Fedkenheuer, Sr., joined the firm in the early thirties, it became known for its stainless steel work. Its Art Deco–style diner interiors were unsurpassed. It patented the split construction method in 1941. It offered an all-stainless-steel-exterior diner before anyone else. Like the other companies that survived into the 1970s, Paramount constructed a complete array of diner-restaurants in every style. Since 1963, the company has been run by Herbert Y. Enyart, who was with Silk City previously.

Paterson Vehicle Company
See Silk City Diners.

Pedco   *P.O. Box 1483, Mesa, AZ 85211, 1987–present*

Pedco, a manufacturer of metal buildings, constructed the prototype for a new chain of franchised old-style diners, the 5 & Diner. The streamlined, two-section unit is reminiscent of 1940s diners on the exterior, recalling a Silk City look. The all-metal interior is somewhat boxy. Pedco is run by Andy and Tony Coscia.

The Pollard Company, Inc.   *463 Chelmsford, Lowell, MA, 1926–1927*

The company was owned by Wilson H. Pollard, who had operated a lunch cart in Lowell, and Joseph E. Carroll, a sheet-metal man. They built a handful of barrel-roofed diners, of which only two are known to exist.

Camille R. Remillard   *53 Wilcox Street, Springfield, MA, 1897–1899*

Remillard took over the lunch wagon–manufacturing business of Wilson Goodrich in 1897 and continued it for a couple of years before opening a restaurant in Springfield.

Roadateria Company, Inc. *4076 Boston Post Road, Bronx, NY, 1929*

Edward J. Tierney was president of this short-lived venture after he was forced out of P. J. Tierney Sons, Inc. The company manufactured a prefab "combination dining car, lunch car and road stand." The unit was vaguely reminiscent of a diner, but had white clapboard siding, casement windows, and a green tile roof. One long window of the building opened up to create a road stand in good weather. It had seats for twenty customers.

Country Club Diner, 1940, Rochester, New York.

Rochester Grills *Rochester, NY, 1940–?*

Little is known about Rochester Grills, which built diners in the style of Bixler. At least one has survived: the Congress Street Diner in Bradford, Pennsylvania.

1910 advertisement.

Schnadig Sales Agency *803 Crilly Block, Chicago, IL, 1909–?*

This company advertised in the *Saturday Evening Post* its horse-drawn restaurant on wheels, which was capable of take-out service only. This small unit was equipped with a stove, burners, coffee urn, waffle irons, and ice-cream-cone irons.

1930s advertising postcard. (Gordon C. Tindall)

Silk City Diners   *Paterson Vehicle Co., East Twenty-seventh Street and Nineteenth Avenue, Paterson, NJ, 1927–1964*

The Paterson Vehicle Company, founded in 1886, was run by the Cooper family, headed by Everett Abbott Cooper. They began as wagon builders in the nineteenth century, but are not known to have made any lunch wagons. Eventually, they made automobile, bus, and truck bodies, and started making "Silk City Diners" in 1927. The name was derived from Paterson's main industry, the silk trade. Irving Brooks Cooper, one of five sons involved in the business, was vice president in charge of design and production for the diner division. Silk City Diners were built as standard production units, six or eight at a time, in different color schemes. Because they were not custom-built, a Silk City was the lowest priced diner you could get, and the company advertised that fact.

Sorge Brothers Company   *Silver Creek, NY, dates of operation unknown*

Sorge Brothers was one of several companies in the Lake Erie region that began building diners following the success of Ward & Dickinson. Little is known about this company.

Starlite Diner's Inc.   *323 Second Street, Holly Hill, FL 32117, 1992–present*

Bill Starcevic founded this new company, which offers a standard diner, finished in polished stainless steel, fourteen feet by seventy-six feet, seating fifty-two. Two larger models have 82 or 102 seats. Their first prefab unit, the Starlite Diner, opened in Daytona, Florida, in 1992. Previously, the company had been in the traditional restaurant and home-building business. In 1990, they opened the Doo Woppa Doo Diners, a chain of five restaurants built on site and located in Florida shopping centers.

Fitzpatrick's Diner, 1941, West Roxbury, Massachusetts. (Daniel J. Fitzpatrick)

Sterling Diners   *J. B. Judkins Company, 18 Main Street, Merrimac, MA, 1936–1942*

John B. Judkins went into the carriage business in 1857. The company switched exclusively to motorcar bodies in 1910 when there was no demand for carriages. Subsequently, the Great Depression nearly ended the call for custom automobile bodies, and J. B. Judkins III entered the diner-building business. They acquired a number of patented designs for a sectionalized construction method. Sterling Diners were manufactured in several different models: the streamliner, with one or both ends configured in a bullet shape; the dinette, a small, scaled-down diner; and the conventional type. Sterling Diners were built completely of wood and were always covered with porcelain enamel. World War II ended all operations of the J. B. Judkins Company.

Suntory Ltd.   Osaka, Japan, 1980s

Suntory, the giant Japanese corporation, built "Up Town Diners," scaled-down versions of Manhattan's Empire Diner. The idea was to occupy small pieces of property that were temporarily dormant between construction projects.

Superior Dining Car Company   Cross Keys Road, Berlin, NJ, 1950s

Superior was a diner-renovating company about which little is known.

Supreme advertisement, 1949.

Supreme Diners   Mountain View, NJ, late 1940s

A small diner-builder whose product greatly resembled that of Master Diners. The standard exterior was stainless steel flutes.

Swingle Diner, late 1950s.

Swingle Diners, Inc.   *300 Lincoln Boulevard, Middlesex, NJ 08846, 1957–1988*

Joseph W. Swingle began his own diner-building operation on August 16, 1957. Previously, he had been in sales with Fodero and Jerry O'Mahony, Inc. Jerry Campora was his shop superintendent, having formerly owned the Campora Dining Car Company and served as shop supervisor at Kullman. Swingle completed 147 jobs in its thirty-one-year history, including mostly new diners, some renovations, and several banks. Swingle built a typical 1950s-style diner before he introduced colonial design on diner interiors. The company also built a significant new, old-style diner, The Dining Car in Philadelphia, in 1981. Their last job was the American Diner, also in Philadelphia, which was a renovation of a late-1940s Paramount diner that had been languishing on the Swingle lot for twenty years.

Patrick J. Tierney   *Post Road near Premium Point Road, New Rochelle, NY, 1905–1917*

Patrick J. "Pop" Tierney operated lunch wagons from 1895 onward and began manufacturing them around 1905 in a small garage behind his house at 27 Cottage Place in New Rochelle. He introduced many improvements to the lunch car of the pre–World War I era, including tile interiors, skylights, and toilets.

Tierney Brothers, Inc.   *Mount Vernon, NY, 1927*

After losing control of P. J. Tierney Sons, Inc., the brothers and their uncle Daniel set up another plant, but did not build any diners. No doubt they would have, but a restraining order was issued forbidding them to use their own name.

Tierney Diners Inc.   *1775 Broadway, New York, NY, 1946*

Edward J. Tierney, shortly before his death on December 29, 1946, launched yet another Tierney diner company, with the hope of a comeback. His incredible streamlined diner, seen only in a rendered view, would have made quite a splash . . . if one had ever been built.

Webster Lunch, 1924, Bronx, New York City. (Pat Fodero)

P. J. Tierney Sons, Inc. *188 Main Street, New Rochelle, NY, 1917–1933*

Edward J. and Edgar T. Tierney succeeded their father after his sudden death. They expanded the business wildly, and for a long time were very successful. They not only manufactured diners, but also operated them. In 1925, when they built their new plant on Main Street, they were cranking out diners at the unbelievable pace of a diner a day. The Tierney diner was a standard car of its time, with a barrel roof, a tile floor and backbar, a marble counter, and usually one or two rows of stools. In the late 1920s, they began to offer tables for ladies. The Tierney sons' expansion program could not keep up with the amount of bad paper they were carrying on their diners.

United Diner Manufacturing Company *609 Central Avenue, Newark, NJ, 1958*

Joe Montano and John Cronk went to work for United, a division of United Advertising Corporation, after liquidating Mahony Diners in 1958. Although mainly a sign company, which specialized in huge signs, they did build two diners.

Uniwest Construction, Inc. *4160 South Four Mile Run Drive, Arlington, VA 22206, 1988–present*

Uniwest started in commercial construction in 1982. Michael D. Collier is the president of this company, which builds in the mid-Atlantic region. They have constructed many restaurants. Following site work and other construction on the Silver Diner prototype in Rockville, Maryland (built by Kullman), Uniwest has built three more Silver Diners in the Washington, D.C., and Baltimore area.

Little Chef Diner, 1940s.

Valentine Manufacturing Company *1020 South McComas, Wichita, KS, 1938–1974*

The company was founded by Arthur H. Valentine. It produced a line of portable steel sandwich shops, including diners, ice cream stands, White Tower restaurants, and a host of other modular buildings. Most of the diners were trucked to locations in the Midwest and West. Valentine had an East Coast sales office operating under the name of National Diner Sales in West Hempstead, New York. The most popular model was the Little Chef, an eight- or ten-stool one-man operation, with take-out service. The diners were finished in porcelain enamel or painted steel and featured integral pylon signage.

Dixie Diner,
1930s.

Miss Toy Town,
1949,
Winchendon,
Massachusetts.
(Dennis P.
Scipione)

Ward & Dickinson   *Silver Creek, NY, 1923–1940?*

This enterprise was begun by Charles Ward and Lee F. Dickinson. The "Ward" dining car was a narrow trolley-inspired diner built on two sets of very low wheels, which were recessed into the car. The standard diner had an off-center front door and one on the end. The monitor roof was employed for most of the company's history. Occasionally, there were four booths in one end.

Wason Manufacturing Company

See J. G. Brill Company

Worcester Deluxe Diner Manufacturing
Company   *477 Park Avenue, Worcester, MA, 1961–?*

Francis Van Slett, sign maker and head of Van Slett Advertising, purchased the inventory of the Worcester Lunch Car Company in 1961 at auction. He started construction on one diner, which was never completed.

Worcester Lunch Car Company   *4 Quinsigamond*
Avenue, Worcester, MA, 1906–May 23, 1961

The Worcester Lunch Car and Carriage Manufacturing Company was founded by Philip H. Duprey and Irving M. Stoddard. They bought out the lunch car–building enterprise of Wilfred H. Barriere and Stearns A. Haynes at 69 Franklin Street in Worcester. The company built 651 diners, beginning with serial number 200 and continuing through 850. When Worcester remodeled one of its diners, it kept its original production number. Worcester was known for a well-built conservative handcrafted diner. Even into the 1950s, the company continued to employ wood trim and booths on the interior. Many Worcester diners sported beautiful graphics in porcelain enamel. They only built one two-section diner in their history, the Vermont Squire, #845, delivered to Brattleboro on June 8, 1954.

Where the Diners Are

The following list is a directory of existing diners open for business when the book went to press. It includes traditional factory-built diners, "homemade" or on-site diners, diners converted from railroad or trolley cars, and "new concept" diner theme restaurants.

This is meant to be used as a guide. Diners change a lot. They change names; they change owners; they even change locations. This happens on a regular basis, so any listing is bound to be out-of-date as soon as it is printed. Don't be discouraged if you have trouble finding some of these diners. They may have been renovated beyond recognition. They may have been demolished.

Once you've found a diner you like, ask the owner where there are others like it. Chances are he'll tell you about one, which might not be on the list. And by all means, if you find a good one I've missed, let me know.

UNITED STATES

Alabama
None

Alaska
None

Arizona
5 & Diner
5220 N. 16th St.
Phoenix
Pedco 1988

5 & Diner
4330 E. Broadway Blvd.
Tucson
1997

5 & Diner
4520 N. Stone Ave.
Tucson

Birth Place Diner
U.S. Rte. 66
Winslow
Valentine

Chaunce's Diner
Santa Fe Ave.
Flagstaff
Valentine 1941

Dot's Diner
Shady Dell
    Campground
1 Douglas Rd.
Bisbee
Valentine 1956

Twin Arrows
Twin Arrows
    Trading Post
Flagstaff
Valentine

Arkansas
Starlite Diner
250 E. Military Dr.
North Little Rock
Starlite

California
Andy's Truckee Diner
10144 West River
Truckee
Kullman 1949

Bert's Diner
8972 Grant Line Rd.
Sheldon
homemade

**Bette's Oceanview
    Diner**
1807A 4th St.
Berkeley
homemade 1980s

Bing's Diner
10961 Merritt St.
Castroville
converted trolley

Dimples Diner
1823 E. Main St.
Visalia
Space Master 1989

Ed Debevic's
134 N. La Cienega
Beverly Hills
homemade 1980s

Fog City Diner
1300 Battery St.
San Francisco
homemade 1985

Grubstake
1525 Pine St.
San Francisco
converted trolley

Max's Diner
311 3rd St.
San Francisco
homemade 1980s

Red Wagon Cafe
Rte. 43
Shafter
converted trolley

Ruby's Diner
2305 E. Pacific Coast
    Hwy.
Corona Del Mar
homemade 1988

Ruby's Diner
No. 1 Balboa Pier
Newport Beach
homemade 1982

Colorado

Chuck's Stop Diner
132 W. Cimarron St.
Colorado Springs
Valentine 1954

Davies' Chuck Wagon Diner
9495 W. Colfax Ave.
Lakewood
Mt. View 1957

Dinky Diner
Rte. 285
Fairplay
Valentine

King's Chef
Costilla St.
Colorado Springs
Valentine

Last American Diner
1955 28th St.
Boulder
homemade 1978

Red Rock Diner
155 Hwy. 133
Carbondale
Starlite

Connecticut

Acropolis Diner
1864 Dixwell Ave.
Hamden

Athena Diner
Rte. 1 N.
Westport

Athena Diner II
320 Washington Ave.
North Haven

Athenian I
1426 Whalley Ave.
New Haven
DeRaffele

Athenian II
864 Washington St.
Middletown
DeRaffele c. 1990

Athenian III
1064 Boston Post Rd.
Milford
DeRaffele 1997

Athenian IV
998 Wolcott St.
Waterbury

Blue Colony Diner
Church Hill Rd.
Newtown

Blue Sky Diner
273 Ferry Blvd.
Stratford

Bridgeport Flyer
245 Bridgeport Ave.
Milford
Swingle 1973

Century Restaurant
1625 Summer St.
Stamford

Charlene's Diner
Main St.
Jewett City
Worcester 1930s

Collin's Diner
Rte. 44, Railroad Sq.
Canaan
O'Mahony 1942

Colonial Diner
1088 Dixwell Ave.
Hamden

Country Diner
High Ridge Rd.
Stamford
DeRaffele

Curley's Diner
62 W. Park Pl.
Stamford
Mt. View 1949

Elm Diner
427 Elm St.
West Haven

Fifty's Diner
Farmington Ave.
Berlin
O'Mahony 1930s

Forbes Diner
189 Forbes Ave.
New Haven
Fodero 1957

Gagain's Parkside Diner
1503 Thomaston St.
Waterbury

Hi Way Diner
95 Water St.
New Haven
Mt. View 1955

Holiday Diner
123 White St.
Danbury

Jimmy's Diner
197 Main St.
Norwalk

Joe's Diner
797 Farmington Ave.
Berlin

Just In Tyme Diner
82 W. Main St.
Meriden
Silk City 1949

Kimberly Diner
459 Boston Post Rd.
Milford
DeRaffele 1960s

Lakeside Diner
1050 Long Ridge Rd.
Stamford

Main Street Diner
40 W. Main St.
Plainville
Master

Makris Diner
1795 Berlin Tpk.
Wethersfield
O'Mahony 1951

Mark Twain Diner
431 Main St.
East Hartford
Master c. 1960

Mellor's Place
S. Colony Rd.
Wallingford

Milford Diner
13 New Haven Ave.
Milford

Miss Washington Diner
10 Washington St.
New Britain
Kullman early 1960s

New Broadway Diner
Broad St. &
    Fairfield Ave.
Bridgeport
c. 1957

New Englander Diner
Railroad Pl. &
    Ives St.
Danbury
DeRaffele c. 1952

New Star Diner
Lombard St.
New Haven
Fodero 1964

New Venice Diner
383 Queen St.
Southington

Ninety-One Diner
420 Middletown Ave.
New Haven

Norm's Diner
171 Bridge St.
Groton
Silk City 1954

O'Rourke's Diner
728 Main St.
Middletown
Mt. View 1946

Old Saybrook Diner
809 Boston Post Rd.
Old Saybrook
DeRaffele 1990s

Olympia Diner
3413 Berlin Tpk.
Newington
O'Mahony 1950s

Olympos Diner
1130 E. Main St.
Meriden

Post Road Diner
312 Connecticut Ave.
Norwalk
Paramount 1947

Quaker Diner
319 Park Rd.
West Hartford
homemade 1931

Rosie's Diner
Kings & Gold
    Star Hwys.
Groton
Silk City 1954

Route 72 Diner
869 Mill St.
East Berlin

Sandy Hook Diner
Churchill Rd.
Sandy Hook
O'Mahony 1920s

Sherwood Diner
901 Post Rd.
Westport

Silva's Diner
Berlin Tpk.
Newington
DeRaffele 1960s

Silver Diner
3780 E. Main St.
Waterbury
Mt. View 1951

Silver Star
210 Connecticut Ave.
Norwalk
Kullman 1980

Sit Down Diner
69 Newtown Rd.
Danbury
Kullman 1985

Skee's Diner
589 Main &
    Elm Sts.
Torrington
O'Mahony c. 1920

**South Windham
    Diner**
881 Rte. 32
South Windham
Bramson

Squeek's Diner
200 E. Main St.
Middletown
Worcester c. 1942

Tony's Diner
46 Columbus St.
Seymour
Kullman late 1940s

Triple A Diner
1209 Main St.
East Hartford
1960s

Trolley Pub
Rte. 66
Willimantic
Ward & Dickinson

Twin Pines Diner
34 Main St.
East Haven

Two Guys Diner
485 Honeyspot Rd.
Stratford

Valley Diner
636 New Haven Ave.
Derby

Washington Diner
Washington St.
Hartford

West Hartford Diner
526 New Park Ave.
West Hartford
Paramount 1960s

Wethersfield Diner
718 Silas Deane Hwy.
Wethersfield
Mt. View 1951

White's Diner
280 Boston Ave.
Bridgeport
DeRaffele 1957

Windmill Diner
245 Danbury Rd.
New Milford

Winsted Grille
496 Main St.
Winsted
Tierney 1931

Zip's Diner
Rtes. 101 & 12
Dayville
O'Mahony 1954

Delaware
Andy's Diner
Rte. 13
Bridgeville
O'Mahony c. 1940

Bridgeville Diner
Rte. 13
Bridgeville
O'Mahony

Ches-Del Diner
St. George
Mt. View 1957

Doyle's Restaurant
Rte. 113
Selbyville
Silk City c. 1950

Hollywood Diner
123 N. Dupont Hwy.
Dover
Fodero c. 1950

Milford Diner
1042 N. Walnut
Milford
Fodero 1955

Seaford Diner
Seaford
Mt. View 1957

Smyrna Diner
Smyrna
Paramount c. 1960

District of
Columbia
American City Diner
5532 Connecticut
    Ave. NW
Kullman 1988

Florida
11th Street Diner
1065 Washington
    Ave.
Miami Beach
Paramount 1949

Angel's Dining Car
Rte. 17
Palatka
converted railroad car
    1932

Ann's 40 Acre Diner
Memorial Blvd.
Lakeland
Worcester 1953

Bumpers Diner
2119 S. Dixie Hwy.
West Palm Beach
Manno 1954

**Denny's Classic
    Diner**
8030 Gladiolus Dr.
Fort Myers
Starlite 1997

**Denny's Classic
    Diner**
Kings Hwy.
Port Charlotte
Starlite 1998

Gourmet Diner
13951 Biscayne Blvd.
Miami
Paramount 1994

**Harrisons Grill &
    Bar**
401 S. Fort Harrison
    Ave.
Clearwater
O'Mahony 1950

**Jack's Hollywood
    Diner**
1031 N. Federal Hwy.
Hollywood
Mt. View 1953

Lester's Diner
250 State Rd. 84
Fort Lauderdale
homemade 1965

Miramar Diner
3101 S. State Rd. 7
Hollywood
c. 1960

Pelican Diner
7501 Gulf Blvd.
St. Petersburg
Mt. View 1951

Scenic 90 Cafe
Scenic Hwy.
Pensacola
Starlite

Schoop's Diner
17 Eagle Ridge Dr.
Lake Wales
Starlite 1996

Starlite Diner
401 N. Atlantic Ave.
Daytona Beach
Starlite 1996

Starlite Diner
6201 N. Andrews Ave.
Fort Lauderdale
Starlite

Starlite Diner
3500 Oakwood Blvd.
Fort Lauderdale
Starlite

Starlite Diner
3902 Cypress Creek
    Rd.
Pompano Beach
Starlite

Toni's Place
1820 Faun Rd.
Venice
Valentine

Village Landing
13001 Gulf Blvd.
St. Petersburg
Mt. View 1953

Georgia

Arirang Korean Restaurant
Rte. 1
Augusta
DeRaffele late 1950s

Bobbie's Diner
Habersham &
E. Anderson Sts.
Savannah
Mt. View c. 1954

Buckhead Diner
3073 Piedmont Rd.
Atlanta
homemade 1987

Fenders Diner
Irvin St.
Cornelia
homemade 1990s

Gabby's Diner
5915 Hamilton Rd.
Columbus
O'Mahony 1938

Gabby's Diner
753 Milgen Rd.
Columbus
homemade

Happy Days Diner
4064 Peachtree Rd.
NE
Atlanta
Happy Days 1990

Landmark Diner
3672 Roswell Rd. NE
Atlanta
DeRaffele 1990s

Silver Dollar Diner
Slappey Blvd.
Albany
Destiny Mobile Home
Builders 1990

Streamliner
Barnard &
W. Henry Sts.
Savannah
Worcester c. 1940

Hawaii

None

Idaho

None

Illinois

An American Original Diner
2941 W. Iles Ave.
Springfield
homemade

Ed Debevic's
640 N. Wells St.
Chicago
homemade

Elite Diner
210 E. Elm
Urbana
Mt. View 1950s

Virginia's Diner
421 14th St.
Moline
Valentine 1940s

Indiana

Boston Grille
1901 E. Old Rd. 30
Warsaw
Starlite 1995

Burch's Family Restaurant
Ridge Rd.
Gary
Mt. View 1951

Cindy's Diner
830 S. Harrison St.
Fort Wayne
Valentine 1954

Connie's Soul Food Diner
38th & Emerson
Indianapolis
Mt. View 1954

Duck-In Diner
U.S. 52 & Hwy. 28
Clarks Hill
Mt. View 1954

Little Chef Diner
147 E. Market
New Albany
Valentine c. 1960

Street Car Diner
Rte. 70 W.
Terre Haute
converted railroad car
1933

The Diner
9762 W. Washington St.
Indianapolis
Mt. View 1954

The Diner on 86th
86th & Allisonville Rd.
Indianapolis
homemade 1987

Iowa

Archie's Diner
723 W. 7th St.
Sioux City
Kullman 1941

Drake Diner
1111 25th
Des Moines
homemade

North End Diner
5055 Merle Hay Rd.
Johnston
homemade

Suzie Q Cafe
142 Northwest
Mason City
Valentine

West End Diner
13731 University
Clive
homemade

Kansas

Bessie's Diner
S. West St. at Pawnee
Wichita
Valentine

Bierrock's
S. Tyler at Maple
Wichita
Valentine

Dyne Quik
11th & N. Broadway
Wichita
Valentine

Kentucky

Cain's Diner
Water St.
Richmond 1946

Louisiana

Hub City Diner
1412 S. College Rd.
Lafayette
1990

Maine

A-1 Diner
3 Bridge St.
Gardiner
Worcester 1946

Bob's Hot Dogs
Waldoboro
Lunch Wagon

Brunswick Diner
101 Pleasant St.
Brunswick
Worcester 1942

Deluxe Diner
29 Oxford Ave.
Rumford
Worcester 1928

Farmington Diner
Intervale Rd.
Farmington
Mt. View c. 1950

Maidee's Cafe International
156 Main St.
Ellsworth
O'Mahony 1932

Miss Portland Diner
49 Marginal Way
Portland
Worcester 1949

Moody's Diner
Rte. 1
Waldoboro
homemade 1927

Palace Diner
18 Franklin St.
Biddeford
Pollard 1927

Wirebridge Diner
Rte. 27
New Portland
Worcester 1932

Maryland

Bel-Loc Diner
Loch Raven Blvd. &
Joppa Rd.
Baltimore
1964

Bunting's English Diner
22nd St. &
Philadelphia Ave.
Ocean City
O'Mahony 1950s

Double T Diner
Rtes. 50 & 2
Annapolis
DeRaffele 1998

Double T Diner
9217 Cornflower Rd.
Baltimore
Kullman 1996

Double T Diner
8302 Pulaski Hwy.
Baltimore
DeRaffele 1959

Double T Diner #1
6300 Baltimore Natl.
Pk.
Catonsville
DeRaffele 1959/1990s

Double T Diner #2
One Mountain Rd.
Pasadena
DeRaffele

Double T Diner #3
10741 Pulaski Hwy.
White Marsh
DeRaffele 1997

English's Diner
Rte. 13 North
Salisbury
Mt. View 1957

English's Diner
Main St.
South Salisbury
O'Mahony 1947

Forest Diner
10031 Baltimore Natl.
Pk.
Ellicott City
Silk City 1947

Frank's Diner
U.S. 1 & Cedar Ave.
Jessup
Kullman c. 1959

Hollywood Diner
400 E. Saratoga St.
Baltimore
Mt. View 1952

Mr. D's Diner
Eastern Ave.
Essex
Starlite 1993

New Ideal Diner
Rte. 40 S.
Aberdeen
O'Mahony 1952

Nick's Diner
11199 Viers Mill Rd.
Wheaton
homemade 1977

Overlea Diner
6652 Bel Air Rd.
Baltimore
Musi 1992

Princess Diner
10071 Baltimore Natl.
Pk.
Ellicott City
Kullman 1998

Silver Diner
Lake Forest Mall
Gaithersburg
Uniwest 2000

Silver Diner–Laurel
14550 Baltimore Ave.
Laurel
Uniwest 1990

**Silver Diner–
Rockville**
11806 Rockville Pk.
Rockville
Kullman 1989

Silver Diner
Towson Town Center
825 Dulaney Valley
Rd.
Towson
Uniwest 1992

Spikes Diner
50 Southlawn Ct.
Rockville
Kullman 1997

Tastee Diner
7731 Woodmont Ave.
Bethesda
O'Mahony 1939

Tastee Diner
118 Washington Blvd.
Laurel
Comac 1951

Tastee Diner
8516 Georgia Ave.
Silver Spring
O'Mahony 1946/7

Time Out Diner
2408 Union Blvd. W.
Wheaton

Tony's Diner
3117 Vera St.
Baltimore

Tony's Diner
8419 Philadelphia Rd.
Rosedale

Massachusetts
1921 Diner
Rte. 140
West Boylston
Worcester c. 1930

50/50 Diner
440 River St.
Fitchburg
Worcester

Adrien's Diner
145 Wahconnah St.
Pittsfield
Sterling 1940s

Agawam Diner
Rtes. 1 & 133
Rowley
Fodero 1954

Airport Diner
108 Lancaster Rd.
Shirley
Worcester c. 1930

Al Mac's Diner
135 President Ave.
Fall River
DeRaffele 1953

Al's Diner
Prospect & Yelle Sts.
Chicopee
Master 1958

Al's Diner
297 S. Broadway
Lawrence
Worcester 1934

**Andy's Rockland
Diner**
1019 S. Main St.
Fall River
Sterling

Angelo's Orchid Diner
805 Rockdale Ave.
New Bedford
O'Mahony 1951

Arsenal Diner
356 Arsenal St.
Watertown
Worcester

Art's Diner
541 W. Boylston St.
Worcester
Worcester

**Arthur's Paradise
Diner**
Bridge St. at
Boott Mill
Lowell
Worcester 1937

Beachmont Roast Beef
629 Winthrop St.
Revere
Worcester 1948

Bel-Aire Diner
Newburyport Tpk.
West Peabody
Mt. View 1953

Betsy's Diner
457 Main St.
Falmouth
Mt. View 1957

Big Dig Diner
Drydock Ave.
Boston
Silk City 1946

Blue Diner
150 Kneeland St.
Boston
homemade

Blue Moon Diner
102 Main St.
Gardner
Worcester 1949

**Blue Point
Restaurant**
6 Dayton St.
Acushnet
Worcester 1939

Bluebonnet Diner
324 King St.
Northampton
Worcester 1950

Bob's Diner
Rawlins Ave.
Marlborough
Worcester 1947

Boulevard Diner
155 Shrewsbury St.
Worcester
Worcester 1936

Breakfast Club
478 W. Housatonic St.
Pittsfield
Ward & Dickinson
1920s

Buddy's Truck Stop
113 Washington St.
Somerville
Worcester 1929

Capitol Diner
431 Union St.
Lynn
Brill 1928

Carl's Oxford Diner
Main St.
Oxford
Worcester 1930s

Casey's Diner
36 South Ave.
Natick
Worcester c. 1922

Central Diner
90 Elm St.
Millbury
Worcester 1933

Chadwick Square Diner
95 Prescott St.
Worcester
Worcester 1928

Charles Diner
218 Union St.
West Springfield
Fodero 1948

Charlie's Diner
344 Plantation St.
Worcester
Worcester 1948

Chet's Diner
Rte. 20
Northboro
Worcester

Chick's Roast Beef
Main St.
Gloucester
O'Mahony 1950s

Chubby's Diner
72 Main St.
Salisbury
O'Mahony/Musi
1940/1996

Club Diner
145 Dutton St.
Lowell
Worcester 1933

Corner Lunch Diner
133 Lamartine St.
Worcester
Musi-reno
1950s/1968

Dave's Diner
390 W. Grove St.
Middleboro
Starlite 1997

Day and Night Diner
456 N. Main St.
Palmer
Worcester 1942

Don's Diner
123 South St.
Plainville
Mt. View c. 1952

Driftwood Diner
94 Foster St.
Peabody
Worcester

Earnshaw's Diner
21 Broadway Ext.
Fall River
O'Mahony

East Coast Diner
149–151 Main St.
Salisbury
Sterling 1930s

East Side Diner
135 Lunenburg St.
Fitchburg
Worcester c. 1925

Edgemere Diner
51 Hartford Pk.
Shrewsbury
Fodero 1948

Emerald Isle
49 Millbury St.
Worcester
O'Mahony 1947

Fillin' Station
Rte. 5–10 S.
Whately
Kullman 1959

Fish Tale Diner
Rte. 1, Ring Island
Salisbury
Worcester 1940

Flying Red Caboose Diner
594 & 1/2 Essex St.
Lawrence
Worcester

Four Sisters Owl Diner
244 Appleton St.
Lowell
Worcester 1940

Full Moon Restaurant
38 Bennett St.
Lynn
Worcester 1952

Green Island Diner
162 Millbury St.
Worcester
Worcester 1929

Henry's Diner
270 Western Ave.
Allston
Worcester 1953

Jake's Diner
114 Alden Rd.
Fairhaven
O'Mahony c. 1952

Jan & Scott's Cameo Diner
715 Lakeview Ave.
Lowell

Jim's Old Colony Diner
Old Colony Rd.
Mansfield
Sterling 1940

Joe's Diner
51 Broadway
Taunton
Sterling 1940

Kathy's Diner
6 Strong St.
Northampton
Worcester c. 1930

Kathy's Little Kitchen
Rte. 12
Leominster
Worcester 1920s

Kelly's Diner
674 Broadway
Somerville
O'Mahony c. 1947

Kenwood Diner
97 Main St.
Spencer
Worcester c. 1933

Liberty Diner
Mass Ave.
Boston
Worcester c. 1930

Lloyd's Diner
184 Fountain St.
Framingham
Worcester 1942

Lou's Diner
100 Chestnut St.
Clinton
Worcester late 1920s

Lou-Roc's
1074 W. Boylston St.
Worcester
Silk City 1953

Main Street Diner
901 Main St.
Woburn
Worcester 1952

Millpond Diner
2571 Cranberry Hwy.
Wareham
O'Mahony c. 1950

Mindy's Diner
Rte. 117
Bolton
Worcester c. 1940

Miss Adams Diner
53 Park St.
Adams
Worcester 1949

Miss Florence Diner
99 Main St.
Florence
Worcester 1941

Miss Worcester Diner
300 Southbridge St.
Worcester
Worcester 1948

Moran Square Diner
6 Myrtle Ave.
Fitchburg
Worcester 1940

My Tin Man Diner
Otis Rotary
Pocasset
Sterling 1940

Nap's Diner
595 S. Main St.
Webster
Worcester 1931

Nest Diner
81 Fairhaven Rd.
Mattapoisett
Mt. View 1951

Nite Owl Diner
1680 Pleasant St.
Fall River
DeRaffele 1956

Parkway Diner
148 Shrewsbury St.
Worcester
Worcester 1930s

Pat's Diner
9 Bridge Rd.
Salisbury
Worcester 1950

Peg's Diner
Main St.
Whitinsville
Worcester c. 1940

Phyllis' Diner
183 Broadway
Everett
homemade

Pig & Whistle Diner
226 N. Beacon St.
Brighton
Mt. View 1952

Pilgrim Diner
4 Boston St.
Salem
Worcester c. 1934

Pizza Pub
2391 Boston Rd.
Wilbraham
DeRaffele 1960

Pizzaria Plus
984 Gorham St.
Lowell
Worcester 1930s

Portside Diner
2 River St.
Danvers
Worcester 1948

Red Wing Diner
Washington St.
Walpole
Worcester 1932

Rose's Lil Red Diner
906 Eastern Ave.
Malden
Worcester 1930s

Rosebud Diner
381 Summer St.
Somerville
Worcester 1941

Route 66 Diner
950 Bay St.
Springfield
Mt. View 1957

Salem Diner
326 Canal St. Ext.
Salem
Sterling 1941

Sam's Steak Out
13 S. Broadway
Lawrence
Worcester

Shawmut Diner
943 Shawmut Ave.
New Bedford
O'Mahony 1953

Sisson's Diner
561 Wareham St.
Middleboro
converted trolley
    Wason Mfg. 1926

Sit Down Diner
458 Russell St.
Hadley
Kullman 2000

South Street Diner
215 South St.
Boston
homemade 1947

Stoughton Diner
659 Washington St.
Stoughton
homemade

Suffolk Diner
275 Lee Burbank
    Hwy.
Revere
homemade c. 1940

Ted's Diner
67 Main St.
Milford
O'Mahony 1920s

**Tex Barry's Coney
    Island**
31 County St.
Attleboro
Worcester 1920s

Tim's Diner
15 Water St.
Leominster
Silk City c. 1949

Town Diner
627 Mt. Auburn St.
Watertown
homemade 1947

Town Square Diner
164 Nahantan St.
Norwood
homemade 1948

Victoria Dining
1024 Massachusetts
    Ave.
Boston
Swingle 1965

**Wendell's Corner
    Snack Bar**
Old Main St.
North Falmouth
Tierney 1920s

Wheelhouse Diner
453 Hancock St.
North Quincy
1960s

Wilson's Diner
507–509 Main St.
Waltham
Worcester 1949

Windsock Diner
Pleasant St.
Southbridge
Master 1958

**Woody's Main Street
    Diner**
311 Main St.
Athol
Worcester

Yankee Diner
Rte. 20
Charlton
Worcester 1930s

Michigan
Al's Diner
U.S. Rte. 235
Alpena
O'Mahony 1955

Central City Diner
6600 Canton
    Center Rd.
Canton
homemade 1997

Delux Diner
4500 14 Mile Rd.
Rockford
Silk City 1952

Fleetwood Diner
300 S. Ashley St.
Ann Arbor
homemade

Lamy's Diner
Henry Ford Museum
20900 Oakwood Blvd.
Dearborn
Worcester 1946

Pal's Diner
Grand Rapids
Manno 1954

Rosie's Diner
4500 14 Mile Rd.
Rockford
Paramount 1946

Varsity Diner
11740 Gera Rd.
Birch Run
O'Mahony 1956

West Bay Diner
Grand Marais
Paramount 1950

Minnesota
Mickey's Dining Car
9th & St. Peter Sts.
St. Paul
O'Mahony 1937

The Band Box Diner
729 S. 30th St.
Minneapolis
homemade 1934

Mississippi
21 Diner
4878 Hwy. 49
Hattiesburg

Missouri
Broadway Diner
218 E. Broadway
Columbia
Valentine 1963

Gooseberry Diner
Hwy. 571 &
    Airport Dr.
Carthage
USA Diners 1999

Montana
None

Nebraska
None

Nevada
Blue Star Cafe
6350 S. Virginia St.
Reno
5 & Diner 1993

Landrum's Cafe
415 S. Rock Blvd.
Sparks
Valentine

Landrum's/Renato's
6770 S. Virginia St.
Reno
homemade

The Chili Cheez
1300 S. Virginia St.
Reno
Valentine 1947

New Hampshire
28 Bar & Grill
282 N. Broadway
Salem
Sterling 1940

Bobby's Girl Diner
Rte. 104
New Hampton
Worcester 1957

Caron's Restaurant
89 Henniker St.
Hillsboro
Kullman early 1950s

Eggie's Diner
127 Plaistow Rd.
Plaistow
Mt. View c. 1951

Four Aces Diner
23 Bridge St.
West Lebanon
Worcester 1952

Gilley's Lunch Cart
175 Fleet St.
Portsmouth
Worcester 1940

Glory Jean's Diner
Rte. 25
Rumney
O'Mahony 1954

Heritage Diner
Main St.
Charlestown
Worcester 1926

Joanne's Kitchen
219 Main St.
Nashua
Worcester 1930

Lindy's Diner
19 Gilbo Ave.
Keene
Paramount c. 1965

Littleton Diner
145 Main St.
Littleton
Sterling 1940

Louis' Diner
Manchester St. &
Airport Rd.
Concord
Worcester 1933

Main Street Station
105 Main St.
Plymouth
Worcester 1946

Miss Wakefield
Diner
Spaulding Tpk.
Wakefield
O'Mahony 1949

Mt. Pisgah Diner
18 Main St.
Winchester
Worcester c. 1930

Paugus Diner
1331 Union Ave.
Laconia
Worcester 1951

Peterboro Diner
10 Depot St.
Peterborough
Worcester 1950

Red Arrow Diner
61 Lowell St.
Manchester
homemade 1922

Riverside Diner
9 S. Main St.
Bristol
Pollard 1927

Ronaldo's Restaurant
Rte. 1A
Hampton Beach

Shirley D's
Elm St.
Manchester
Worcester 1920s

Sunny Day Diner
Rte. 3
Lincoln
Master 1958

Tilt'n Diner
Rte. 93, Exit 20
Tilton
O'Mahony 1950s

Tumble Inn Diner
1 Main St.
Claremont
Worcester 1941

New Jersey
21 Egg Plate Diner
10th at 18th St.
Paterson
Paramount 1930s

295 Diner & Truck
Stop
Exit 7 off Rte. 295
Pedricktown
DeRaffele

46 Diner
Rte. 46
Lodi

5 Star Diner
Rte. 206
Branchville
Paramount/Silk City

54 Diner
Rte. 54 at Weymouth
Rd.
Buena
Mt. View 1952

Absecon Diner
200 White Horse Pk.
Absecon
Fodero late 1960s

Act III Diner
Rte. 35
Eatontown

Al's Diner
873 Communipaw
Ave.
Jersey City

Alexis Diner
3130 Rte. 10 W.
Denville
Paramount 1990s

American Diner
179 Nassau St.
Princeton
Kullman 1950s

Americana Diner
Rtes. 130 & 571
East Windsor
Musi-reno
1970s/1996

Americana Diner
1160 Hwy. 35
Shrewsbury
Kullman 1997

Amwell Valley Diner
Rte. 31 S.
West Amwell
Swingle-reno
1959/1988

Angelo's Diner
26 N. Main St.
Glassboro
Kullman 1951

Angie's Bridgeton
Grille
Rte. 49
Bridgeton
Silk City

Arena Diner
250 Essex St.
Hackensack
c. 1979

Atco Diner
Rte. 30
Atco

Athens Diner
Harrison Ave.
Harrison
Fodero 1940s

Avenel Diner
Rte. 1
Avenel
Silk City 1940s

Bay Avenue Diner
32 E. Bay Ave.
Manahawkin
O'Mahony 1947

Bay Diner
11 MacArthur Blvd.
Somers Point

Bendix Diner
Rte. 17 &
   Williams Ave.
Hasbrouck Heights
Master 1947

Berlin Diner
Main St.
Berlin
Kullman 2000

Betsy Ross Diner
537–545 Morris Ave.
Elizabeth

Big "E" Diner
267 Closter Dock Rd.
Closter
Fodero 1952

Billy's Diner
20th Ave. &
   Straight St.
Paterson
Silk City 1930s

Blairstown Diner
Rte. 8
Blairstown
Paramount 1949

Bloomfield Diner
Bloomfield Ave.
Bloomfield
O'Mahony 1948

Blue Diamond Diner
275 S. Pomona Rd.
Pomona

Blue Tower Diner
Bloomfield Ave.
Bloomfield
Mt. View 1954

Bobby-Q's Diner
Livingston Mall
Livingston
Kullman 1994

Boonton Diner
909 Main St.
Boonton
Manno

Bound Brook Diner
502 E. Main St.
Bound Brook
Fodero c. 1948

Broadway Diner
1081 Broadway
Bayonne

Broadway Diner
43 Monmouth St.
Red Bank
DeRaffele 1950s

Broadway Diner
55 River Rd.
Summit

Brooklawn Diner
Rte. 130
Brooklawn Circle
Brooklawn
DeRaffele c. 1977

Burlington Diner
Rte. 130 & High St.
Burlington
DeRaffele 1927

Candlewyck Diner
179 Paterson Ave.
East Rutherford
Kullman 1969

Cannon China
Rtes. 1 & 9
Elizabeth
Kullman 1950s

**Captain John's Mr.
   Breakfast**
19th St.
Ship Bottom
O'Mahony 1950s

Century Diner
1140 Tilton Rd.
Pleasantville
Paramount 1988

Chappy's Diner
W. Railroad Ave. &
   Gould Ave.
Paterson
Silk City 1950s

Chester Diner
Main St.
Chester
Kullman-reno 1993

Circle Diner
Rtes. 202–31–12
Flemington

Club Diner
Rte. 168
Bellmawr
Kullman early 1960s

Colonial Diner
560 Rte. 18
East Brunswick
Swingle 1968

Colonial Diner
27 Orient Way
Lyndhurst
mid-1950s

Colonial Diner
Rte. 1
Princeton

**Conlon's Deluxe
   Diner**
1807 45th St.
North Bergen
DeRaffele 1980s

Cookstown Diner
Rte. 528 Spur
Cookstown
Paramount/Mt. View
   late 1930s

Country Club Diner
705 Haddonfield-
   Berlin Rd.
Vorhees

Country Diner
Rte. 130
Windsor
Kullman 1960s

Country Squire Diner
Black Horse Pk.
Cardiff Circle
Cardiff

Crossroads Diner
Rte. 46
Bridgeville
Campora 1957

Crystal Diner
Madison Ave.
Dumont
O'Mahony c. 1930

Dakota Diner
4 Rte. 46 W.
Pine Brook

Delrando Diner
130 Fairview St.
Delran

Diamond Diner
Rte. 70 & Grove St.
Cherry Hill
DeRaffele 1960s

Don's Diner
666 Nye Ave.
Irvington

Double S Diner
155 Glenwood Ave.
Hamburg
Silk City

Dover Star Diner
Rte. 46
Dover

Dynasty Diner
117 E. Main St.
Tuckerton
   1970s

**East Orange Gaslight
   Restaurant**
18–20 Washington St.
East Orange
Swingle 1963

Echo Queen Diner
1079 Rte. 22 E.
Mountainside
Paramount

Egg Platter Diner
Getty Ave. &
   Crooks Ave.
Paterson
Paramount/Master
   1940/1950

El Matador Diner
Rte. 9
Madison Township

Elgin Diner
621 Mt. Efraim Ave.
Camden
Kullman 1958

Elizabethtown Diner
663 Bayway Ave.
Elizabeth
Swingle 1984

Empress of Fairlawn
13–48 River Rd.
Fairlawn
Manno 1967

Ernie's Diner
3801 Atlantic Ave.
Wildwood
Mt. View/Paramount
   1956

Felix #9 Diner
Rte. 22
Bridgewater
1985

Fiesta Hut Diner
Rte. 17
Paramus
Mt. View 1954

Forked River Diner
Rte. 9
Forked River
Kullman c. 1960

Fort Lee Diner
1645 Lemoine Ave.
Fort Lee

Four Seasons Diner
Rtes. 130 & 30
Collingswood

Fred's Beach Haven Diner
4th & Bay Ave.
Beach Haven
Mt. View 1954

Freeway Diner
Rte. 41
Deptford
Superior/Mt. View/
Kullman

Galloway Diner
235 White Horse Pk.
Pomona

Glenn Miller's
Asbury Park Cir.
Asbury Park
Manno c. 1957

Golden Bell Diner
Rte. 9 &
Adelphia Rd.
Freehold

Golden Coach Diner
Hwy. 130
Hightstown

Golden Coach Diner
224 Third Ave.
Long Branch

Golden Dawn Diner
E. Park
Edgewater
Kullman

Greenwood Manor Diner
801 U.S. 1
Iselin
c. 1979

Hackettstown Diner
Rte. 46
Hackettstown

Harris Diner
21 N. Park St.
East Orange
O'Mahony 1953

Harvest Diner
2602 Rte. 130
Cinnaminson
Kullman

Heritage Diner
72 E. Mt. Pleasant
Ave.
Livingston

Hightstown Diner
Mercer St.
Hightstown
DeRaffele late 1940s

Island Diner
3212 Bayshore Ave.
Brigantine

Jackson Hole Diner
362 Grand Ave.
Englewood
homemade 1995

Joe's Chadwick Diner
Rte. 35 N.
Chadwick Beach

Joe's White Diamond
Belleville Tpk.
Belleville
1938

Kelly's Diner
Rte. 31
Washington
1950s

Key City Diner
600 Memorial Pkwy.
Phillipsburg
Mt. View 1957

Kless Diner
1212 Springfield Ave.
Irvington

L & M Diner
Ocean Township

Lamp Post Diner
6 Weeks Ave.
North Wildwood
Paramount c. 1939

Linden House Diner
200 W. St. George
Ave.
Linden

Little Falls Diner
9 Paterson Ave.
Little Falls
Master 1940s

Lukas' Last American Diner
Rte. 22 E.
Branchburg
Starlite 1999

Madison Diner
1570 Rte. 38
Mt. Holly

Madison IV Diner
Madison Ave. at Getty
Paterson
1941

Majestic Diner
9201 Bergen Blvd.
North Bergen

Malibu Diner
14th St. & Park Ave.
Hoboken
Erfed c. 1964/1988

Marina Diner
St. Hwy. 36
Middletown
Kullman c. 1992

Mark Twain Diner
1601 Morris Ave.
Union
Kullman 1962/1989

Mastoris Diner
144 Rte. 130
Bordentown
late 1960s

Matthews Colonial Diner
430 S. Washington
Ave.
Bergenfield

Matthews Colonial Diner
4 Franklin Tpk.
Waldwick

Max's Grille
731 Harrison Ave.
Harrison
O'Mahony 1927

Medport Diner
Rte. 70
Medford
DeRaffele 1960s

Metro Diner
Oak Tree Rd.
Iselin
Kullman 1987

Midas Touch Diner
W. Westfield Ave. &
Locust
Roselle Park

Middlesex Diner
Rte. 1, 130 Cir.
North Brunswick

Millbrook Diner
Rte. 34
Matawan

Monmouth Queen Diner
Asbury Park
Kullman 1962

Monmouth Queen Diner
Rte. 35 & Wyckoff Rd.
Eatontown

Mustache Bill's
8th & Broadway
Barnegat Light
Long Beach Island
Fodero 1958

Nautilus Diner
95 Main St.
Madison
Kullman 1997

Nevada Diner
293 Broad St.
Bloomfield
late 1980s

New Dunellen Diner
390 North Ave.
Dunellen
O'Mahony c. 1950

New Fair Lawn Star Diner
39–10 Broadway
Fair Lawn
late 1970s

New Grand Street Diner
246 Grand St.
Paterson
Silk City 1930s

New Lido Diner
Rte. 22 E. &
    Lawrence Rd.
Springfield
Paramount 1960

**New Market Tower
    Diner**
671 Market St.
Newark

New Sherros Diner
Rte. 130
Pennsauken

New Sunset Diner
1 Bloomfield Ave.
Fairfield
Mt. View 1956

New Tri-Boro Diner
Essex & Porter Sts.
Paramus
Fodero 1960s

**New Vincentown
    Diner**
Rtes. 206 & 38
Vincentown
c. 1979

**New Woodbridge
    Diner**
680 Amboy Ave.
Woodbridge
c. 1979

Newark Ave. Diner
361 Newark Ave.
Jersey City
Sterling

Nicholas Diner
88 E. Railway Ave.
Paterson
homemade/Erfed
    1960s

**Nico's Heritage
    Diner**
80 River St.
Hackensack
Manno 1960s

North Star Diner
Rte. 23
Wayne

Oakland Diner
72 Ramapo Valley Rd.
Oakland

Ocean Bay Diner
Rtes. 35 & 88
Point Pleasant

Ocean Diner
108 W. Brigantine
    Ave.
Brigantine
Mt. View 1955

Ocean Queen Diner
Laurelton Cir.
Bricktown

Olga's Diner
16th & Federal Sts.
Camden
Mt. View 1952

Olga's Diner
Rtes. 70 & 73 Cir.
Marlton
Kullman/Fodero

Oliver's Diner
E. State St.
Trenton
Mt. View 1952

Olympia Diner
Rtes. 1 & 9
Elizabeth
Paramount

Olympic Diner
The Circle
Black Horse Pk.
Pleasantville
Fodero

Omer's Diner
Rte. 130 &
    New Albany Rd.
Cinnaminson
Kullman-reno 1991

Ormos Diner
45 New St.
Irvington

**P & B Colonial
    Diner**
420 N. Delsea Dr.
Glassboro
Swingle 1963

Pallas Diner
Rte. 73, the Circle
Berlin

Palmyra Diner
Rte. 73
Palmyra

Par-Troy Diner
1315 Rte. 46
Parsipanny
Kullman 1970s/1992

Park Ridge Diner
125 Kinderkamack Rd.
Park Ridge

Park West Diner
Rte. 46
Little Falls
Kullman 1996

Parsonage Diner
Rte. 27 at Parsonage
    Rd.
Edison

Pat's Diner
1300 S. Broad St.
Trenton
1950s/60s

Pat's Riverview Diner
Rte. 35
Belmar
Fodero 1956

Paul's Diner
Rte. 46
Parsippany
Fodero

Penn Queen Diner
Rte. 130
Pennsauken
DeRaffele 1960s

Penn Villa Diner
Rte. 130 &
    Drexel Ave.
Pennsauken

Phil's Pizza Palace
Rte. 130
Robbinsville
Comac

Phily Diner
31 S. Black Horse Pk.
Runnemede
DeRaffele 1980s/1994

Phoenix Diner
Rte. 202
Oakland

Pier 13 Steak Joynt
Rte. 49
Pennsville

Pilgrim Diner
82 Pompton Ave.
Cedar Grove
Manno 1965

Ping's Diner
291 Clark Ave.
Clark
Silk City 1955

Plaza 17 Diner
400 Rte. 17
Upper Saddle River

Plaza Diner
2066 Rte. 27
Edison

Plaza Diner
2045 Lemoine Ave.
Fort Lee

Point Diner
MacArthur Blvd. &
    Circle Dr.
Somers Point

Pollonia Diner
122 Causeway
South River
O'Mahony 1955

**Pompton Queen
    Diner**
666 Rte. 23
Pompton Plains

Ponzio's
Rte. 130 & Browning
    Rd.
Brooklawn
DeRaffele 1970s

Ponzio's Restaurant
Rte. 70, Ellisburg Cir.
Cherry Hill
DeRaffele 1970s

Pop & Joe's Diner
Main St.
Clifton
1930s

Premium Diner
Rtes. 1 & 9
Avenel
Fodero 1951

Presidential Diner
Delsea Dr. & Landis
    Ave.
Vineland

Primrose Diner
Rte. 46 & Clove Rd.
Little Falls

Princetonian Diner
Rte. 1, Princeton Rd.
Princeton

**Queen Elizabeth
    Diner**
Rtes. 1 & 9
Elizabeth

Raritan Manor
Rtes. 202 & 28
Somerville Cir.
Raritan
c. 1979

Red Lion Diner
Rtes. 70 & 206
Southampton

Red Oak Diner
2191 Fletcher Ave.
Fort Lee
Kullman 1971

Red Oak Diner
Rte. 35
Hazlet

Red Tower Diner
864 Rte. 22 E.
North Plainfield
Kullman 2000

Regent Diner
Rte. 9
Lakewood
Swingle 1960s

Renaissance Diner
Rte. 22
North Plainfield

Reo Diner
392 Amboy Ave.
Woodbridge
Musi 1970s

River Star Diner
14 Rte. 57
Hackettstown

Riverview Diner
Rte. 18
Middlesex
Swingle/PMC-reno
1967/1980

Riverview Diner
River St.
Piscataway

Roadside Diner
Rte. 33
Wall
Silk City c. 1950

Royal Diner
Rte. 22
Whitehouse
O'Mahony 1950s

Rustic Mill Diner
109 North Ave.
Cranford

Saddle Brook Diner
30 Market St.
Saddle Brook
c. 1979

Sage Diner
1170 Rte. 73
Mt. Laurel
1980s

Salem Oak Diner
W. Broadway at
Oak St.
Salem
Silk City 1955

Salleo Diner
1419 Irving St.
Rahway
Kullman c. 1960

Sandy Hook Diner
Rte. 36
Leonardo

Scotchwood Diner
1934 Rte. 22 E.
Scotch Plains
Kullman 2000

Service Diner
935 River Dr.
Garfield

Seville Diner
1035 Rte. 18
East Brunswick

Shamrock Diner
1887 Rte. 35
Middletown

Sherban's Diner
222 Front St.
South Plainfield

Short Stop Diner
315 Franklin St.
Bloomfield
Kullman/Manno-reno
1953

Silver Coin Diner
Hwy. 206 & White
Horse Pk.
Hammonton

Silver Diner
2131 Rte. 38
Cherry Hill
Uniwest 1997

Skyline Diner
5914 Park Ave.
West New York

Snuffy's II
Rte. 22
Somerville
Swingle 1961

Snuffy's III
87 Sip Ave.
Jersey City

Somerset Diner
1045 Easton Ave.
Somerset

**Spinning Wheel
Diner**
Rte. 22
Lebanon
Kullman 2000

State Diner
567 Valley Rd.
West Orange

State Line Diner
Rte. 46
Bridgeville
Kullman-reno 1993

Suburban Diner
1475 Rte. 1 S.
Edison
Kullman 1970s/1997

Suburban Diner
Rte. 17
Paramus

Summit Diner
Summit Ave. &
1 Union Pl.
Summit
O'Mahony 1938

**Sunset Colonial
Diner**
Rte. 22 E.
Green Brook
Swingle 1965

Sussex Cafe
Hamburg Ave.
Sussex
Silk City late 1940s

Swingle's Diner
Rte. 22
Springfield
Swingle 1960

The Fireplace Diner
152 Rte. 46
Rockaway

The Forum Diner
Rte. 4 at Forest Ave.
Paramus

The Hop Diner
Rte. 54 &
Railroad Ave.
Hammonton
Kullman

**The Original Six
Brothers Diner**
Rte. 46 & Clove Rd.
Little Falls
1990s

Tick Tock Diner
281 Allwood Rd.
Clifton
Kullman 1994

Tiffany Diner
1045 Rte. 17
Ramsey

Time Out Diner
2050 Hwy. 50
Tuckahoe
Silk City 1940s

Tom Sawyer Diner
550 Bergen Blvd.
Ridgefield

Tom's Diner
Rte. 46
Ledgewood
Silk City c. 1940

Tom's Diner
Rte. 8 S.
New Berlin
Kullman 1950s

Toms River Diner
Rte. 37
Toms River

**Tony's Freehold
Grille**
59 E. Main St.
Freehold
O'Mahony 1947

Town Center Diner
322 Kinderkamack
Rd.
Westwood

**Town & Country
Diner**
Rtes. 130 & 206
Bordentown
Fodero 1960s

Town & Country Diner
Rtes. 206 & 70
Vincentown
1960s

Town Square Diner
Wharton
Paramount c. 1987

Triangle Diner
Wagarow-Hawthorne
& Goffle Rds.
Paterson

Trojan Diner
Rte. 22
Phillipsburg

Truck Stop Diner
Rte. 1 &
Hackensack Ave.
South Kearny
Kullman 1940s

Tunnel Diner
12th St.
Jersey City
Paramount c. 1940

Twin Oaks Diner
350 Rte. 17 N.
Paramus

Union Plaza Diner
Rte. 22, Center Island
Union
Fodero/Kullman
1960s/1987

Vegas Diner
14th &
New Jersey Aves.
North Wildwood
Fodero

Versailles Diner
516 Rte. 46
Fairfield
c. 1979

Vicki's Diner
110 E. Broad St.
Westfield
Kullman 1997

Webers Diner
136 White Horse Pk.
Audubon

West Side Diner
324 Rte. 46
Denville
Silk City 1950

Westfield Diner
309 North Ave.
Westfield
Swingle 1983

White Circle Diner
Bloomfield Ave.
Bloomfield
Manno 1957

White Crown Diner
2019 S. Wood Ave.
Linden
Comac

White Crystal Diner
Center Ave.
Atlantic Highlands
Kullman 1960

**White Diamond
Hamburgers**
1208 E. Grand St.
Elizabeth

**White Mana
Hamburgers**
Tonnele & Manhattan
Aves.
Jersey City
Paramount 1939

**White Manna
Hamburgers**
358 River St.
Hackensack
Paramount late 1930s

White Rose System
154 Woodbridge St.
Highland Park
Paramount 1960s

**White Rose System
Hamburgers**
E. 1st Ave at
Walnut St.
Roselle
Kullman c. 1960

White Star Diner
715 W. Front St.
Plainfield
Kullman

Whitehouse Diner
Rte. 22
Whitehouse
Silk City 1930s

Wildwood Diner
4005 Atlantic Ave.
Wildwood
O'Mahony

Williamstown Diner
Rte. 42
Williamstown
Mt. View c. 1957

Willie's Diner
9 State St.
Bloomfield
Fodero 1954

Windsor Diner
Rte. 38 & Cooper
Landing Rd.
Cherry Hill
1960s

Windsor Diner
1030 Raritan Rd.
Clark

Woodstown Diner
Rte. 40
Woodstown
1960s

Zikos Diner
610 Delilah Rd.
Pleasantville

New Mexico
Dad's Diner
4395 Largo St.
Farmington
Starlite 1997

Rio Grande Diner
Belen
Starlite 1997

Route 66 Diner
Rte. 66
Albuquerque
homemade

The Diner
Rtes. 285 & 64
Tres Piedras
Valentine

Tic Toc Diner
601 Osuna NE
Albuquerque
Valentine

New York
209 Diner
Rte. 209
Ellenville
Silk City 1952

2nd Avenue Diner
670 2nd Ave.
Brooklyn
Paramount

84 Diner
Rte. 52
Fishkill
DeRaffele 1997

Acropolis Diner
829 Main St.
Poughkeepsie
Paramount 1982/1993

Adams Diner
Rte. 22
Wingdale
DeRaffele late 1950s

Airport Diner
3760 Veterans Hwy.
Bohemia, L.I.

Alexis Diner
Rte. 4
East Greenbush
DeRaffele 1999

Americana Diner
6501 7th Ave.
Brooklyn
DeRaffele

Americana Diner
Rtes. 23 & 30
Grand Gorge
Fodero c. 1952

Apollo Diner
630 Merrick Ave.
East Meadow, L.I.
Kullman c. 1962

Arch Diner
1866 Ralph Ave.
Brooklyn
DeRaffele

Argento Cafe
301 Halstead Ave.
Harrison
DeRaffele c. 1940

Auburn Diner
State & Garden Sts.
Auburn
Bixler 1935

Augie's Diner
375 Orisikany Blvd.
Whitesboro
Silk City 1940

Baldwin Coach Diner
Sunrise Hwy. &
Central Ave.
Baldwin, L.I.

**Baldwin Townhouse
Diner**
785 Merrick Rd.
Baldwin
DeRaffele c. 1960

Bel Aire Diner
31–91 21st St.
Astoria
c. 1960

Bellerose Diner
248–27 Jamaica Ave.
Bellerose, L.I.

Belmont Diner
247 Hempstead Tpk.
Elmont, L.I.

Bill Gates Diner
Adirondack Museum
Blue Mountain Lake
converted trolley 1937

Blauvelt Coach Diner
Rte. 303
Blauvelt
c. 1979

Blue Bird Diner
4914 Glenwood Rd.
Brooklyn
Mt. View

Blue Dawn Diner
1860 Veterans
    Memorial Hwy.
Central Islip

Blue Dolphin Diner
175 Katonah Ave.
Katonah
Kullman late 1930s

Blue Point Diner
145 Main St.
Blue Point
Mt. View 1953

Blue Ribbon Diner
1801 State St.
Schenectady

Bob's Diner
27 Main St.
Brewster
O'Mahony 1955

Bolton Diner
Lake Shore Dr.
Bolton Landing
Worcester 1946

Bonwit Inn
Vanderbilt Pkwy. &
    Commack Rd.
Commack, L.I.

Boulevard Diner
69–20 Queens Blvd.
Woodside, L.I.

Broadway Diner
563 Broadway
Menands

Broadway Inn Diner
590 S. Broadway
Yonkers

By-Pass Diner
Albany Post Rd.
Peekskill

Cairo Diner
Main St.
Cairo
1928

Canastota Dinerant
Main St.
Canastota
Silk City 1958

Candlelight Diner
56 Veterans Hwy.
Commack, L.I.
Kullman 1997

Cape May Cafe
Main St.
Clarence
Ward & Dickinson

Carol's Diner
Rte. 4
Stillwater
Silk City

Carolina Diner
248–58 Rockaway
Rosedale, Queens

Casey's Bar & Grill
1255 Castleton Ave.
Staten Island

Center Diner
13 Bank St.
Peekskill
O'Mahony 1938

**Center Raceway
    Diner**
833 Yonkers Ave.
Yonkers
DeRaffele c. 1960

**Charlie's Northway
    Diner**
256 Wolf Rd. Ext.
Colonie
Silk City

Cheyenne Diner
411 Ninth Ave.
NYC
Paramount

Chez Sophie Bistro
Saratoga Springs
Fodero c. 1951

Circle Diner
813 Loudon Rd.
Latham
Kullman 1998

Circle E Diner
Rte. 17
Hancock
Mt. View

City Limits Diner
200 Central Ave.
White Plains
homemade 1994

City Limits Diner
125 Westchester Ave.
White Plains

Coliseum Diner
1019 Front St.
Uniondale, L.I.

Colonial Diner
8–10 Dolson Ave.
Middletown

Colonial Diner
767 New York Ave.
Huntington, L.I.
Swingle 1961

Colonie Diner
1890 Central Ave.
Albany

Colonnade Diner
2001 Hylan Blvd.
Staten Island

Colony Diner
2019 Hempstead Tpk.
East Meadow, L.I.

Columbia Diner
717 Warren St.
Hudson
O'Mahony c. 1950

Comfort Diner
214 E. 45th St.
NYC
homemade 1996

Comfort Diner #2
86th & Lexington
NYC
homemade 1998

Concord Diner
99 Fourth St.
Valley Stream
Kullman 1992

Connie's Diner
Rte. 20
Waterloo
Manno 1960s

Corfu Diner
18th & 10th Aves.
NYC
Kullman c. 1940

Country Club Diner
2270 Clove Rd.
Staten Island

Countryside Diner
Rtes. 9 & 20
Castleton-on-Hudson
Silk City 1941

Crazy Dog Diner
123 Montauk Hwy.
Westhampton Beach,
    L.I.
Mt. View/Fodero
    1950s

**Cross Island Inn
    Diner**
243–03 Merrick Blvd.
Rosedale, Queens

**Croton Colonial
    Diner**
Rtes. 9A & 129
Croton-on-Hudson

Croton North Diner
49 N. Riverside Ave.
Croton-on-Hudson
Bixler

Cutchogue Diner
Main Road
Cutchogue
Kullman c. 1940

D-B Diner
Rte. 9 W.
Middlehope
c. 1960

Dakota Diner
921 Richmond Ave.
Staten Island
Kullman

Danny's Diner
151 Main St.
Binghamton
Sterling 1939

Del Rio Diner
166 Kings Hwy.
Brooklyn
DeRaffele

Dewey's Diner
Fullerton Rd.
Colonie
Kullman c. 1950

Dewey's Diner
Kingston
Fodero

Dine-Asty Diner
Greenwood Lake
Master c. 1947

Diner
85 Broadway
Brooklyn
Kullman late 1920s

**Doc's Little Gem
Diner**
832 Spencer St.
Syracuse
Fodero 1956

**Dominico's
Restaurant**
E. Brighton Ave.
Syracuse
O'Mahony late 1930s

Duanesburg Diner
Rtes. 7 & 20
Duanesburg
Bixler 1930s

Dutchess Diner
799 South Rd.
Poughkeepsie
Paramount 1994

**East Greenbush
Diner**
751 Columbia Tpk.
East Greenbush
Paramount mid 1970s

East Market Diner
2592 Atlantic Ave.
Brooklyn

**Eddie's Paramount
Diner**
414 W. Dominick St.
Rome
O'Mahony 1940

El Greco Diner
1821 Emmons Ave.
Brooklyn
DeRaffele

El Tropico Inn
Main St.
Port Jefferson Station
Silk City 1957

Embassy Diner
4280 Hempstead Tpk.
Bethpage, L.I.
DeRaffele late 1980s

Embassy Diner
758 S. Fulton Ave.
Mt. Vernon

Empire Diner
100 W. Albany St.
Herkimer
Mt. View 1952

Empire Diner
210 Tenth Ave.
NYC
Fodero 1946

Eveready Diner
540 Albany Post Rd.
Hyde Park
Paramount 1995

Expressway Diner
666 Motor Pkwy.
Hauppauge, L.I.

Floridian Diner
2301 Flatbush Ave.
Brooklyn
Kullman

Foursome Diner
3070 Avenue U
Brooklyn

**Frank & Mary's
Diner**
10 Port Watson St.
Cortland
homemade

Gager's Diner
327 Broadway
Monticello
1950s

Galaxy Diner
Jericho Tpk.
New Hyde Park
DeRaffele late 1950s

Gateway Diner
899 Central Ave.
Albany
DeRaffele early 1960s

Gateway Diner
Washington Ave.
Kingston

Georgia Diner
86–55 Queens Blvd.
Elmhurst, Queens

Gibby's Diner
Rte. 7
Quakerstreet
Mt. View 1953

Golden Dove Diner
3281 Richmond Ave.
Staten Island
DeRaffele

Golden Star Diner
267 Saw Mill
River Rd.
Elmsford

Greasy Spoon Diner
20 North Hwy.
Southampton, L.I.
Silk City

Green Arch Diner
41 W. Main St.
Brocton
Mulholland 1931

**Greenpoint Ave.
Deli-Diner**
255 Greenpoint Ave.
Brooklyn
Kullman

Halfmoon Diner
Rte. 9
Halfmoon
DeRaffele

Highland Park Diner
960 S. Clinton Ave.
Rochester
Orleans Mfg. 1948

Hilltop Diner
Rte. 12
Green

Historic Village Diner
39 N. Broadway
Red Hook
Silk City 1951

Holbrook Diner
980 Patchogue-
Holbrook Rd.
Holbrook

Holiday Grill Diner
Montauk Hwy.
Southampton, L.I.

Homestyle Eatery
412 Oliver St.
North Tonawanda
Tierney 1920s

Honest Diner
74 Montauk Hwy.
Amagansett
Kullman/Silk City

Houselight Diner
Wantagh
Kullman 1962

Hunter Dinerant
18 E. Genesee St.
Auburn
O'Mahony 1951

**Hunter's Points
Golden Fountain**
49th Ave. & 21st St.
Long Island City
Mt. View 1952

Hyde Park Diner
Rtes. 9 & 9-G
Hyde Park

Imperial Diner
63 W. Merrick Rd.
Freeport, L.I.

Imperial Diner
Rte. 9
Wappingers Falls

J.R.'s Diner
Wolf St.
Syracuse
Bixler 1930s

Jack & Jill's Diner
Crystal Run Mall
Middletown
Kullman 1992

Jack's Diner
547 Central Ave.
Albany
Comac 1949

Jackson Hole Diner
3501 Bell Blvd.
Bayside
1998 reno

**Jackson Hole
Wyoming Airline
Diner**
69–35 Astoria Blvd.
Jackson Heights
Mt. View 1952

Jay's Diner
2612 W. Henrietta Rd.
Rochester
Swingle 1966

Jen's Diner
455 Court St.
Watertown
Bixler

Jimmy D's Pizza Royale
Rtes. 20 & 22
New Lebanon
Fodero 1964

Jimmy's Diner
285 Broadway
Newburgh

Johnny D's Diner
909 Union Ave.
New Windsor
Kullman 1996

Johnny's Diner
603 Flushing Ave.
Brooklyn
Kullman

Jones' Diner
371 Lafayette St.
NYC
DeRaffele

Kellogg's Diner
514 Metropolitan Ave.
Brooklyn

King's Arms Diner
500 Forest Ave.
Staten Island

King's Plaza Diner
4124 Avenue U
Brooklyn

Kings Villa Diner
419 Old Country Rd.
Westbury, L.I.

La Salle Diner
98–22 Queens Blvd.
Forest Hills

Larchmont Diner
399 Boston Post Rd.
Larchmont
DeRaffele 1995

Lexus Diner
411 Rte. 9W
Newburgh
homemade 1990

Lighthouse Diner
3240 Sunrise Hwy.
Wantagh, L.I.

Lindenwood Diner
2870 Linden Ave.
Brooklyn
DeRaffele

Lloyd's of Lowville Diner
7405 S. State St.
Lowville
homemade 1930s

Majestic Diner
Rte. 9
Wappinger Falls

Mamaroneck Inn
405 Boston Post Rd.
Mamaroneck

Manos Diner
357 Elmira Rd.
Ithaca
Swingle 1977

Mario's Diner
628 S. Main St.
North Syracuse
Silk City

Market Diner
9th Ave. & 33rd. St.
NYC
Kullman

Market Diner
572 11th Ave.
NYC
DeRaffele 1962

Martindale Chief Diner
Rte. 23
Craryville
Silk City 1958

Mary's Diner
163 Shear Hill Rd.
Mahopac

Marybill Diner
14 Merrick Ave.
Merrick
Silk City

Massapeaqua Diner
4420 Sunrise Hwy.
Massapeaqua, L.I.

Max Hart's Diner
20 Flint Rd.
Amherst
homemade

Maybrook Diner
Rte. 208
Maybrook
Mt. View 1954

Mayville Diner
7 W. Chautauqua St.
Mayville
Sorge 1930s

Merrick Town House Diner
2160 Sunrise Hwy.
Merrick
1979

Metro 20 Diner
1709 Western Ave.
Guilderland
DeRaffele 1998

Michael's Diner
Ulster Ave. Mall
Kingston

Midway II Diner
Rte. 11
Polkville
Kullman early 1960s

Mike's Diner
630 Utica Ave.
Brooklyn
DeRaffele

Mike's Place
140 New Dorp Ln.
Staten Island
Paramount

Mike's Silver Diner
Mineola
Silk City c. 1950

Millbrook Diner
Rte. 44
Millbrook
O'Mahony c. 1950

Mineola Diner
138 Jericho Tpk.
Mineola
Mt. View c. 1947

Mirage Diner
717 Kings Hwy.
Brooklyn
Swingle 1980

Miss Albany Diner
901 Broadway
Albany
Silk City 1941

Miss America Diner
322 West Side Ave.
Jersey City
O'Mahony 1950s

Miss Johnstown Diner
28 E. Main St.
Johnstown

Miss Oneida Diner
Phelps St.
Oneida
Ward & Dickinson

Miss Port Henry Diner
3 Church St.
Port Henry
Ward & Dickinson

Miss Troy Diner
626 Pawling Ave.
South Troy
Brill/Swingle 1929

Miss Williamsburg Diner
206 Kent Ave.
Brooklyn
Silk City 1940s

Mo's Place 2
Rte. 12
Watertown

Moondance Diner
80 6th Ave.
NYC

Mountaintop Diner
Hunter
Kullman c. 1959

Munson Diner
600 W. 49th St.
NYC
Kullman c. 1950

Nautilus Diner
5523 Merrick Rd.
Massapequa, L.I.

Nebraska Diner
2939 Cropsey Ave.
Brooklyn
DeRaffele 1999

Neptune Diner
5001 St. Hwy. 23
Oneonta
Kullman 2000

New Brighton Diner
827 Main St.
Poughkeepsie

New Empire Diner
N. Jerusalem Ave. &
    W. John St.
Hicksville

New Harvest Diner
41 Lafayette Ave.
Suffern
DeRaffele 1960

Newark Diner
246 E. Union St.
Newark
Sterling 1939

Northampton Diner
Rte. 30
Northville
O'Mahony late 1930s

**Nowhere Bound
    Diner**
Rte. 415
Avoca
Silk City early 1950s

**O.K. Corral
    Restaurant**
Rte. 12
Remsen
Fodero 1940s

O'Donnell's
Greenport, L.I
Kullman 1920s

Ocean Harbor Diner
2756 Long Beach Rd.
Oceanside, L.I.

Omega Diner
1809 Lakeville Rd.
New Hyde Park, L.I.

On Parade Diner
Jericho Tpk.
Woodbury, L.I.

Palace 55 Diner
Rte. 55, off Taconic
    Pkwy.
Poughkeepsie

Palace Lunch
62 S. Main St.
Gloverstown
O'Mahony 1923

Papa's Family Diner
209 Delaware St.
Walton
Paramount 1993

Parthenon Diner
192 Washington St.
Poughkeepsie

**Patti's Lakeview
    Diner**
43 Lake St.
Geneva
Bixler 1930s

Patty's Place
918 Wolf St.
Syracuse
Bixler

Pearl Diner
212 Pearl St.
NYC
Kullman c. 1960

Pelican Diner
508 W. Manlius St.
East Syracuse

Penn Yan Diner
131 E. Elm St.
Penn Yan
Galion Dining Car
    Co. 1925

Peter Pan Diner
Sunrise Hwy.
Bay Shore–
    Brightwaters
DeRaffele 1954

Petrino Diner
8430 New Utrecht
    Ave.
Brooklyn
DeRaffele

Pioneer Diner
5 Raceway
Monticello 1950s

Pleasant Valley Diner
251 Dutchess Tpk.
Poughkeepsie
DeRaffele 1972/1992

Pompey's Take-Out
457 E. Delavan Ave.
Buffalo
Ward & Dickinson

Port Jervis Diner
E. Main St.
Port Jervis
Silk City

**Prospect Mountain
    Diner**
Canada St.
Lake George
Silk City 1950

Quintessence Diner
11 New Scotland Ave.
Albany
Fodero 1949

Red Coach Diner
4010 Austin Blvd.
Island Park

Red Fox Diner
138 N. Central Ave.
Elmsford

Red Robin Diner
Johnson City
Mt. View c. 1950

Redwood Diner
E. Manlius St.
East Syracuse
Ward & Dickinson

Reel Diner
357 West St.
NYC
Kullman 1962

Restop Diner–Motel
Rte. 17 Quickway
Parksville
Paramount 1950

Ridge Diner
7404 5th Ave.
Brooklyn
DeRaffele

River Diner
452 11th Ave.
NYC
Kullman 1930s

Riverdale Diner
Broadway & 282nd
    St.
NYC
O'Mahony
    1950s/1980s

Riverhead Grill
85 E. Main St.
Riverhead, L.I.
1932

Rochelle Diner
272 Main St.
New Rochelle
DeRaffele 1950

Roscoe Diner
Rte. 17
Roscoe

Royal Coach Diner
670 Fulton Ave.
Hempstead

Royal Diner
495 Old Country Rd.
Hicksville, L.I.

Royal Diner
Rte. 28
Kingston
Mahoney

Royal Palace Diner
1601 Utica Ave.
Brooklyn
DeRaffele

Ruby's Silver Diner
167 Erie Blvd.
Schenectady
converted railroad car

Sage Diner
80–26 Queens Blvd.
Elmhurst

Sam Chinita
19th St. & 8th Ave.
NYC
Master c. 1950

Saravan Diner
146–01 Northern
    Blvd.
Flushing
c. 1980

Sautter's Diner
53 E. Main St.
Morrisville
Silk City late 1950s

Saw Mill Diner
337 Saw Mill Rd.
Yonkers

Scarsdale Diner
878 Scarsdale Ave.
Scarsdale

**Scobee Little Neck
    Diner**
Northern Blvd.
Little Neck, Queens

Sea Coral Diner
579 Veterans Hwy.
Hauppauge, L.I.

Seacrest Restaurant
4 Glen Cove Rd.
Old Westbury, L.I.

Seasons Diner
556 Driggs Ave.
Brooklyn

Seaview Diner
2136 Rockaway Pkwy.
Brooklyn
Kullman

Seville Diner
231–10 Northern
Blvd.
Douglaston, Queens
Kullman 1971/1990

**Sheepshead Bay
Diner**
3165 Emmons Ave.
Brooklyn
DeRaffele c. 1960

Sherwood Diner
311 Rockaway Tpk.
Lawrence, L.I.
DeRaffele 1987

Silver Moon Diner
Union Tpk. &
Lakeville Rd.
Queens
Kullman 1987

Silver Star Diner
Rte. 22
Patterson
Silk City 1958

Six Brothers Diner
2153 White Plains
Rd.
Bronx

Skyliner Diner
Strong Museum
One Manhattan Sq.
Rochester
Fodero 1956

**Sonny's Walden
Valley Diner**
23 Orange Ave.
Walden
homemade 1976–77

South Main Diner
S. Main St.
Wellsville
O'Mahony

**Southampton
Princess Diner**
32 Montauk Hwy.
Southampton

Spa Diner
Rte. 9
Ballston Spa

Sparta Diner
101 Herricks Rd.
New Hyde Park, L.I.

Spartan Diner
Rte. 110 &
Conklin St.
Farmingdale

**Speedway Family
Diner**
Rte. 20
West Lebanon
Bixler 1930s

Spicy's BBQ
225 W. Main St.
Riverhead, L.I.
Kullman

Square Diner
33 Leonard St.
NYC
Kullman 1940s

Square Diner
Kingston St.
Wurtsboro

**St. George Clipper
Diner**
Staten Island
Kullman 1962

Stagecoach Diner
858 Hoosick Rd.
Brunswick
Swingle 1988

Star Diner
66 1/2 E. Post Rd.
White Plains
Silk City c. 1950

Starlight Diner
3156 Hempstead Tpk.
Levittown

Starlight Diner II
4812 Sunrise Hwy.
Massapequa Park,
L.I.

State Diner
428 W. State St.
Ithaca
homemade 1947

**Suburban Skyliner
Diner**
Rtes. 11 & 41
Cortland
2 Silk City diners

Sullivan's Diner
Rte. 273
Horseheads
Silk City 1941

Tappan Coach Diner
203 Rte. 303
Orangeburg

Terrace Diner
585 Sunrise Hwy.
West Babylon, L.I.

The 50s Diner
Broadway & Kieffer
Ave.
Depew
Silk City 1954

The Forum Diner
Montauk Hwy.
Bay Shore, L.I.

The Golden Coach
111 Main St.
East Rockaway

The Pantry Diner
Long Beach &
Merrick Rds.
Rockville Centre
1949

Thru-Way Diner
810 Main St.
New Rochelle
DeRaffele 1991

Tick Tock Diner
481 8th Ave.
NYC
Kullman 1996

Tiffany Diner
397 Main St.
Beacon
O'Mahony c. 1946

Tiffany Diner
9904 Fourth Ave.
Brooklyn
DeRaffele

Tilly's 50s Diner
off Rte. 17
Monticello

Toomey's Diner
252 Empire Blvd.
Brooklyn

Tops Diner
351 Duanesburg Rd.
Rotterdam
Paramount c.1960

**Town & Country
Diner**
312 Jericho Tpk.
Syosset, L.I.

Trolley Stop
258 E. Water St.
Syracuse
Bixler

Twin Maple Diner
Sawmill River Rd.
Elmsford
Swingle 1961

Unadilla Diner
57 Main St.
Unadilla
Master c. 1947

**Uncle Milty's
Glenmont Diner**
Rte. 9W
Glenmont
Silk City 1960

Unicorn Diner
2944 Victory Blvd.
Staten Island
Swingle 1980

Val-Brook Diner
160 E. Merrick Rd.
Valley Stream

Victory Diner
1781 Richmond Ave.
Staten Island
Kullman

Village Diner
Main St.
Millerton
Silk City 1958

West Market Diner
659 131st St.
NYC
Mt. View late 1940s

**West Taghkanic
Diner**
Rte. 82 & Taconic
Pkwy.
West Taghkanic
Mt. View 1954

Westfield Main Diner
40 E. Main St.
Westfield

White Plains Diner
50 Westchester Ave.
White Plains
DeRaffele 1960s

Wolff's Diner
Rte. 4
Stillwater
Kullman 1942

Woodrow Diner
655 Rossville Ave.
Staten Island

North Carolina
Four Corners Diner
100 E. Fort Macon
  Rd.
Atlantic Beach
1950s

Gypsy's Shiny Diner
1550 Buck Jones Rd.
Cary
Starlite 1997

Gypsy's Shiny Diner
335 Tryon Rd.
Garner
Starlite 1999

Mel's Diner
29 Hickory Hills Dr.
Grandy
Starlite 1996

Mel's Diner
1286 Hwy. 105 S.
Boone

Owens' 501 Diner
1500 N. Fordham
  Blvd.
Chapel Hill
homemade 1992

Rockin' Comet Diner
11637 Hwy. 70 W.
Clayton
Diner-Mite 1998

North Dakota
None

Ohio
**Annabelle's '50s
  Diner**
8637 Twinbrook Rd.
Mentor
Mt. View 1954

Brookfield Diner
524 St. Rte. 7 SE
Brookfield

Charlie's Restaurant
Brook Park &
  Broadview Aves.
Cleveland
Valentine 1950s

Crosser Diner
127 W. Lincoln Way
Lisbon
Sterling 1940

Eddie's Diner
Liberty Air Museum
Port Clinton
DeRaffele 1954

Emerald Diner
825 N. Main St.
Hubbard
O'Mahony 1930s

Gazebo Diner
Medina
O'Mahony late 1930s

George's Diner
920 W. Tuscawaras
  Ave.
Canton
Kullman 1958

Harley Diner
23105 Aurora Rd.
Cleveland
Worcester 1946

Jerry's Diner
205 S. Water St.
Kent
O'Mahony 1920s

John's Diner
18260 Detroit Ave.
Lakewood
Worcester 1941

Lester's Diner
233 S. Main St.
Bryan

Little Chef Diner
2169 Parkwood Ave.
Columbus
Valentine

**Michael J's Classic
  Diner**
634 Warren St.
Sandusky
O'Mahony c. 1938

**Ruthie & Moe's
  Diner**
4002 Prospect Ave.
Cleveland
O'Mahony/Kullman
  1940/1966

Steel Trolley Diner
140 E. Lincoln Hwy.
Lisbon
O'Mahony 1956

**The Diner on St.
  Clair**
101 S. St. Clair St.
Dayton
Mt. View c. 1952

**The Diner on
  Sycamore**
1203 Sycamore St.
Cincinnati
Mt. View 1954

Village Diner
Rtes. 18 & 58
Wellington
1930s

Oklahoma
Abraham's Diner
4900 N. Western Ave.
Oklahoma City
Valentine

Abuelita Rosas
1220 N. Hudson
Oklahoma City
Valentine

El Meson
2701 S. Walker
Oklahoma City
Valentine

Oregon
Blue Moon Diner
20167 SW Tualatin
  Valley Hwy.
Aloha
Starlite 1997

Pennsylvania
209 Diner
5139 Milford Rd.
Marshalls Creek
O'Mahony c. 1940

401 Diner
401 Fayette St.
Conshohocken

9th & Marion Diner
1200 N. 9th St.
Reading
Silk City 1958

Ace Diner
5517 Lancaster Ave.
Philadelphia
Silk City 1940s

Adamstown Diner
Willow St. &
  Lancaster Pk.
Adamstown
Silk City 1941

Airport Diner
15110 Kutztown Rd.
Kutztown
Silk City 1960

American Diner
4201 Chestnut St.
Philadelphia
Paramount/Swingle
  1947/1988

**American Dream
  Diner**
1933 Herr St.
Harrisburg
DeRaffele 1953

**Andy's River Road
  Diner**
335 N. River St.
Plains
Silk City 1956

**Angelo's Family
  Restaurant**
321 S. Main St.
Sellersville
1960s

**Angie's Brookside
  Diner**
1360 Eisenhower
  Blvd.
Harrisburg
Kullman 1956

**Angie's Family
  Restaurant**
Rtes. 11 & 15 N.
New Buffalo
Kullman 1954

Anna's Pizza
6211 Lancaster Ave.
Philadelphia
Fodero 1954

Aramingo Diner
3356 Aramingo Ave.
Philadelphia
Musi/DeRaffele
  1970/1976

Arlington Diner
834 N. 9th St.
Stroudsburg
Silk City 1940s

Astor Diner
609 Sumneytown Pk.
Lansdale
Musi 1970

B & D Diner
Rte. 6
Wysox
homemade

Baby's Diner
131 S. Garner St.
State College
Silk City 1959

Beacon Diner
Rtes. 309 & 54
Hometown
Paramount 1941

Beaver's Diner
Rte. 11
Hallstead
O'Mahony c. 1956

Berk's Family Restaurant
Rtes. 61 & 73
Leesport
Silk City 1955

Besecker's Diner
1427 N. 5th St.
Stroudsburg
Silk City 1958

Billy's Pocono Diner
Rte. 611
Tannersville
Kullman

Blue Bird II
Rtes. 6 & 11
Factoryville
Mt. View 1948

Blue Comet Diner
43 S. Church St.
Hazelton
Mt. View 1957

Blue Fountain Diner
2029 E. Lincoln Hwy.
Langhorne
Fodero 1963

Bob's Diner
6053 Ridge Ave.
Philadelphia
O'Mahony 1947

Bowmanstown Diner
642 White St.
Bowmanstown
Fodero/Silk City
1952/1960

Broad Street Diner
1135 S. Broad St.
Philadelphia
1960s

Broadway Diner
11650 Roosevelt Blvd.
Philadelphia
Kullman 1985

Cappy's Diner
185 Main St.
Eldred
Ward & Dickinson
1930s

Cauvel's Diner
408 12th St.
Franklin
1930s

Center City Diner
601 Linden St.
Allentown
Kullman 1953

Chaplin's Family Restaurant
223 E. Drinker St.
Dunmore
1940s

Charcoal Diner
1804 Tilghman St.
Allentown
Silk City 1957

Charge's Diner
4700 Birney Ave.
Moosic
Mt. View 1955

Charlie's Diner
7619 1/2 Penn Ave.
Wilkinsburg
National 1940

Charlie's Pizza & Subs
1401 W. Market St.
Pottsville
Paramount 1951

Chef's Place
81 W. Lancaster Ave.
Downingtown
Silk City c. 1962

Chestnut Hill Diner
Rte. 209
Brodheadsville
Fodero/Swingle
1964/1984

Chick's Diner
1032 Moosic Ave.
Scranton
Mt. View 1951

China Buddha Restaurant
175 E. Lancaster Ave.
Wayne
Mt. View 1955

Chio's Diner
3447 Richmond St.
Philadelphia

Chris's Family Restaurant
922 Union Blvd.
Allentown
O'Mahony 1955

Chris's Family Restaurant
5635 Tilghman St.
Allentown
Swingle 1983

Chung Sing
210 E. Lancaster Ave.
Ardmore
Fodero 1952

Clearfield Diner
207 E. Locust St.
Clearfield
Bixler c. 1930

Clearview Diner
Rte. 230
Elizabethtown
Paramount 1948

Cloister Diner
607 W. Main St.
Ephrata
Silk City 1950

Club House Diner
2495 Street Rd.
Bensalem

Coach Diner
149 2nd St.
Fredonia
converted trolley
1910/1948

Compton's Pancake House
105 S. Park Ave.
Stroudsburg
Paramount/Fodero/
Nicholas
1948/1950/1992

Continental Diner
181 Market St.
Philadelphia
Fodero 1963

Country Club Restaurant
1717 Cottman Ave.
Philadelphia
Fodero 1968

Country Squire Diner
2560 West Chester Pk.
Broomall
Musi 1963

Court Diner
140 E. Baltimore Pk.
Media
Kullman 1964

Coventry Diner
1435 Hanover St.
Pottstown
Silk City c. 1962

Crestmont 2 Diner
1323 E. Lincoln Hwy.
Coatesville
Paramount c. 1950

Crossroads Dinor
101 Plum St.
Edinboro
converted trolley

Crystal Palace
Rte. 22 W. &
   Mountain Rd.
Harrisburg
Kullman 2000

D-K Diner
608 E. Gay St.
West Chester
Mt. View 1954

D'Alexander's Diner
1352 Cumberland St.
Lebanon
Fodero 1960

Daddypop's Diner
232 N. York Rd.
Hatboro
Mt. View 1953

Dallas Diner
7025 Rte. 13
Levittown

Dean's Diner
2175 Rte. 22 W.
Blairsville
Fodero 1954

Decoven Diner
1913 State Rd.
Duncannon
O'Mahony 1955

DeGrand Diner
5627 U.S. Rte. 13
Bristol
Kullman 1952/1970

Deluxe Restaurant
2295 W. Lancaster Pk.
Shillington
Swingle 1960/1981

Dempsey's American Kitchen
800 Eisenhower Blvd.
Harrisburg
DeRaffele 1980s

Dempsey's Restaurant
1128 E. Main St.
Hummelstown
Swingle 1966/1976

Dempsey's American Kitchen
1725 Lancaster Ave.
Lancaster
Kullman 1950s

Denny's Classic Diner
Rte. 30
Breezewood
Starlite 1999

Dick's Diner
4200 William Penn Hwy.
Murrysville
O'Mahony 1946

Dina's Diner
736 Tilghman St.
Allentown
Silk City 1940s

Diner 22
Rte. 22
Alexandria
converted railroad car 1919

Dobb's Country Kitchen
Exit 68 off I-81
Hallstead
Manno 1960s

Domino Diner
5110 Umbria St.
Philadelphia
O'Mahony/Swingle 1948/1963/1995

Double Tt Diner
1765 DeKalb Pk.
Blue Bell
Kullman c. 1960

Dutch Kitchen Diner
433 S. Lehigh Ave.
Frackville
Silk City 1959

Dutch Valley Diner
554 Shoemakersville Ave.
Shoemakersville
Fodero 1956

East Shore Diner
711 S. Cameron St.
Harrisburg
O'Mahony 1953

Eat Well Diner
1539 E. Cumberland St.
Lebanon
Kullman 1956

Eddie's Place
577 Fox Hill Rd.
Plains
Fodero c. 1948

Edy's Bistro
Rtes. 209 & 115
Brodheadsville
Silk City mid-1950s

Effort Diner
Rte. 115
Effort
homemade 1936

Emmaus Diner
1418 Chestnut St.
Emmaus
Paramount 1957

Eric's Diner
641 Gap-Newport Pk.
Avondale
Mt. View/Kullman 1952/1961

Espresso Cafe
2400 N. Reading Rd.
Denver
Kullman 1939

Fegely's Restaurant
4860 Perkiomen Ave.
Birdsboro
1930s

Felty's Diner
Rte. 25
Fountain
converted railroad car

Fifth St. Diner
5336 N. 5th St. Hwy.
Temple
Silk City 1959

Flamingo Diner
Rte. 11
West Nanticoke
Paramount c. 1948

Forks Diner
3315 Sullivan Trail
Easton
1970s

Frazer Diner
189 W. Lancaster Ave.
Frazer
O'Mahony 1938

Gabe's Diner
1680 N. Keyser Ave.
Scranton
Kullman early 1950s

Gap Diner
Rtes. 30 & 41
Gap
Kullman 1959

Gap Diner
1041 S. Broadway
Wind Gap
Paramount

Garden Restaurant
3455 Centre Ave.
Reading
1950s

Garfield Diner
402 W. Market St.
Pottsville
Kullman 1954

Gateway Diner
2215 Macdade Blvd.
Holmes
1970s

Gateway Diner
2540 Ridge Pk.
Jeffersonville
Fodero 1950

Gatto's Cycle Diner
139 E. Sixth Ave.
Tarentum
O'Mahony 1946

Girard Dinor
222 W. Main St.
Girard

Glider Diner
890 Providence Rd.
Scranton
Mt. View 1951

Golden Dawn IV
7115 New Falls Rd.
Levittown
Kullman 1985

Golden Eagle II
300 Bath Rd.
Bristol
DeRaffele/Kullman 1974/1993/1999

Golden Gate Diner
1318 Union Blvd.
Allentown
Manno 1964

Golden Sword Diner
4210 Whitaker Ave.
Philadelphia
Fodero 1970s

Great China Restaurant
1126 Schuylkill Ave.
Reading
1960

Grove City Diner
108 E. Main St.
Grove City
Silk City 1938

Grubb's Diner
4th St. & Rte. 22
Huntingdon
Swingle 1964

Haggerty's Diner
1930 W. 26th St.
Erie
Silk City 1948

Hamilton Diner
2027 Hamilton St.
Allentown
Fodero 1959

Hawley Diner
302 Main St.
Hawley
Mt. View 1954

Heisey's Diner
1740 Rte. 72 N.
Lebanon
O'Mahony 1951

Highspire Diner
255 Second St.
Highspire
Silk City 1952

Home Plate Diner
2 Lonsome Rd.
Moosic
O'Mahony 1940s

Hong Luck
Rte. 13
Bristol
Swingle 1960s

Hula Hoops
745 Main St.
Stroudsburg
Paramount/Fodero
1948/1950

Huntingdon Valley Diner
1051 County Line Rd.
Huntingdon Valley
1997

Ingleside Diner
3025 Lincoln Hwy.
Thorndale
Fodero 1956

Jaden's Family Dining
4727 William Penn
Hwy.
Monroeville
Swingle 1979

Jennie's Diner
2575 Lincoln Hwy. E.
Ronks
Silk City 1959

Johnnie's Diner
709 Lincoln Way E.
McConnellsburg
1920s

Kay's Italian Restaurant
Rte. 435
Daleville
O'Mahony 1920s

Kennett Diner
719 Old Baltimore Pk.
Kennett Square
O'Mahony 1920s

Key City Diner
1947 W. Main St.
Stroudsburg
1970s

Kumm Esse Diner
101 W. Lincoln Ave.
Myerstown
DeRaffele 1960

Kuppy's Diner
Brown & Poplar Sts.
Middletown
Ward & Dickinson
1938

Lancer's Diner
858 Easton Rd.
Horsham
1970s

Laverne's Diner
113 S. Main St.
Pittsburgh
Silk City 1959

Lee's Diner
4320 W. Market St.
York
Mt. View 1951

Lehigh Pizza
306 Broadway
Bethlehem
Silk City 1954

Lehigh Valley Diner
1162 MacArthur Rd.
Allentown
Silk City 1956

Limerick Diner
411 W. Ridge Pk.
Limerick
Swingle 1969

Lincoln Diner
32 Carlisle St.
Gettysburg
Silk City 1954

Littleton's Diner
8001 Ogontz Ave.
Philadelphia
Paramount 1958

Llanerch Diner
Township Line Rd.
Havertown
Swingle 1968

Lyndon City Line Diner
1370 Manheim Pk.
Lancaster
DeRaffele 1997

Lyndon Diner
665 Lancaster Rd.
Manheim
DeRaffele 1990

Marcus Hook Diner
10th and Green Sts.
Marcus Hook
1950s

Marlene Diner
7260 Marshal Rd.
Upper Darby
O'Mahony 1949

Mayfair Diner
7373 Frankford Ave.
Philadelphia
O'Mahony 1954/1956

Meadowbrook Diner
Rte. 209
Brodheadsville
Swingle 1974

Mel's Diner
8 E. Cumberland St.
Lebanon
O'Mahony 1955

Melrose Diner
1501 Snyder Ave.
Philadelphia
Paramount 1956

Michael's Restaurant
Rte. 422 W.
Douglassville
Kullman early 1960s

Middlesex Diner
462 Sharon Rd.
West Middlesex
Ward & Dickinson
1926

Mil-Lee's Luv-Inn Diner
5717 Rising Sun Ave.
Philadelphia
O'Mahony
1930s/1960s

Milford Diner
Rtes. 6 & 209
Milford
Manno 1972

Miller's Diner
1205 Main St.
Northampton
Silk City 1950s

Minella's Main Line Diner
320 Lancaster Ave.
Wayne
1964

Miss Oxford Diner
233 S. 3rd St.
Oxford
Silk City 1955

Morgan's Eastland Diner
127 Oneida Valley Rd.
Butler
Mt. View 1957

Mount Bethel Diner
Rte. 611 N.
Bethel

Mountain City Diner
10 W. Oak St.
Frackville
1950s

Mountainhome Diner
Rte. 191
Mountainhome
Mt. View 1953

Nazareth Diner
Rte. 258 & S. Broad St.
Nazareth
1950s

Neptune Diner
924 N. Prince St.
Lancaster
Mt. View 1951

New City View Diner
1831 MacArthur Rd.
Whitehall
DeRaffele 1960/1992

Norwin Diner
10640 Rte. 30
Irwin
Kullman 1976

Oak Lane Diner
6528 N. Broad St.
Philadelphia
Paramount 1950

Olympic Diner
142 E. Baltimore Pk.
Clifton Heights
Mt. View 1953

Oregon Diner
302 Oregon Ave.
Philadelphia
c. 1960

**Paradise Family
   Restaurant**
Rte. 61 S.
Schuylkill Haven
Silk City 1950s

Park Classic Diner
3893 William Penn
   Hwy.
Monroeville
Kullman 1999

Park Dinor
4019 Main St.
Erie
Silk City 1948

**Paul's Gyro
   Restaurant**
37 N. 7th St.
Allentown
1930s

Peggy's Diner
Rte. 220
Claysburg
1970s

Pennsburg Diner
321 Pottstown Ave.
Pennsburg
Silk City/Swingle
   1959/1968

Penrose Restaurant
20th & Penrose Aves.
Philadelphia
DeRaffele 1963

Pioneer Diner
508 Belmont Ave.
Mt. Pocono
Swingle 1968

Pip's Diner
1900 Woodville Ave.
Pittsburgh
Tierney 1920s

Pipher's Diner
Rtes. 6 & 187
Wysox
homemade

**Plain & Fancy
   Restaurant**
Rte. 309
Quakertown
DeRaffele 1960

Poodle Skirt Diner
911 S. 5th St.
Allentown
Silk City 1956

Preston Diner
Governor Printz Hwy.
Essington
Silk City/Kullman
   1958/1960s

Prospect Diner
Columbia Ave.
Columbia
Kullman 1954

Quaker Diner
7241 Rising Sun Ave.
Philadelphia
O'Mahony 1939

Queen City Diner
1801 Lehigh St.
Allentown
Kullman c. 1970

R & J Family Diner
22 Wyoming Ave.
Wyoming
1953

**R & S Keystone
   Restaurant**
4714 Bethlehem Pk.
Telford
c. 1950

R-Way Diner
880 Baltimore Pk.
Springfield
homemade 1955

Ray's Dining Car
1968 W. Main St.
Jeffersonville
Silk City c. 1962

**Reading Family
   Restaurant**
2725 Centre Ave.
Reading
1950s

Red Robin Diner
6330 Frankford Ave.
Philadelphia
Fodero 1960s

Rise 'n' Shine Diner
Rte. 222
Ephrata
Silk City 1940s

Risser's Diner
Rte. 422
Stouchsburg
Fodero 1954

Ritter's Diner
5221 Baum Blvd.
Pittsburgh
Fodero 1976

Royal Diner
80 High St.
Pottstown
DeRaffele 1961

Royann Diner
1318 Rte. 309
Sellersville

Sand Trap Cafe
4417 Castor Ave.
Philadelphia
1950s

Saville's Diner
830 E. Philadelphia
   Ave.
Boyertown
Swingle/Paramount
   1961/1968/1977

Saylor's Restaurant
701 N. 19th St.
Allentown
Paramount 1946

**Schmeck's Family
   Restaurant**
16515 Pottsville Pk.
Hamburg
Wingard Dining Car
   Co.

Scotrun Diner
Rte. 611
Scotrun
c. 1970

Silk City Diner
1640 N. Reading Rd.
Stevens
Silk City/Paramount
   1957

Silver Star Diner
845 Linden St.
Allentown
DeRaffele 1960

Six East Restaurant
1611 Rte. 6
Dickson City
Mt. View 1949

Skyline Diner
200 W. Lincoln Hwy.
Penndel
Paramount 1956

**Skyline Family
   Restaurant**
7510 Allentown Blvd.
West Hanover
Silk City 1945

Skyliner Diner
4118 Birney Ave.
Moosic
O'Mahony 1955

Smethport Diner
423 W. Main St.
Smethport
Ward & Dickinson
   1937

Snydersville Diner
Bus. Rte. 209
Stroudsburg
Mt. View/Swingle
   1955/1970

Stadium Restaurant
1925 Centre Ave.
Reading
Silk City 1954

Starlite Restaurant
Rtes. 22 & 100
Fogelsville
Kullman 1957

Suburban Diner
14 W. Street Rd.
Feasterville
1940s

Sullivan Trail Diner
6221 Sullivan Trail
Nazareth
1960s

Summit Diner
760 Rte. 422 E.
Butler
DeRaffele 1948

Summit Diner
791 N. Center Ave.
Somerset
Swingle 1960

Sunrise Diner
1401 S. 4th St.
Allentown
DeRaffele 1960

Sunrise Diner
3 Hazard Sq.
Jim Thorpe
O'Mahony 1947

Sunset Diner
Rte. 209
Kresgeville
O'Mahony 1930s

Tamaqua Diner
39 Center St.
Tamaqua
Bixler

Tannersville Diner
Rte. 715 at I-80
Tannersville
Fodero/Swingle
    1960s/1982

**The Dining Car &
    Market**
8826 Frankford Ave.
Philadelphia
Swingle 1981

The Silk City Diner
435 Spring Garden St.
Philadelphia
Silk City 1959

Tic Toc Restaurant
2510 Northampton
    St.
Easton
Kullman 1957

Tiffany Diner
9010 Roosevelt Blvd.
Philadelphia
1970s

Tom Sawyer Diner
4455 Hamilton Blvd.
Allentown
DeRaffele 1962

Top Diner
1019 Union Blvd.
Allentown
Silk City 1953

Town House Diner
920 Main St.
Honesdale
Mt. View 1957

Trail Diner
Rte. 11
New Milford
Mt. View c. 1950

Trivet Diner
4549 Tilghman St.
Allentown
DeRaffele 1980s

Trolley Car Cafe
15 E. Market St.
Lewistown
O'Mahony

Two Guys Diner
Rte. 222 N.
Adamstown
Silk City c. 1930

Union City Dinor
48 N. Main St.
Union City
Mulholland 1926

Vale-Rio Diner
114 Nutt Rd.
Phoenixville
Paramount 1948

Venus Diner
5313 William Flynn
    Hwy.
Gibsonia
Fodero 1958

Village Diner
Rtes. 6 & 209
Milford
Mt. View 1956

Wellsboro Diner
19 Main St.
Wellsboro
Sterling 1938

West Reading Diner
411 Penn Ave.
West Reading
DeRaffele mid-1960s

West Shore Diner
1011 State Rd.
Lemoyne
Silk City c. 1940

White Diner
Rte. 309
Tamaqua
1950s

**White Haven Family
    Diner**
302 Main St.
White Haven
Paramount 1950s

**Willow Street
    Restaurant**
Rtes. 272 & 222
Willow Street
Kullman early 1960s

Wolfe's Diner
624 Rte. 15 S.
Dillsburg
O'Mahony early 1950s

Yakkitty-Yak Diner
1219 Rte. 56 E.
North Apollo
O'Mahony 1956

Yankee Doodle Diner
5000 Milford Rd.
Marshalls Creek
Kullman 1960s

**Ye Olde College
    Diner**
126 W. College Ave.
State College
1920s

Zinn's Diner
2270 N. Reading Rd.
Denver
Paramount/Fodero
    1949/1969/
    1973/1976

Zoto's Diner
Rte. 309 & Hilltown
    Pk.
Line Lexington
Fodero 1973

Rhode Island
4th Street Diner
184 Admiral Kalfbus
    Rd.
Newport
O'Mahony 1950

Alexion's Diner
Rte. 1A
Pawtucket
DeRaffele c. 1972

China Star
Newport Ave.
East Providence
DeRaffele c. 1950

El Faro
581 Atwells Ave.
Providence
Kullman 1946

**Haven Brothers
    Diner**
Fulton St. at City Hall
Providence
homemade 1946

Hope Diner
742 Hope St.
Bristol

**Jenn's Elmwood
    Diner**
777 Elmwood Ave.
Providence
Worcester 1947

Jigger's Diner
145 Main St.
East Greenwich
Worcester 1950

Johnny B's
1388 Cranston St.
Cranston
Worcester 1920s

Mike's Diner
675 Valley St.
Providence
DeRaffele 1966

Modern Diner
364 East Ave.
Pawtucket
Sterling 1941

Prairie Diner
Prairie & Public Sts.
Providence
Tierney 1927

**Purple Cat
    Restaurant**
Rtes. 44 & 102
Chepachet
converted trolley

Seaplane Diner
307 Allen Ave.
Providence
O'Mahony late 1940s

Silver Top Diner
13 Harris Ave.
Providence
Kullman 1941

Snoopy's Diner
4001 Quaker Ln.
North Kingstown
Silk City 1940s

State Line Diner
Rte. 6
Foster Center
Worcester 1955

Tommy's Deluxe Diner
159 E. Main Rd.
Middletown
O'Mahony 1941

Veterans Square Diner
Rte. 117
Coventry
converted trolley

Wampanaug Diner
2800 Pawtucket Ave.
East Providence

Wickford Diner
64 Brown St.
Wickford

South Carolina
Seaboard Diner
1201 Lincoln St.
Columbia
homemade 1951

South Dakota
Market Diner
Louise Ave.
Sioux Falls
Starlite 1998

Tennessee
Summit Diner
137 S. Central St.
Knoxville
homemade 1993

Texas
59 Diner
3801 Farnham
Houston
homemade 1987

Avalon Diner
2417 Westheimer
Houston
homemade 1938

Majestic Diner
1806 Barton Springs
Austin
homemade 1990

Prince's Diner
8808 Westheimer
Houston
O'Mahony 1948

Utah
Westerner Grill
331 N. Main St.
Moab
Valentine 1954

Vermont
Birdseye Diner
Main St.
Castleton
Silk City 1940s

Chelsea Royal
West Brattleboro
Worcester 1938

Cosmos Diner
1110 Shelburne Rd.
South Burlington
Worcester 1954

Delaney's Country Girl Diner
Rtes. 103 & 11
Chester
Silk City c. 1950

Henry's Diner
155 Bank St.
Burlington
O'Mahony 1925

Jad's Family Restaurant
107 Canal St.
Brattleboro
Kullman 1930s

Libby's Blue Line Diner
1 Roosevelt Hwy.
Colchester
Worcester 1953

Martha's Coventry Diner
Rtes. 5 & 14
Coventry
Fodero 1953

Mid Mountain Cafe
Stratton Mt. Ski Area
Manchester
O'Mahony c. 1935

Miss Bellows Falls
90 Rockingham
Bellows Falls
Worcester 1941

Miss Newport Diner
E. Main St.
Newport
Worcester 1950

Oasis Diner
189 Bank St.
Burlington
Mt. View 1954

Parkway Diner
1696 Williston Rd.
South Burlington
Worcester 1953

Ray's Diner
45 Canal St.
Brattleboro
Worcester 1920s

Shanghai Garden
Hwy. 11
Springfield
Worcester

Sonny's Blue Benn Diner
102 Hunt St.
Bennington
Silk City 1948

T. J. Buckley's Uptown Diner
132 Elliot St.
Brattleboro
Worcester 1920s

Windsor Diner
135 Main St.
Windsor
Worcester 1952

Yankee Diner
Timber Village
Rte. 4
Quechee
Worcester 1946

Virginia
29 Diner
10536 Lee Hwy.
Fairfax
Mt. View 1947

Amphora Restaurant
377 Maple Ave.
Vienna

Amphora's Diner Deluxe
1151 Elden St.
Herndon
DeRaffele 1997

Bill's Diner
1 Depot St.
Chatham
converted trolley
1940s

Blue Star Diner
9955 Warwick Blvd.
Newport News
Manno-reno 1959

Burnett's Diner
19 S. Main St.
Chatham
converted trolley
1940s

Comet Diner
1718 Shenandoah Ave.
Front Royal
Mt. View c. 1957

Exmore Diner
Main St.
Exmore
Silk City 1940s

Fox Diner
20 South St.
Front Royal
homemade 1955

Frost Diner
55 Broadview Ave.
Warrenton
O'Mahony 1955

Gary's Diner
Rte. 11
Roanoke
Valentine 1957

Hillsville Diner
525 Main St.
Hillsville
O'Mahony 1920s

L & S Diner
255 N. Liberty St.
Harrisonburg
homemade 1947

Little Chef
200 E. City Point Rd.
Hopewell
Valentine

Little Chef Diner
2337 N. Main St.
Danville
Valentine early 1950s

Mama's Restaurant
9715 Lee Hwy.
Fairfax

Marion Diner
Rtes. 11 & 16
Marion
Silk City/Paramount 1950s

Metro 29 Diner
4711 Lee Hwy.
Arlington
Uniwest/DeRaffele 1995

Silver Diner–
Clarendon
3200 Wilson Blvd.
Arlington
Uniwest 1996

Silver Diner–
Fair Oaks
12251 Fair Lakes
Pkwy.
Fairfax
Uniwest 1995

Silver Diner–
Merrifield
8150 Porter Rd.
Merrifield
Uniwest 1997

Silver Diner–
Potomac Mills
14375 Smoketown Rd.
Dale City
Uniwest 1991

Silver Diner–Reston
11951 Killingsworth
Ave.
Reston
Uniwest 1997

Silver Diner–
Springfield
6592 Springfield Mall
Springfield
Uniwest 1997

Silver Diner–
Tyson's Corner
8101 Fletcher St.
McLean
Uniwest 1995

Silver Diner–
Virginia Beach
4401 Virginia Beach
Blvd.
Virginia Beach
Uniwest 2000

Triangle Diner
27 W. Gerrard St.
Winchester
O'Mahony 1948

Walker's Diner
307 N. Main St.
Farmville
Valentine late 1950s

Washington
Andy's Diner
16200 W. Valley Hwy.
Renton
converted railroad car

Andy's Diner
2963 4th St. S.
Seattle
converted railroad cars
1949

Blue Water Diner
305 Madison Ave.
Bainbridge Island
Fodero 1947

West Virginia
Bev's Diner
10 E. Main St.
White Sulphur
Springs
Valentine 1950

Mountain State
Diner
Rural Rte. 5
Morgantown

Wisconsin
Frank's Diner
508 58th St.
Kenosha
O'Mahony 1920s

Monterey Jack's
Sun Prairie
Valentine

Wyoming
Starlite Diner
Exit 89, I-80
Green River
Starlite

ARGENTINA
Dixie Diner
Av. R. Obligado y J.
Salguero S/N
Buenos Aires
homemade 1996

Dixie Diner
Carlos Pelligrini 1594
Buenos Aires
homemade 1997

CANADA
Capital City Diner
460 Hunt Club Rd.
West Ottawa, Ontario
homemade 1996

Flo's Diner
10 Bellair St.
Toronto
homemade 1987

Le Galaxie Diner
4801, rue St. Denis
Montreal
Mt. View 1950s

ENGLAND
Fatboy's Diner
Spitalfields Markets
London
Worcester 1955

Rock Island Diner
Tamworth
Mt. View c. 1950

GERMANY
Excellent Diner
Aalen
O'Mahony 1947

Gateway Diner
Oberhausen
Silk City 1950

Mel's Diner
Hildesheimer Strasse
83 Hannover/
Laatzen
Starlite 1996

Mercer Diner
Stuttgart
O'Mahony 1953

Sam Kullman's Diner
Linthe
Kullman 2000

Tom's Diner
Karlsruhe
Paramount c. 1940

RUSSIA
Starlite Diner
Tverskaya Şt.
Moscow
Starlite 1995

Starlite Diner II
Oktyabrskaya
Moscow
Starlite 1996

SPAIN
Woody's Diner
Arturo Soria 66
Madrid
Fodero 1948

Index

Note: Page numbers in italics refer to illustrations and captions.